IMAGES
of America

SEBASTICOOK VALLEY

IMAGES
of America

SEBASTICOOK VALLEY

Brenda Seekins

ARCADIA

ISBN 0-7385-3584-2

First published 2004

Published by Arcadia Publishing
Charleston SC, Chicago IL, Portsmouth NH, San Francisco CA

Printed in Great Britain

Library of Congress Catalog Card Number: 2004101702

For all general information, contact Arcadia Publishing:
Telephone 843-853-2070
Fax 843-853-0044
E-mail sales@arcadiapublishing.com
For customer service and orders:
Toll-free 1-888-313-2665

Visit us on the Internet at www.arcadiapublishing.com

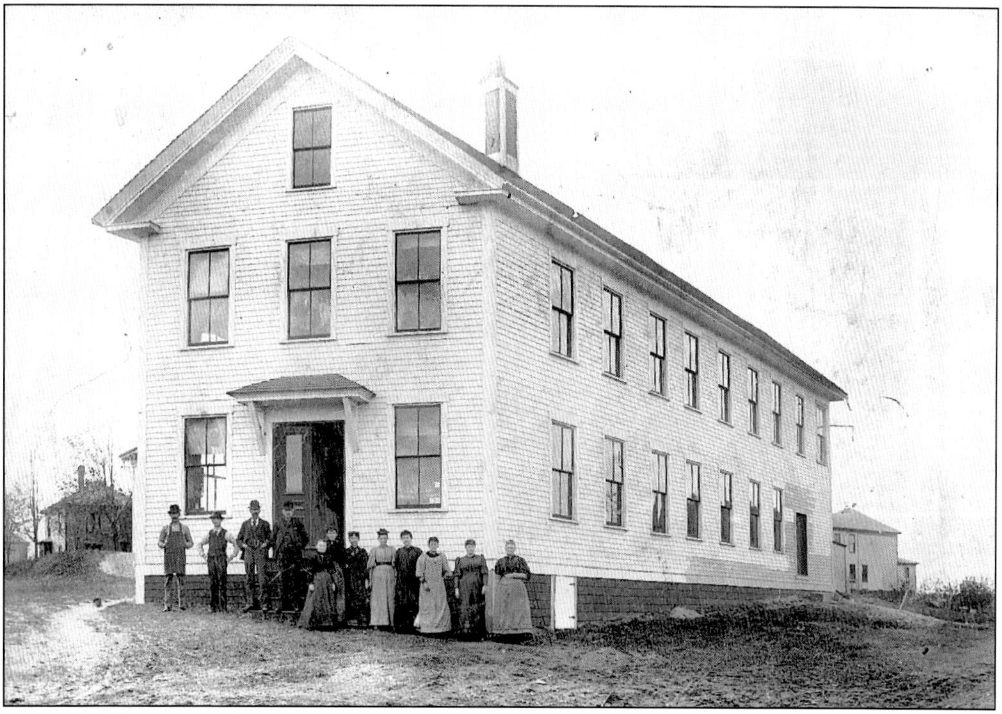

In Pittsfield *c.* 1900, the Conant Pant Factory was an early entry in the manufacturing history of the community and an example of the self-sufficiency that each community in the valley developed in its history. The company was located on Railroad Street in the vicinity of the current post office.

Contents

ACKNOWLEDGMENTS

This book would not have been possible without the assistance of historical societies in Hartland, Newport, Pittsfield, and St. Albans. Individuals who contributed to the photograph collection and accompanying data include Don and Gwen Emery and Evangeline and Max Matijczyk, Newport; Wendell and Marjorie Bubar and Darrell Butler, St. Albans; Douglas I. Fernald and Anna F. Fernald, Detroit; Don Hallenbeck, Lois S. Braley, Virginia S. Agostinelli, Scott and Carol Millett, Francine Mayhew, and Ed and Polly Nichols, Pittsfield; Hilda E. Nutter, Myrtle L. Marble, Meredith Randlett, B. J. Childs Frosch, Shirley Humphrey, and Peggy Morgan, Hartland; Mary Ellen Bossom, Scarborough; Eunice Harper, Sally Withee, Dan Weeks, Pam Weeks, and Pat White, Palmyra; and Donna Ferrucci, Southington, Connecticut.

My personal interest in history was fostered long ago by elderly relatives who shared their experiences of 19th and early 20th century lifestyles with me, allowing me to understand that the "modern" conveniences I enjoyed in the 1950s and 1960s were miracles beyond their childhood experiences. I was fortunate to know these people, and I treasured their active minds and the tales of their experiences; they were so willing to share with an inquisitive, if not nosy, child. My curiosity continued to grow with the help of two high school history teachers who always knew the stories behind the stories in the driest of textbooks. And, ultimately, I have to credit my good fortune to have worked for so long with the talented editorial staff of Maine's largest daily newspaper, a group of people whose curiosity demanded accuracy, clarity, and thoroughness of detail to continue recording history.

No acknowledgment would be complete without a sincere thank you to my family members for their patience, assistance, and, most of all, for believing in me and my ultimate goal.

—Brenda J. Thompson Seekins

INTRODUCTION

Long before the English or other white settlers discovered the fields, hills, wetlands, and woodlands of Sebasticook Valley, an area defined by the flow of the east and west branches of the Sebasticook River, Maine's native tribes were navigating the rivers and lakes, settling seasonally at strategic points to fish and hunt. The "people of the dawn land," the Abenaki, are thought to have been among the original inhabitants of the valley, along with their brethren, the Penobscots and other members of the Wabanaki Confederation, who sought the abundance of fish, fowl, and mammals in the valley. The native people were regular travelers in Sebasticook Valley, using it as a meeting place and crossing point between two of Maine's great river valleys, the Kennebec and the Penobscot. Many white settlers in the first century of Sebasticook Valley's development would follow these same routes by land and water to find permanent homesites in the area.

Over the past 200 years of "civilized" development, many discoveries in the Sebasticook region have told the story of earlier native villages and encampments along the shores, but fail to tell us where and who those native peoples' descendants, if any, might be today.

It wasn't until after the Revolutionary War that organized settlements appeared in the area that would one day become Detroit, Hartland, Newport, Pittsfield, Palmyra, and St. Albans. Land in neighboring Corinna was also part of the original land grants and purchases.

In 1792, Ephraim Ballard and Samuel Weston were the first surveyors of record in the region, labeling most of the area as "3rd and 2nd Range of townships north of the Waldo Patent." It was another 28 years before the land became part of a state known as Maine. Much of Maine's population at that time lived along the coast or on the lower reaches of the major rivers. A few rugged souls were pioneering in the Sebasticook Valley region and apparently were not here long enough to lay permanent claim to the land.

Many of the early residents came from settlements to the south and west of the valley to purchase land from the original developers. Dr. John Warren of Revolutionary War fame was one of the earliest landowners, but it was his descendants that eventually moved to the region to oversee Dr. Warren's investment from a large home on Warren Hill in Palmyra, originally Township No. 5.

South of the Palmyra-Hartland-St. Albans development, General William Shepard and the trustees of Monmouth Academy were selling lots that would later become Detroit and other villages to its south. The early 1800s were a busy era of development for the entire valley.

Newport was designated as Township No. 4 in the third range of townships north of the Waldo Patent, and until 1800 it was only trappers that made their way up the Sebasticook to harvest the natural resources of the region. James Houstin, a single trapper, is recognized as the first Newport settler. Houstin was alone until he was joined in 1807 by Dea. John Ireland, who moved with his family from Bloomfield (now Skowhegan) to live in the region that would be known as North Newport. Ireland's descendants still reside in the North Newport area.

Early settlers in Hartland and St. Albans, Townships No. 3 and 4 in the range, were emigrants from several New Hampshire communities. These early settlements began in what is now West Hartland and on St. Albans Mountain. It was years later that entrepreneurs took settlements to the lake and river shores to harness waterpower.

In Pittsfield, it was Moses Martin who traveled east with a Norridgewock hunting party and ultimately settled shortly before 1800 on Peltoma Point on the Sebasticook, just south of today's village and near the confluence of the east and west branches of the river. Other Norridgewock neighbors eventually followed Martin to settle more of the region.

Sebasticook Valley's location, between the Kennebec and Penobscot valleys and large industrial and governmental sites at Bangor, Waterville, Skowhegan, and Augusta, fostered its early development and continues to spur continued growth today at the "crossroads" or "hub" of Maine's major transportation routes.

Like Maine's earliest settlers, those who followed were men of vision and industry, women of strength and resolve, and children offering promise for the future growth of the region. Industry and business have waxed and waned throughout the centuries and continue to today.

This book is not intended as an authoritative history of the region, but as a small indication of what has been part of its history, its lifestyles and livelihoods, and how it has changed.

—Brenda J. Thompson Seekins

One
PITTSFIELD

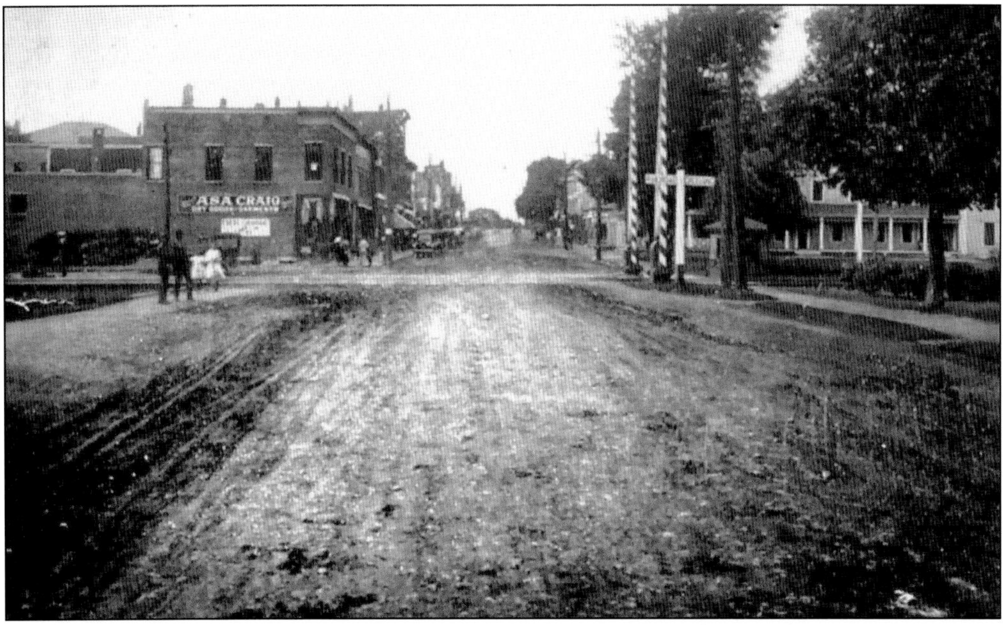

By the time of Pittsfield's centennial in 1919, Main Street had a thriving business community. The famed Lancey House was newly rebuilt after a devastating fire in 1906. The railroad was long established in the region and located prominently at the foot of Main Street in Pittsfield. The previous century was a busy time in Pittsfield's early history, beginning in 1800 when George Brown from Norridgewock followed his former neighbor Moses Martin to the area. It was Brown who chose the advantageous spot that would become Pittsfield village. Brown apparently settled at the intersection of Main and Easy Streets, seen in the background of this photo. It was an elevation that could likely have given him a clear view upriver and down on the Sebasticook with the apparently barren landscape of the time. Martin, who came in 1795, settled in pioneering style farther south on the river, making his home on the west branch of the Sebasticook at Peltoma Point long before there were established roads or paths other than those forged by his friends the Norridgewocks, members of the Abenaki nation.

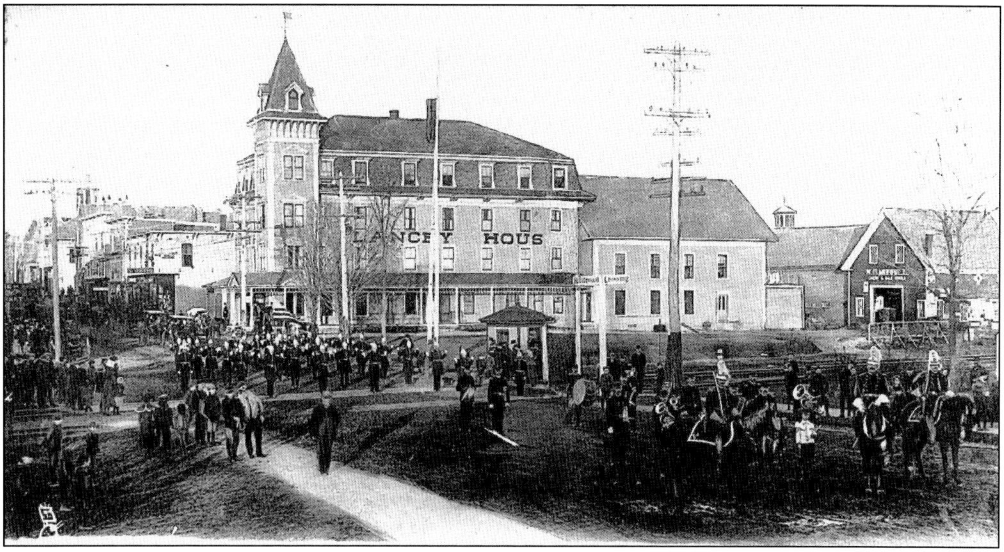

Pittsfield's grand hotel, the Lancey House, survived 101 years and suffered through three destructive fires before finally meeting its end in 1965. Begun as a tavern and inn farther north on Main Street, the historic structure that stood at the corner of Main Street and Hunnewell Avenue was built in 1864 by Isaac Lancey, son of Col. William Lancey. It was the elder Lancey who operated the original tavern, beginning in 1830. Until 1906, it was one story taller than the size it remained at for the rest of its history.

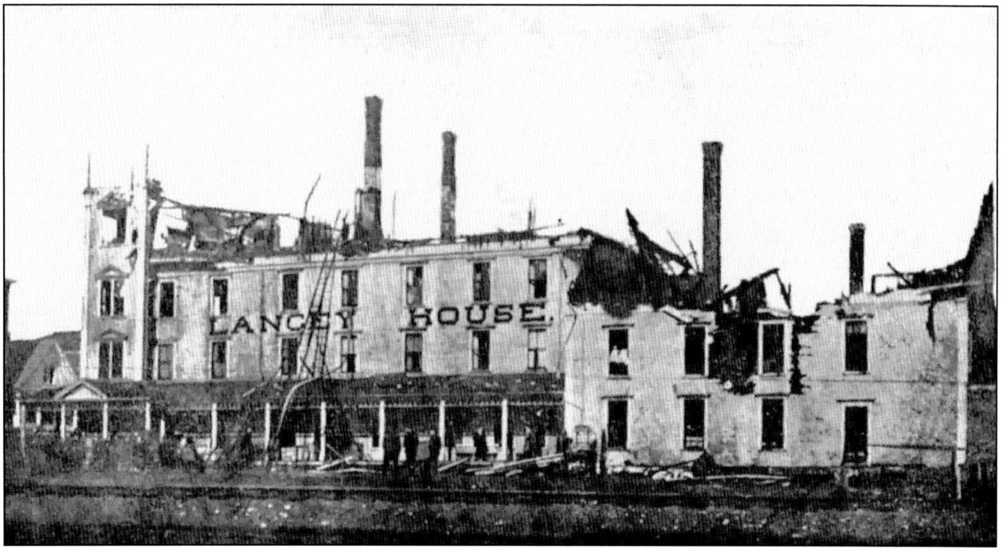

In October 1906, fire destroyed the famed hotel, beginning in the pastry room and sweeping up through the entire building. The fire department was hampered by a lack of water to fight the blaze, but managed to save enough of the building's shell for it to eventually be rebuilt. When the telephone exchange inside the hotel was knocked out by the fire, firefighters telegraphed Waterville for a steam pumper, which arrived too late to assist. It was five long years before anyone attempted to reconstruct the hotel, which had an estimated $25,000 in damage. Eventually, progress-minded citizens joined forces to finance the project to benefit the local economy. That type of foresight was employed many more times to propel Pittsfield business forward in the 20th century. When the building was rebuilt, it flourished for another 60 years.

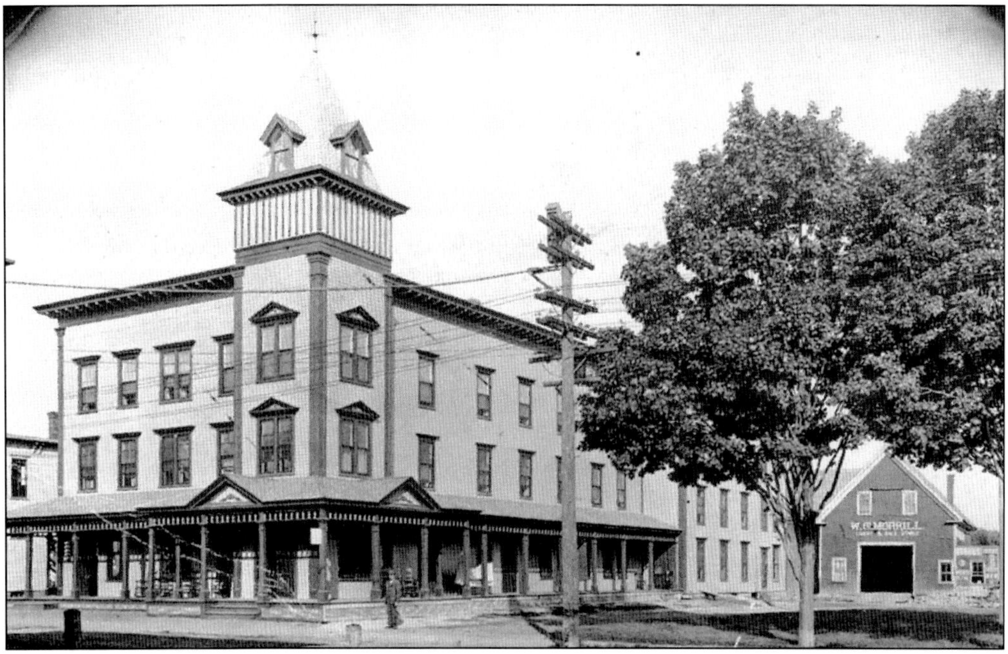

By 1911, the hotel was operational again. However, the mode of transportation was changing as the 20th century added motoring to the mix. Col. William Morrill's livery stable in the rear was not needed for many more years. The hotel was home to many "drummers" (traveling salesmen) during the week, and on weekends it was a popular destination for the chauffeured elite from throughout the state, who traveled to Pittsfield to dine on duck, roast goose, or seasoned steak. At the center of the community, it was a logical headquarters for many historic Pittsfield events, including Memorial and Flag Day tributes and a visit from Pres. Dwight D. Eisenhower during a well-planned fishing trip to Maine.

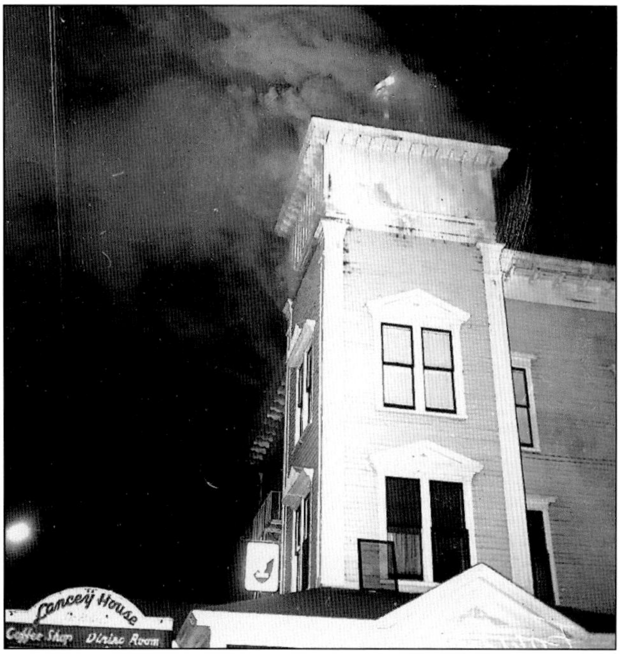

By October 1965, however, the heyday of grand hotels was coming to an end. Although the dining room and coffee shop were ever-popular places for locals and travelers, the state of the local economy and the damage of the last fire were too much for the old building, and it was removed. Well-known Pittsfield photographer William Fowlie captured this scene from the 1965 fire. A branch of the Peoples Heritage Bank is located on the Lancey House site today.

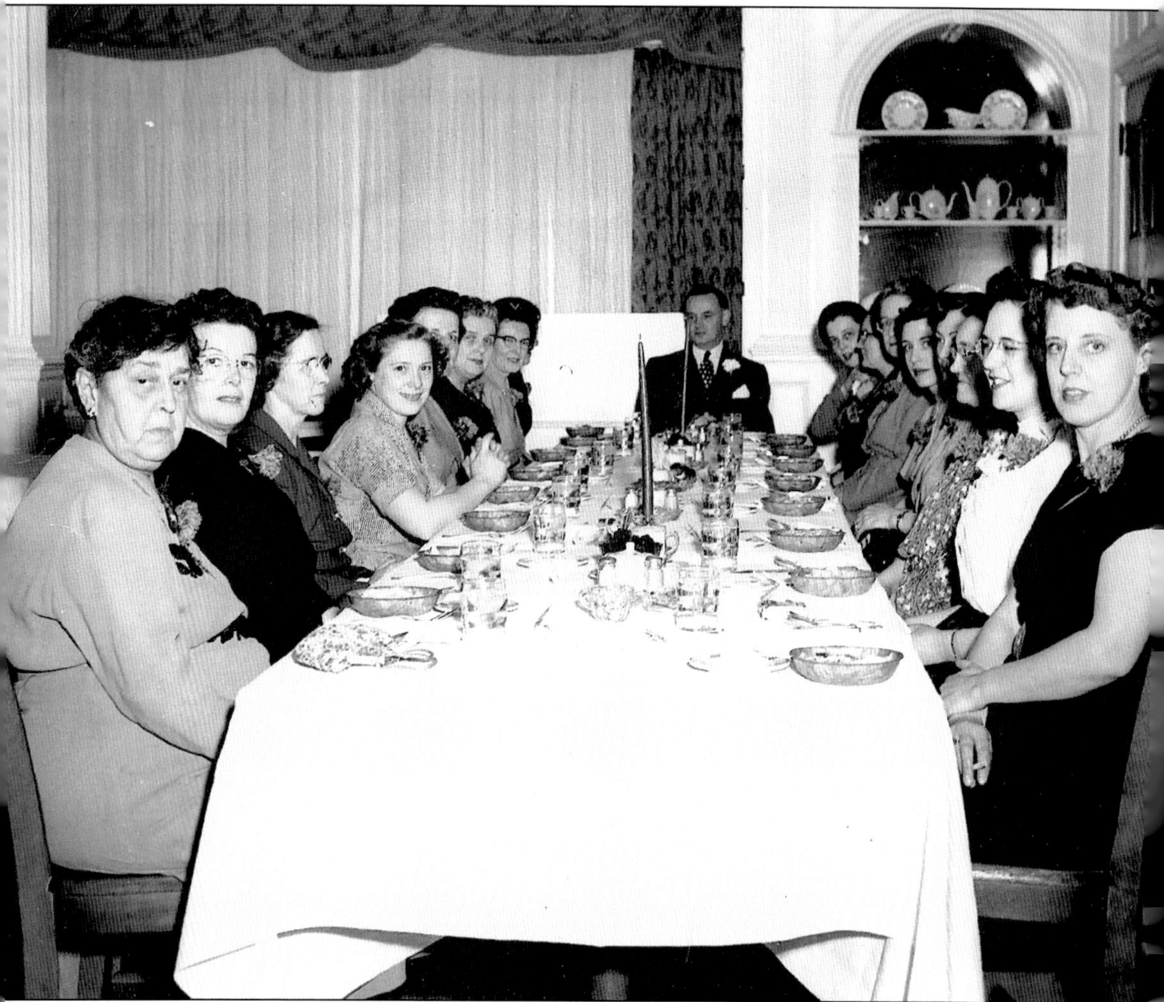

Pittsfield has long been a town of multiple organizations, which provided socialization for their members and services for the community. With the loss of the old Lancey House, groups like the R. N. Club, an organization of area nurses, had to find new meeting places. Members at this c. 1955 gathering are, from left to right, as follows: Elizabeth Walker, Julia Lehr, Fannie Gilman, Jeannette Fitts, Marion Stein, Mabel Sallinen, Jean Maden, Dr. Ernest Stein, unidentified, Elizabeth Field, Katherine Aker, Phoebe Krause, unidentified, Marie Bradford, Eunice Harper, and Rowena Fields.

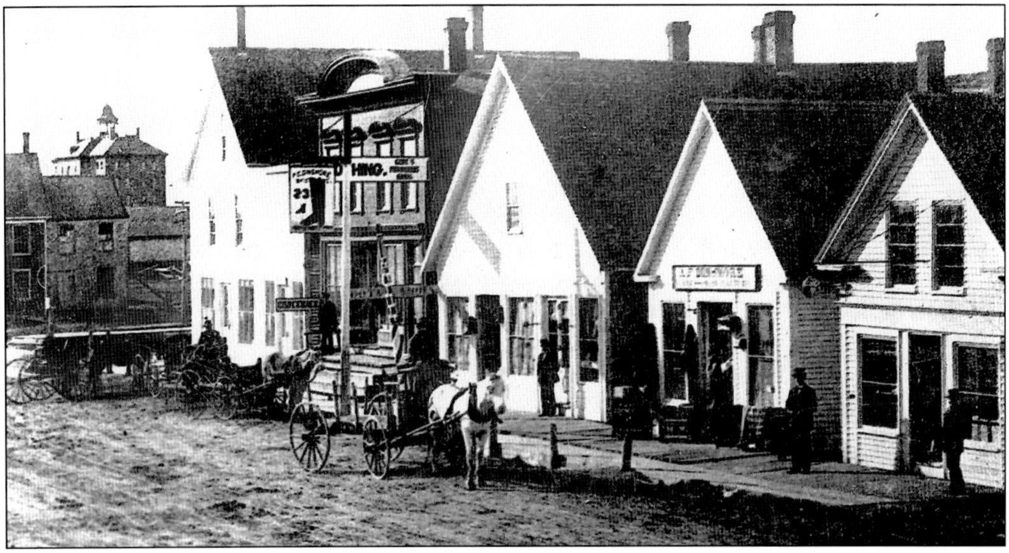

The west side of Main Street has seen many changes over the past century. The Main Street of 1875 has little similarity to Main Street today. A fire in 1881 wiped out most of the buildings on that side of the street. The railroad had not yet arrived to divide Main Street from South Main Street, and Maine Central Institute (MCI), still relatively new, can be seen in the distance. A crowded residential district between Main Street and MCI prevents that view today.

In 1881, the first of many fires to plague downtown Pittsfield struck a severe blow to the city, wiping out most of the west side of Main Street. The boy shown here is standing on the corner of Park and Middle Streets where the Pittsfield Municipal Building stands today. In 1883, just a year after this photograph was taken, a new municipal building, Union Hall, and a fire station were constructed and opened on the corner.

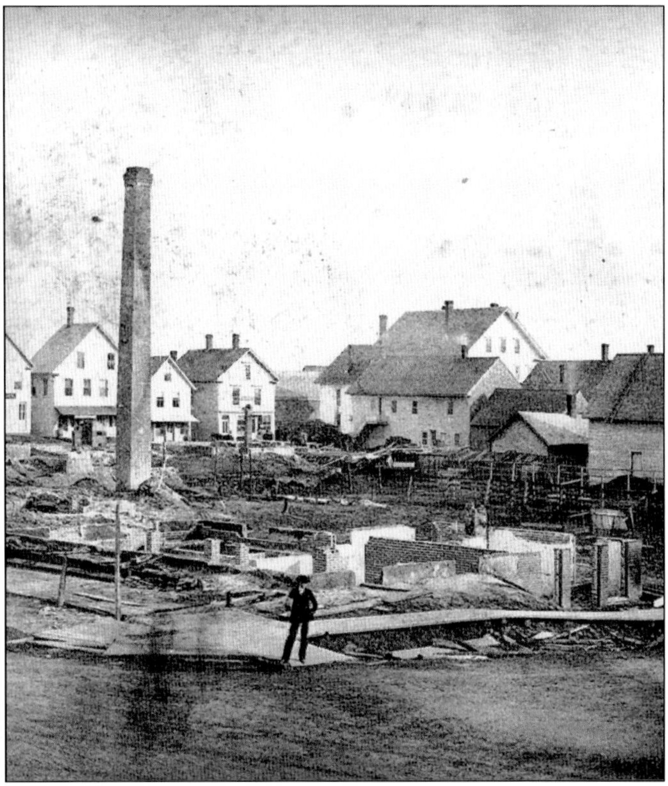

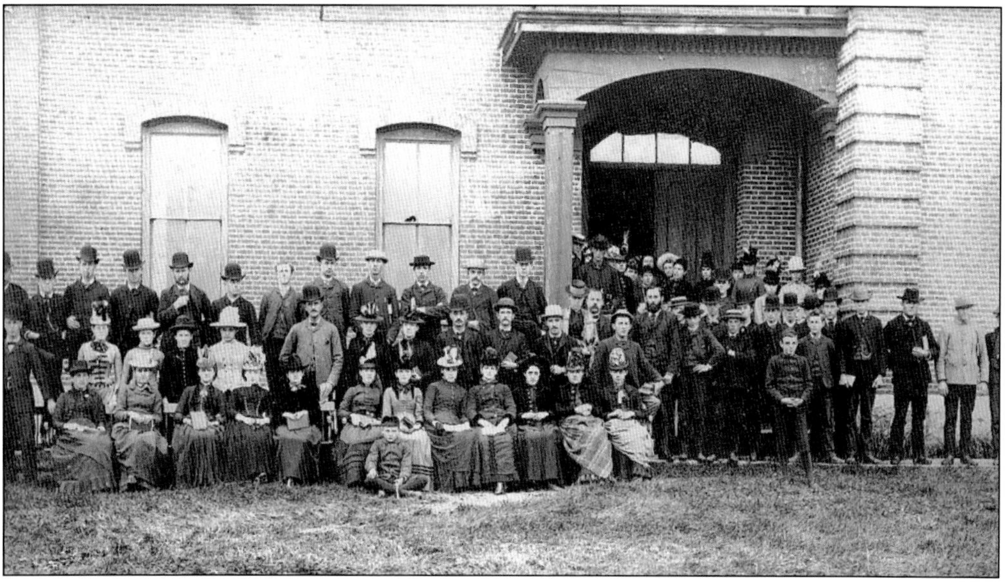

In February 1866, several prominent Pittsfield businessmen gathered to incorporate a new secondary school initially intended to prepare students for continued education at Bates College in Lewiston. The first term met in August 1866 with 83 students in attendance at a local schoolhouse. The main building, now "Founders Hall," wasn't ready for use until 1869, when the student body had grown to 130. Going Hathorn, one of the school's founders, was so eager to see the building completed that he created a brickyard near the campus and furnished bricks for the project. This c. 1885 group of students is pictured outside the main building, which still looks the same today. In 1979, it was named to the National Register of Historic Places.

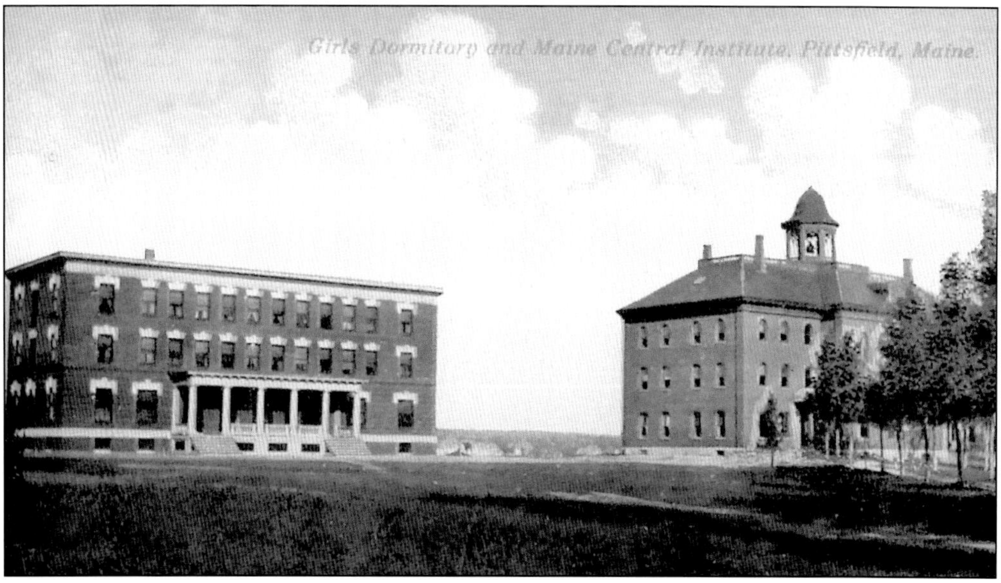

By the early 1900s, the MCI campus grew again with the addition of a girls' dormitory. In later years, the building became Weymouth Hall. The porch was torn off and eventually restored to its original design in the 1980s, when the school's administrative offices were moved into the building.

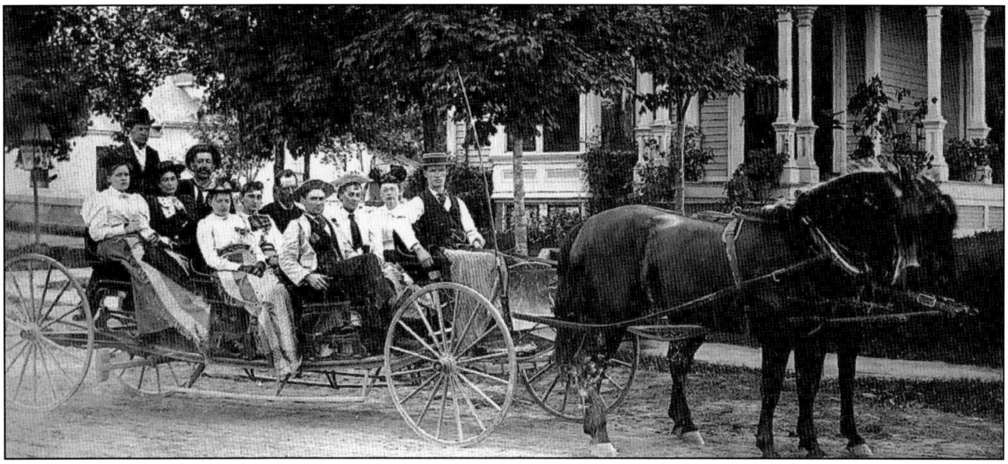

The Maine Central Institute class of 1884 demonstrated early on how far-reaching the school's attraction might be. Students in this group were from throughout central Maine and beyond. Some of the class members were Harry Briggs, Houlton; William M. Getchell, Pittsfield; Frank W. Hovey, Houlton; William L. Pushor, Hartland; Floral Boyd, East Newport; Alice M. Clark, Pittsfield; May E. Fernald, Dixmont; Alice M. Pushor, Pittsfield; Ella Stafford, Harmony; Katie Bridgham, East Corinth; Alice E. Chase and Nettie A. Chase, Canaan; Lizzie E. Fischer, Pittsfield; Ella F. Mayo, Hermon; Gertrude Sawyer, Pittsfield; Abbie W. Sylvester, Etna; and Albert E. Taylor, Delaware.

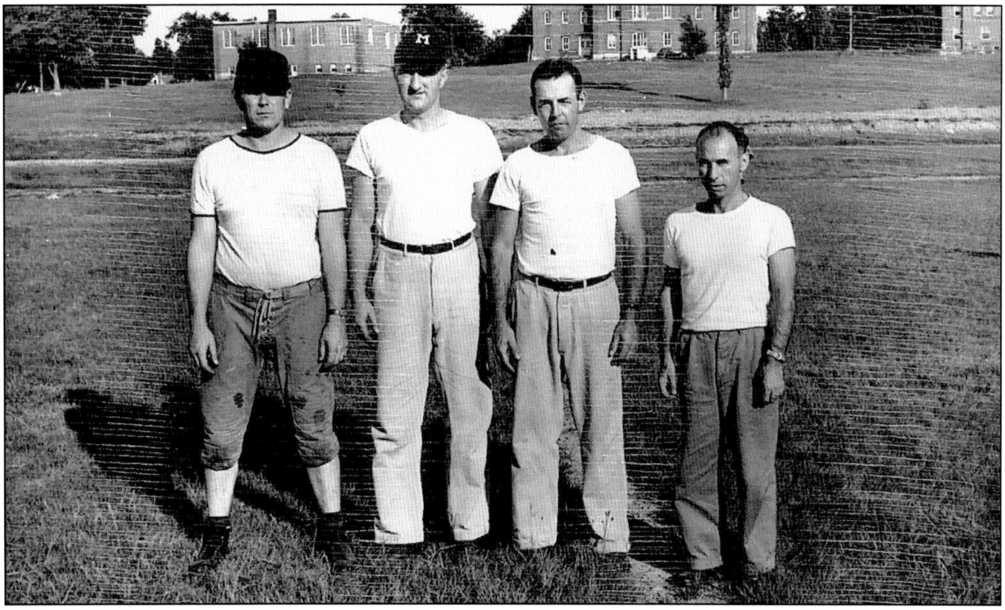

By 1947, the MCI campus had added more buildings, and two members of this still-young coaching staff were on their way to becoming legends at the school. Shown here are, from left to right, as follows: C. Nelson Corey, football coach and math instructor; Lawrence J. Muzrall, assistant football coach and math instructor; Roderic L. Smith, Director of Athletics and biology instructor; and Paul Legge, assistant football coach and science instructor. Smith and Legge were important contributors to Pittsfield athletic programs and MCI for many years after this picture was taken. Both retired from the school. They witnessed many changes on campus during their tenure and into retirement.

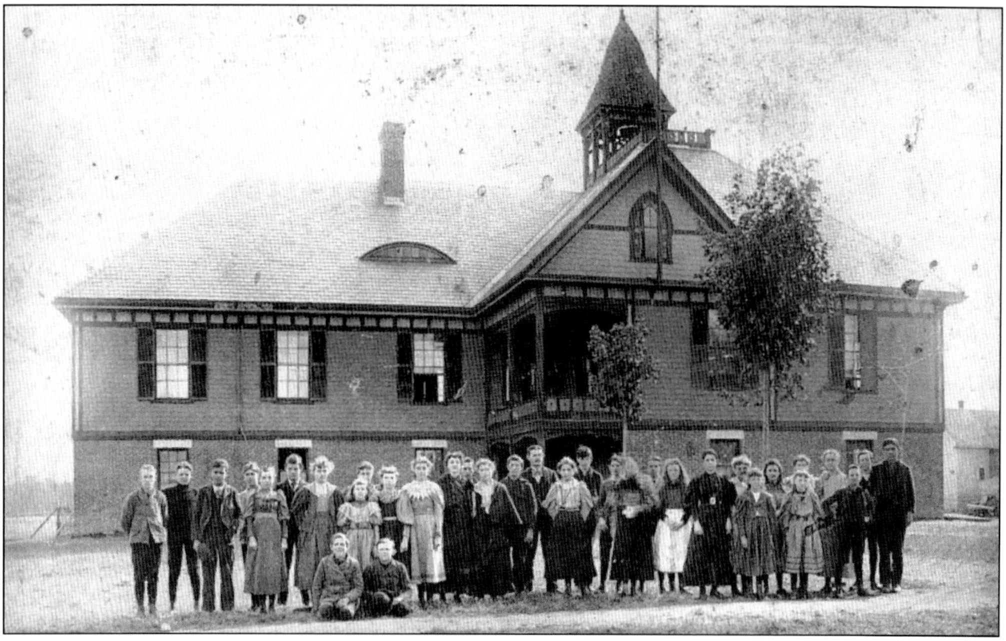

In 1895, the Lancey Street School was a prominent part of the local school system. It disappeared forever in 1967. In the late 1950s, it was still in use as a primary school with grades kindergarten through third, and the school system's hot lunch program was housed on the first floor. Fourth and fifth graders walked to lunch from the Manson Park School, built in 1952, and sixth through eighth graders were bussed to lunch from the Vickery School, which opened in 1958.

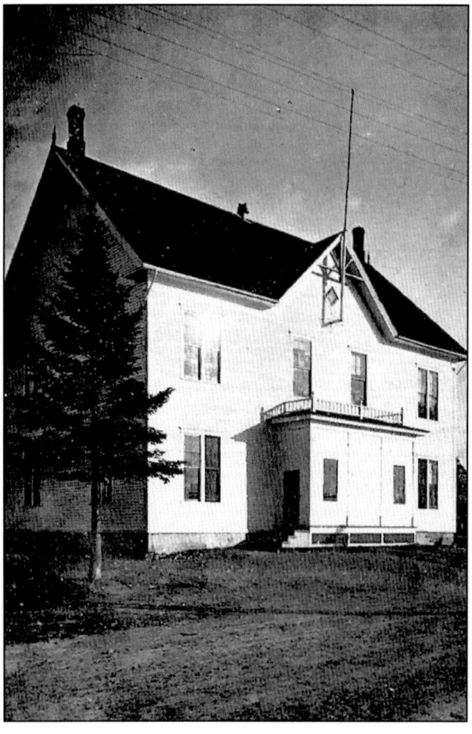

The Riverside Grammar School on North Main Street was abandoned in the 1950s and has since become an apartment house. The building is located near the site of Pittsfield's first school on the ledges on the river.

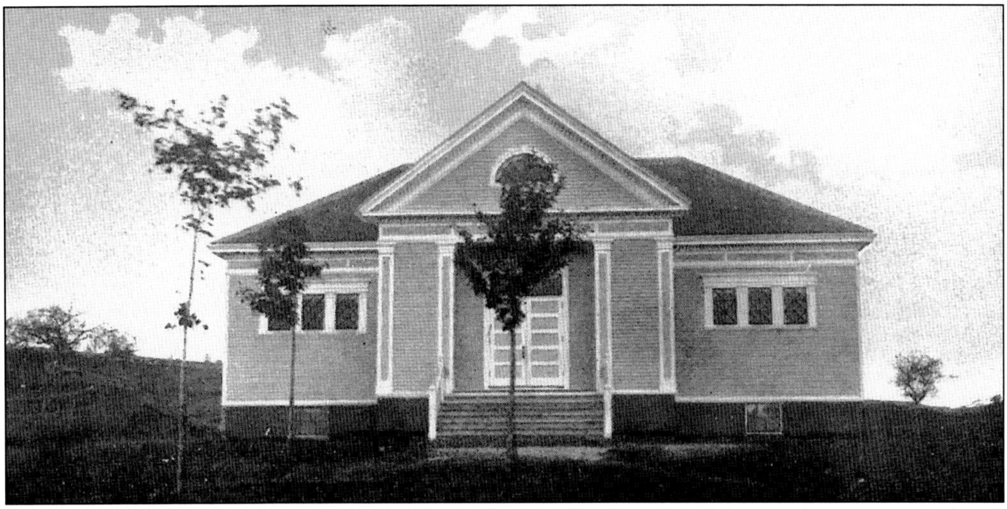

The two-room Hartland Avenue School is still in use by the school district, but not as a school. In the 1950s and early 1960s, it housed kindergarten and first-grade classes, serving as a neighborhood school. When it was abandoned, the Sebasticook Association for Retarded Children took it over for several years, until legislation aimed at providing a public education for developmentally delayed children caused the school district to reacquire it. As special education classes and mainstreaming became the norm in the district, the separate school was no longer needed, and the staff and superintendent of schools for Maine School Administrative District 53 moved in.

The Grammar School is another building that is used differently today. More commonly known as 3 North Lancey, it was renovated and restored in the 1980s to house office space. Used as a primary school in the early 1900s, it was built to consolidate many of the rural one-room schoolhouses in Pittsfield. Its location in this early photograph shows a far different Pittsfield than a photograph from the same viewpoint today might. The Pittsfield Grange Hall is seen to the back, and there are no other buildings, parking lots, or paved roads visible as there might be currently. Like many Pittsfield scenes of the early 1900s, this photograph also shows how Pittsfield got its name in 1824. The landscape here and in much of the village area was nearly void of trees. The town was named for William Pitt of Belgrade, who was a large landowner in town at the time. Before that time, the town had been called Sebasticook, Plymouth Gore, and Warsaw before taking Pitt's name.

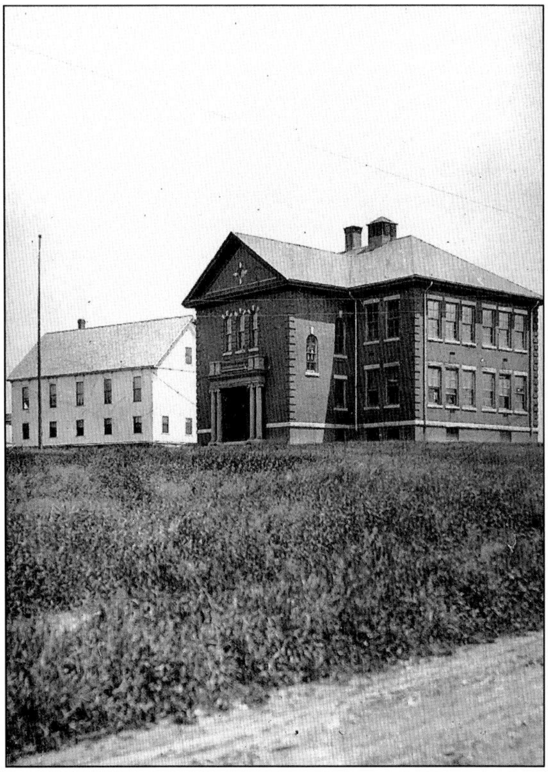

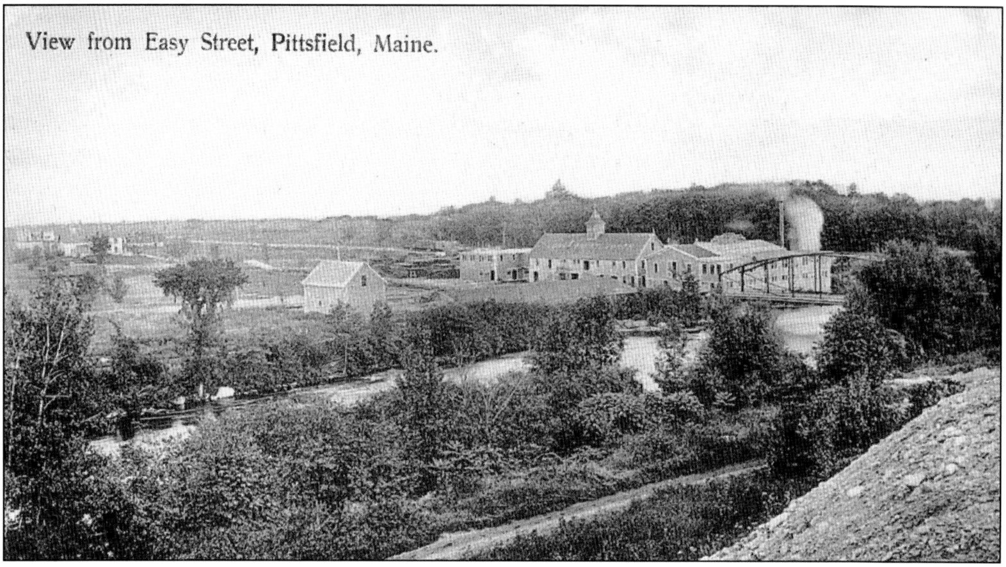

Another telling photograph shows the view behind the Grange Hall and Grammar School as seen from the end of Easy Street. Today, that area would be heavily wooded, and the view of the river or Hunnewell Avenue would be obscured. The gravel road in the foreground is now part of the parking lot at EST (Edwards Systems Technology), and the buildings on the east shore of the river and along Hunnewell Avenue have been replaced by Cianbro Corporation.

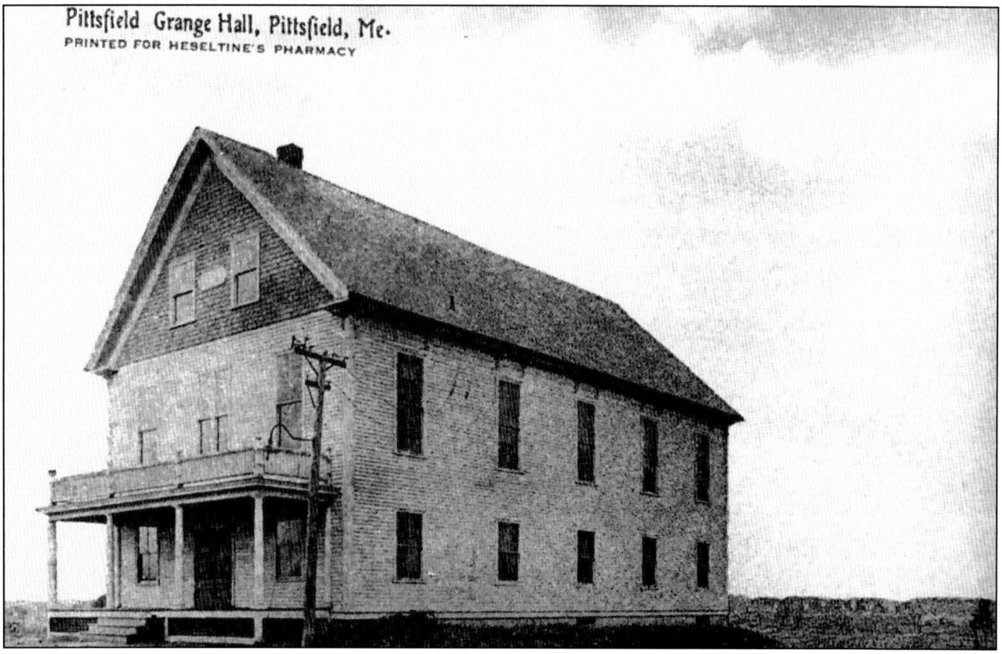

The Pittsfield Grange Hall must have been as impressive, before the 20th century, as its organization was revered. The building stood on one of the highest points over the river in the village, with little to obstruct the view in all directions. Other smaller communities in the valley were able to maintain longer ties to a farming lifestyle and the organization that championed it, but Pittsfield's grange declined in the 1960s, and the building was given up and demolished in the 1970s.

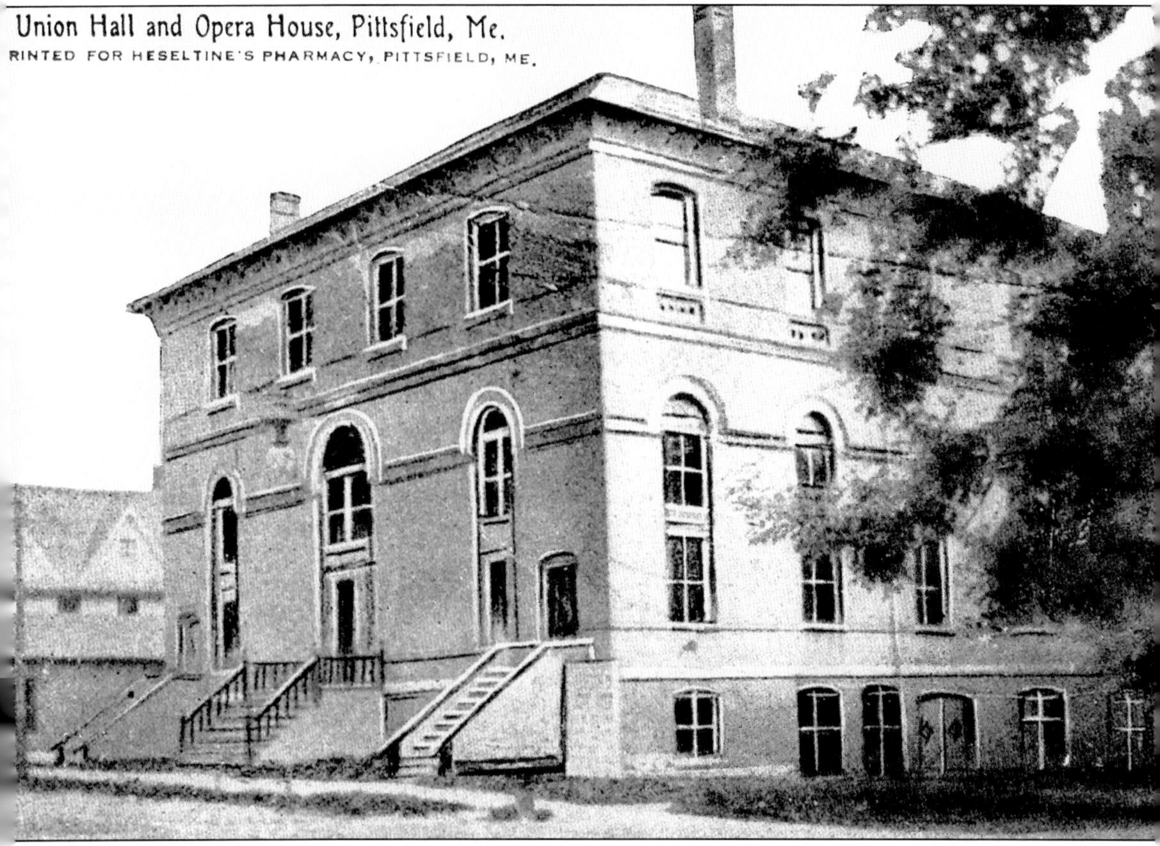

The location of Pittsfield's government offices has not changed, although the building is not the same. In 1882, shares were sold to enable the town to build a hall, initially to be known as Engine Hall, that would house a fire station, meeting hall, and opera house. By the time the building was ready to open in 1883, it was known as Union Hall, and it was called that until it was partially demolished in the 1970s. A grant project from the federal government enabled the town to dismantle the aging structure and reconstruct it as a fire station. A subsequent grant project provided funds to add new municipal offices and meeting rooms to the east side of the building and connect them with narrow halls through the old foundation and walls. Union Hall was home to the town office, the fire and police departments, the local fraternal organizations, and countless events for nearly 90 years. The granite arches from the original building now grace the lawn at the Pittsfield Fraternal Hall on Hamilton Drive.

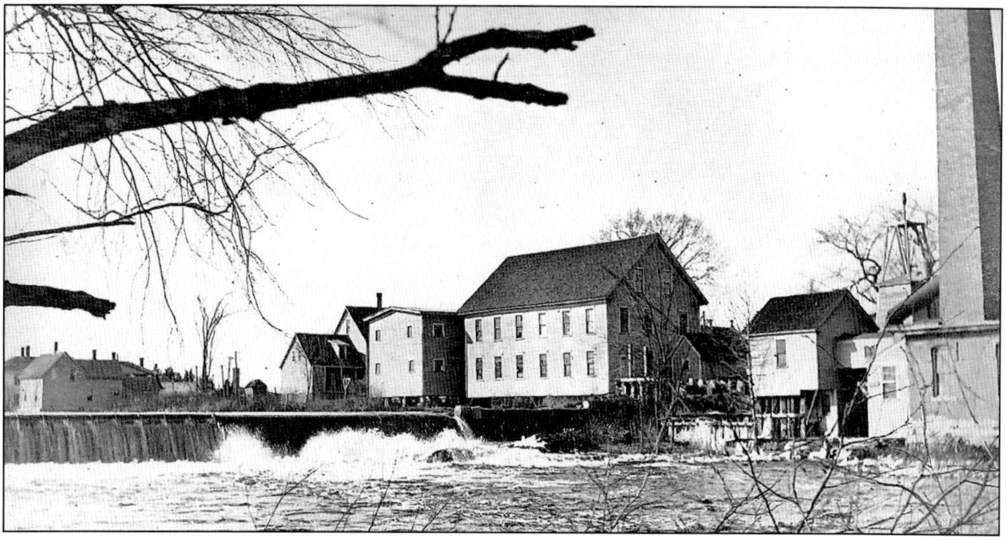

A log dam on the Sebasticook River was removed in 1867 and replaced with a granite and concrete structure around the same time the Pioneer Mill construction began just below it. The Pioneer Dam has seen many uses and owners. It is currently owned by the town and leased by a private company that continues to generate electricity. The buildings at the far side of the dam have been gone for many years.

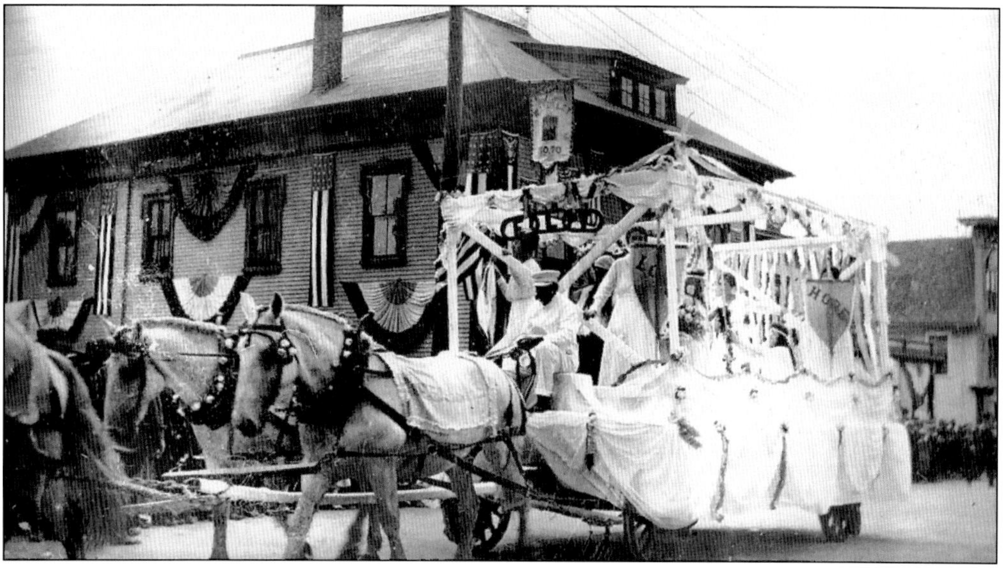

In 1919, the Waverly Rebekahs had one of many floats in the centennial parade. The entire town was decked out in patriotic bunting and flags. The grand parade began at MCI, marching to Main Street, Waverly Avenue, Hartland Avenue, Park Street, and back to Main Street to the library, where a dedication ceremony was held for a memorial tablet in honor of the veterans of World War I. Afternoon events included games, activities, and a longtime Pittsfield favorite: harness racing. Col. Walter G. Morrill brought harness racing to town after his famed Civil War service with the 20th Maine Regiment and the well-known Gen. Joshua Chamberlain. Morrill operated a livery stable for the Lancey House and also ran his own Union Park race track at the present location of the municipal airport. He was known throughout the state for nearly 50 years for his horse racing knowledge.

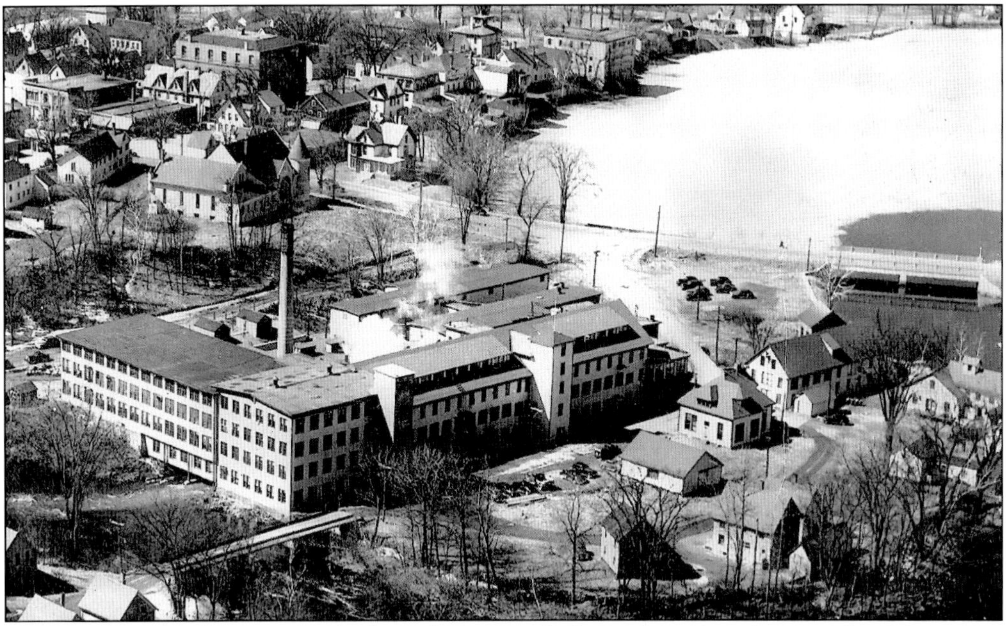

The textile industry in Maine had not begun its decline when this photograph of American Woolen's Pioneer Mill at Pittsfield was taken in 1935. Even the flood of 1936 (below) failed to diminish the mill's strong hold on the economy in the area. In the 1940s, the Waverly Mill upstream closed, and Pittsfield businessmen were searching for a new occupant. The solution came in the form of shoe manufacturing. The shoe manufacturers remain at the site today in a more modern facility. By 1953, the Pioneer Mill also closed, and Pittsfield again was searching for a new occupant. By 1956, the Edwards Company (now Edwards Systems Technology), a manufacturer of alarms and signaling devices, had taken up residence in the mill and was on its way to becoming a major Pittsfield employer. It remains at the location; many renovations and transformations have made it into a modern electronics firm.

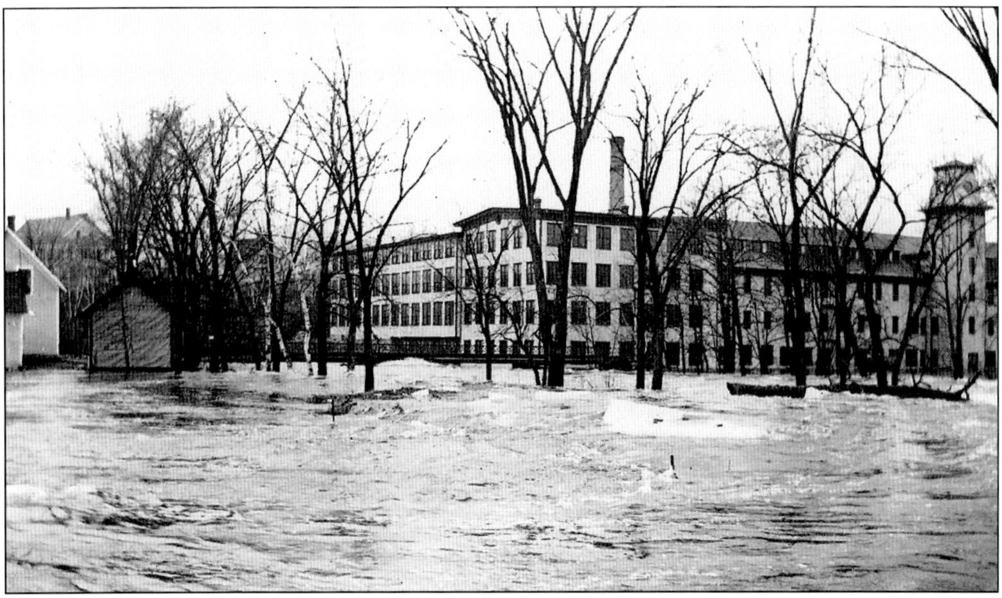

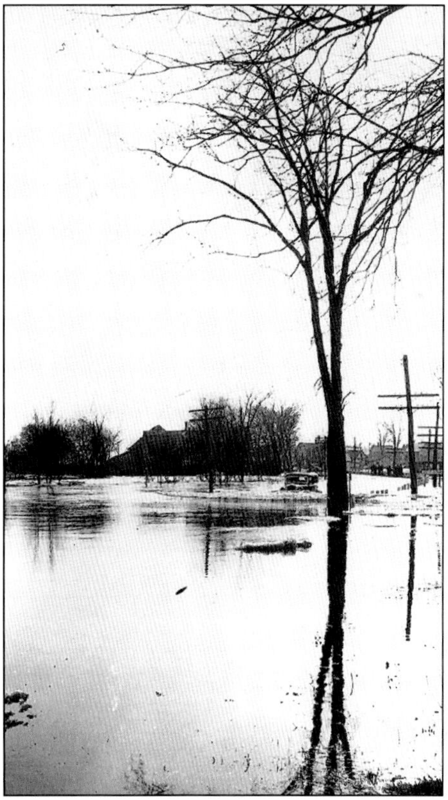

The flood of 1936 was devastating to many along the Sebasticook. And, like any natural disaster, it posed a challenge to many along its banks. Pittsfield resident and amateur photographer Merton Withee captured this intrepid traveler as he attempted to make his way through the flood waters. The exact location of the scene is difficult to determine.

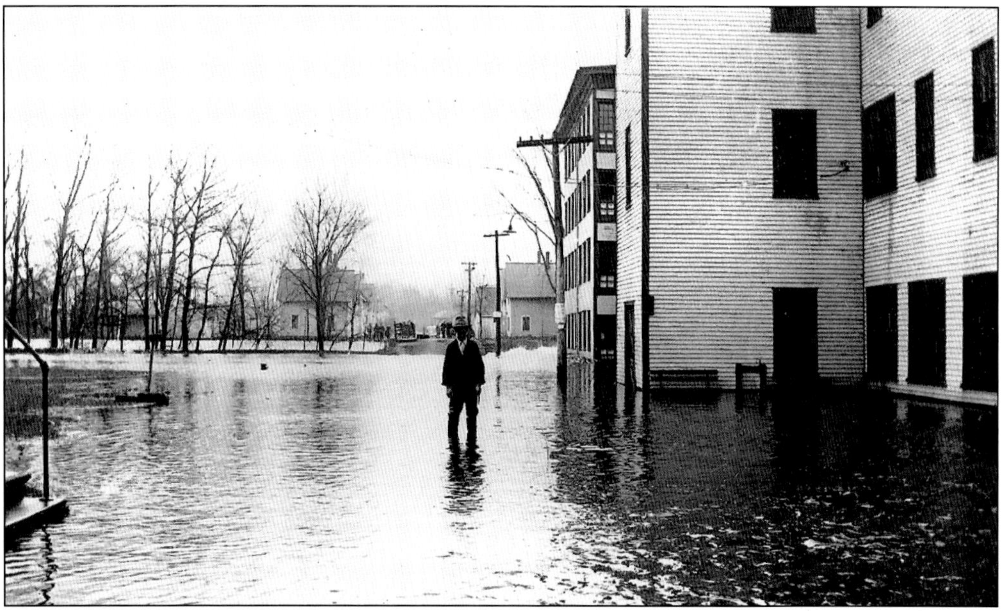

The river flooded the woolen mills on both sides of the river off Main Street and Detroit Avenue and washed out the bridge that originally connected the mill to Mill Street, pictured at the back of this photograph.

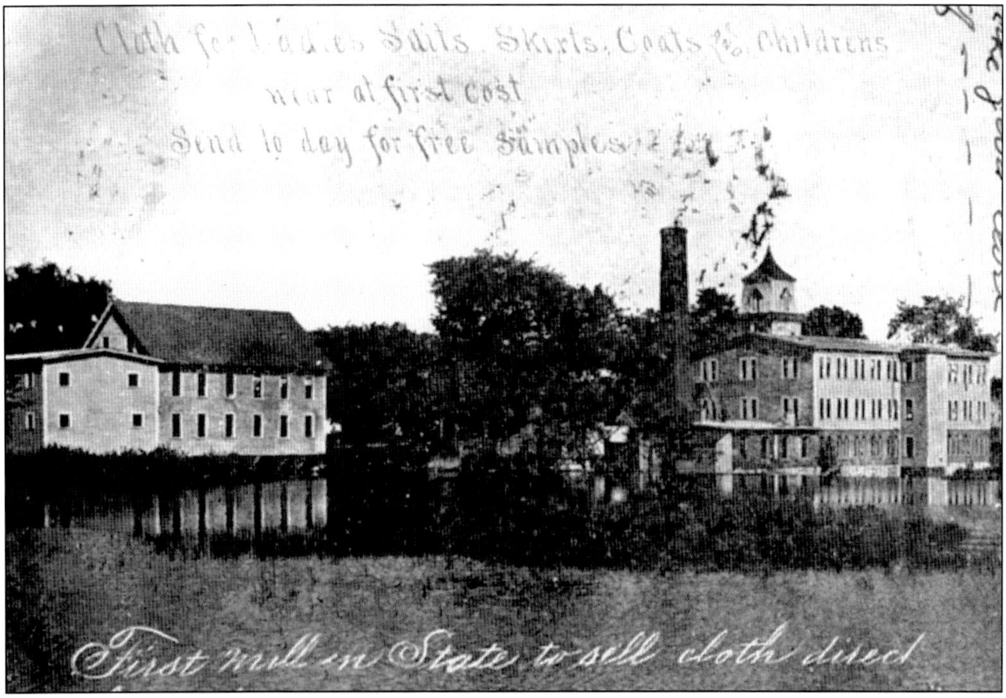

In 1906, Riverside Woolen Company promoted itself as the only woolen mill selling "cloth direct from loom to wearer." The mill was located on the opposite side of the Sebasticook River from the American Woolen Mill. The mill was commonly known as the "Shoddy Mill" in later years. After it was abandoned, it was used for many years as a warehouse. It burned in 1997.

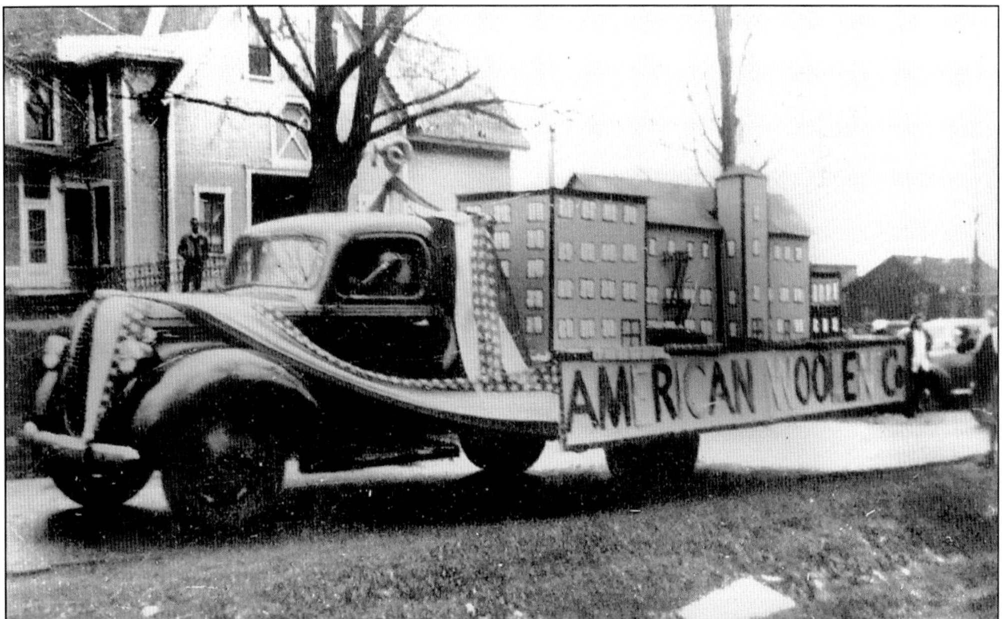

In 1946, American Woolen demonstrated its prominence and participation in the community with this float in the Armistice Day parade.

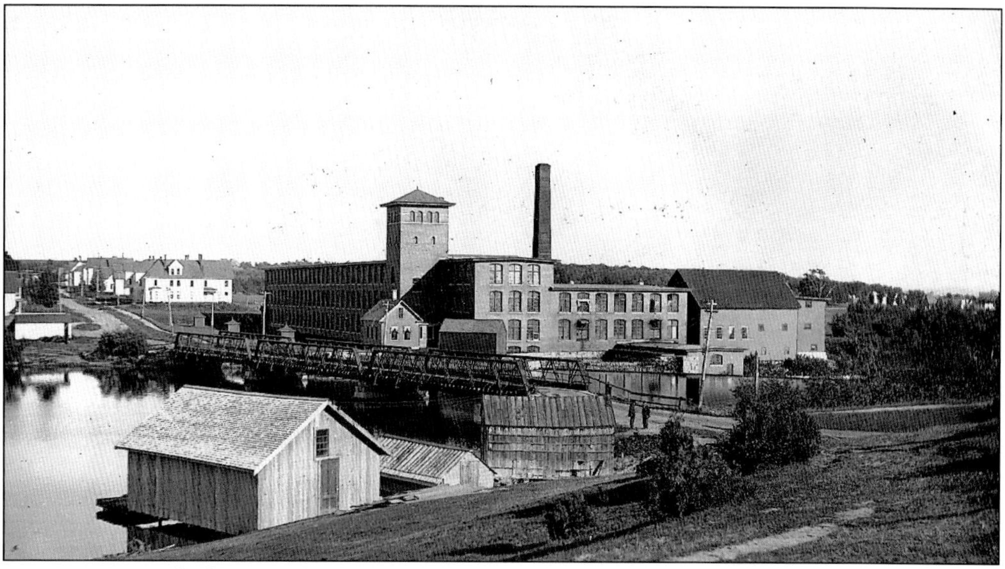

In 1893, a special edition of the *Pittsfield Advertiser* marked the opening of a new era of Pittsfield development, including the opening of the new Waverly Mill upriver from the village and other manufacturing facilities. That year saw the addition of the new mill, more than 31 new homes, a large storehouse at Bryant and Osborne Woodworking on Hunnewell Avenue, two new stores on the corner of Hunnewell and Main, a boarding home for Waverly employees, and a proposal for a Pittsfield waterworks. The Waverly Mill closed in 1929 and did not reopen until 1943, when the first of several successive shoe manufacturers came to town. Today, it is part of the successful San Antonio Shoe Company complex.

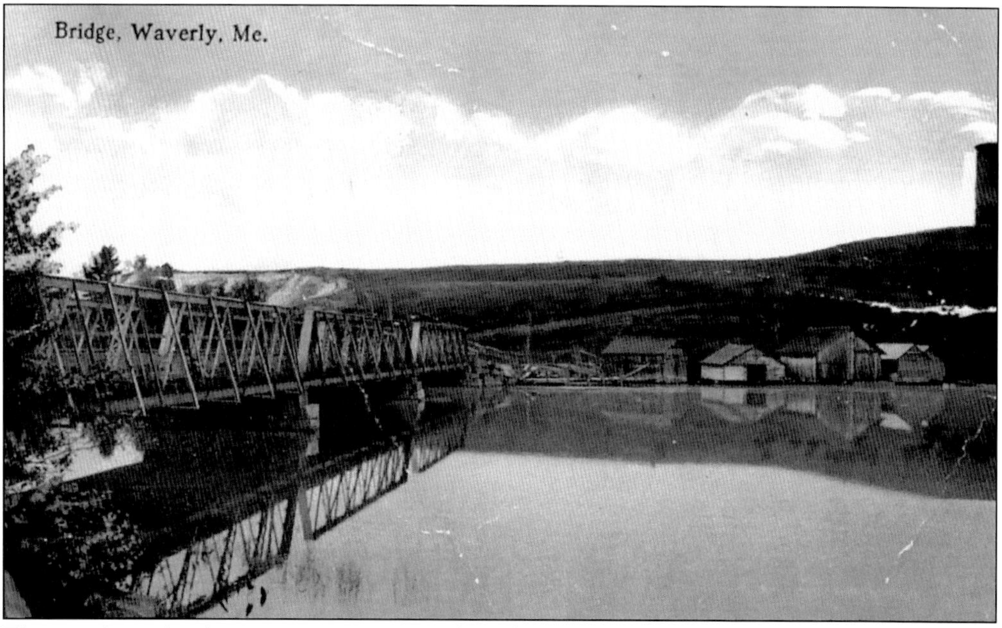

The standpipe for the water company stood on the Pinnacle for nearly 100 years before it was taken down for safety reasons in the 1980s. The boathouses on the river at the Waverly Bridge site were presumably used for river traffic headed upriver to Ringwood Park, Hartland, and Palmyra.

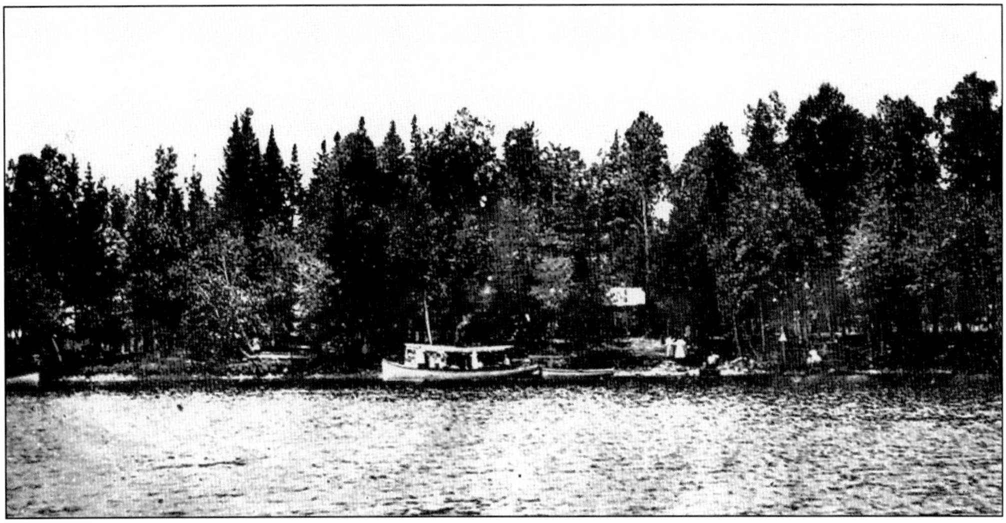

In 1903, Captain Parsons, who operated the small steamer *Winthrop* on the upper Sebasticook River, announced plans to expand facilities at Ringwood Park. The park, located on Douglas Pond in Palmyra, was a popular site for boating parties and picnics. Parsons announced plans to construct a dancing pavilion at the park. The new pavilion opened in July of that year. Parsons used his steamer to make daily trips to Hartland and half-hourly trips to and from the landing at Waverly. The pavilion was open afternoons and evenings, with 50 to 100 couples attending at any given time.

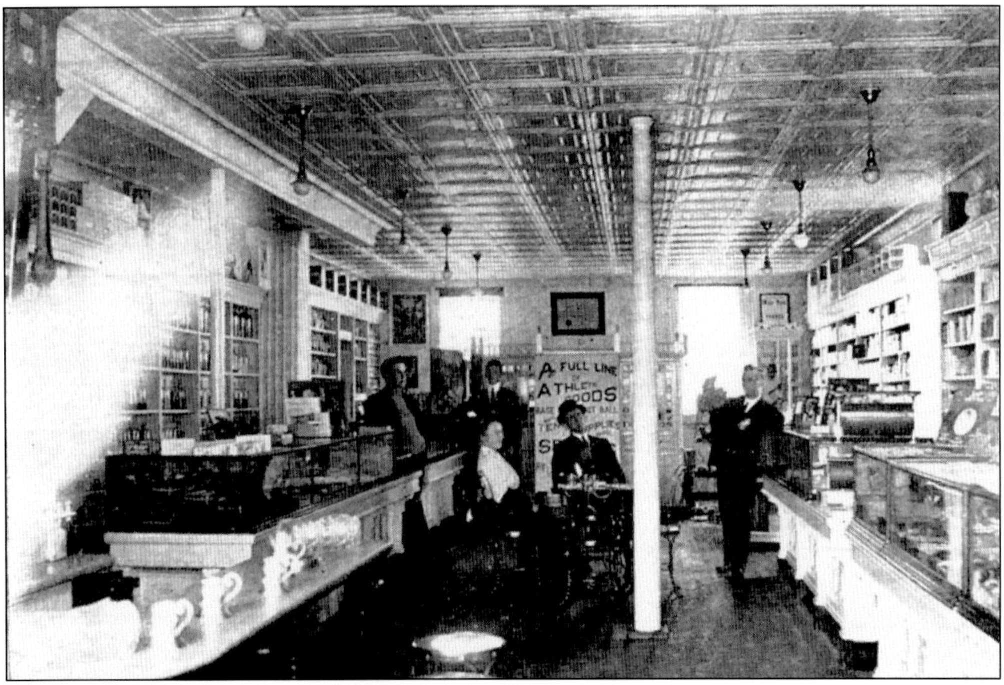

The Pittsfield Drugstore, owned and operated by H. H. Nutter on Main Street, was not just a locally popular spot in the early 1900s. Nutter saw to it that his store was known far and wide with the production of this postcard for circulation outside the region.

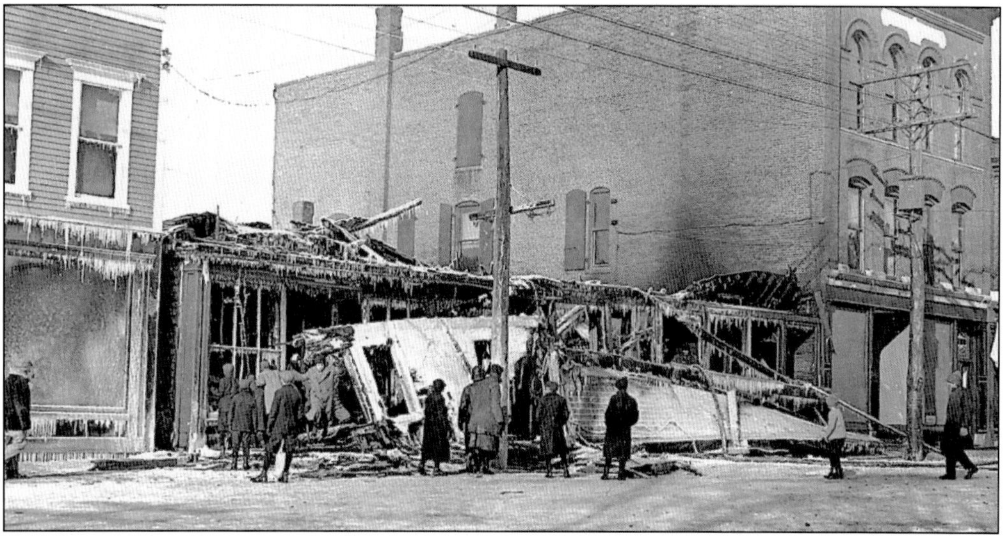

A fire in 1911 took out a business block on the west side of Main Street, in the present location of the Pittsfield Community Theater. A postcard photograph of the scene at the time relayed that "Tom Getchell's store was not burned any. A gallon of paint will make it as good as new. The others show for themselves." The card was signed by "Alf" and mailed to Independence, Kansas.

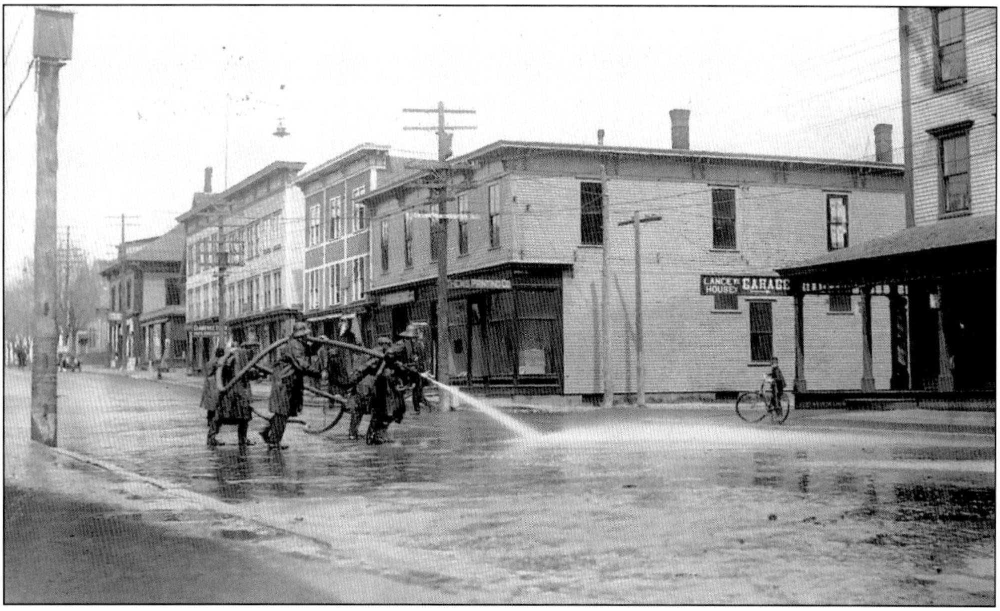

The east side of Main Street was undamaged and apparently prospering when fire crews cleaned up after yet another fire, possibly in 1911. The Lancey House was open again, and local businesses were reaping the benefits of a good economy.

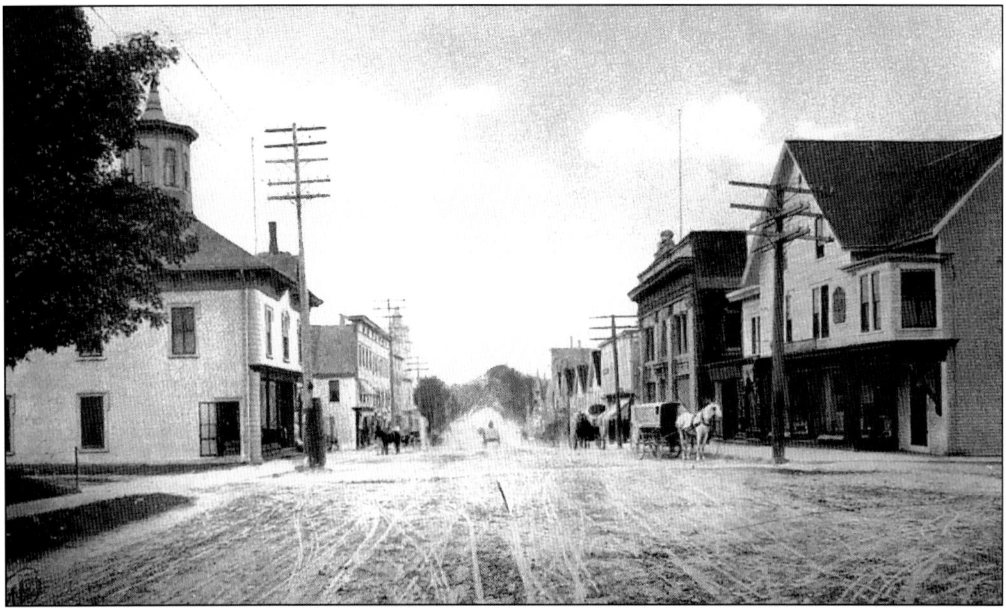

Main Street c. 1904 bears little resemblance to Main Street in 2004. The east side of the business district disappeared due to fires and the economy. Pittsfield's federal Urban Development Action Grant of the 1970s took what little was left of the east side of Main Street. Paving was not a necessity when horses ruled the road.

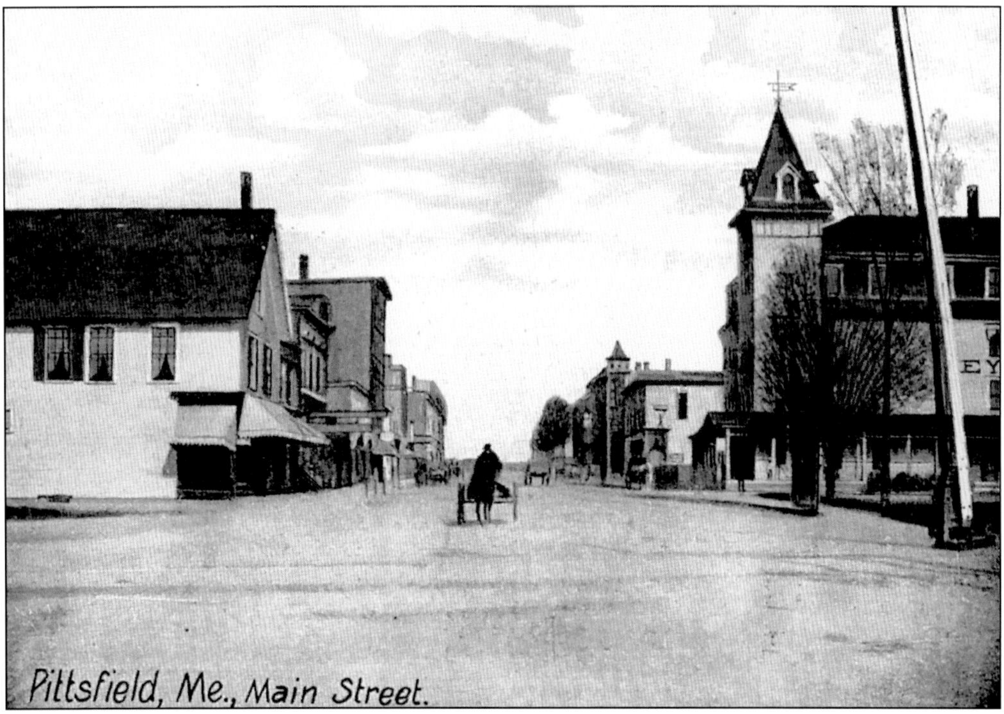

Another shot of Main Street, looking north, shows more of what is not there anymore. This scene was captured on a souvenir plate for Pittsfield's celebration of its "sesqui-triquarter centennial," a 175th birthday, in 1994.

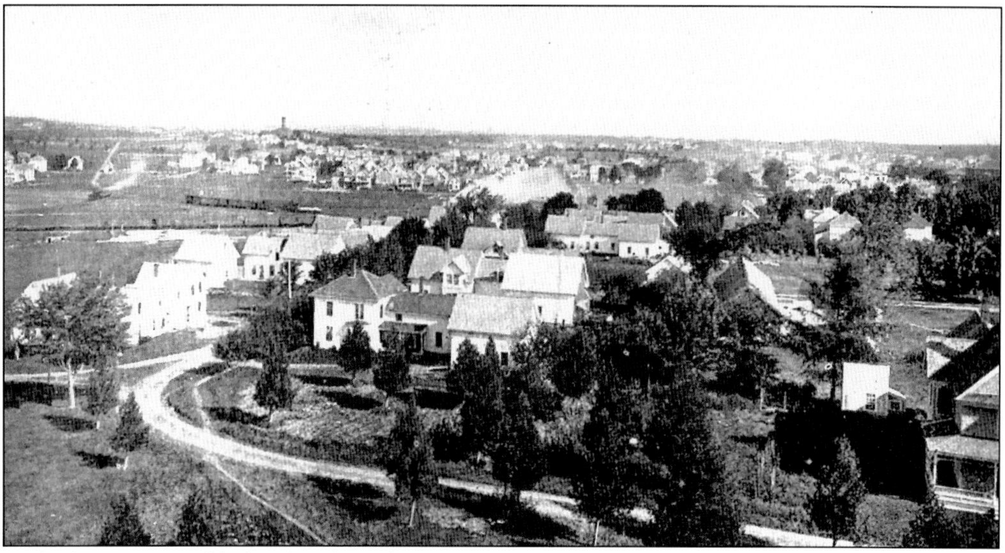

A "bird's-eye view," likely taken from the MCI bell tower in the early 1900s and looking northwest, shows just how much Pittsfield grew in its first century and how much has changed since.

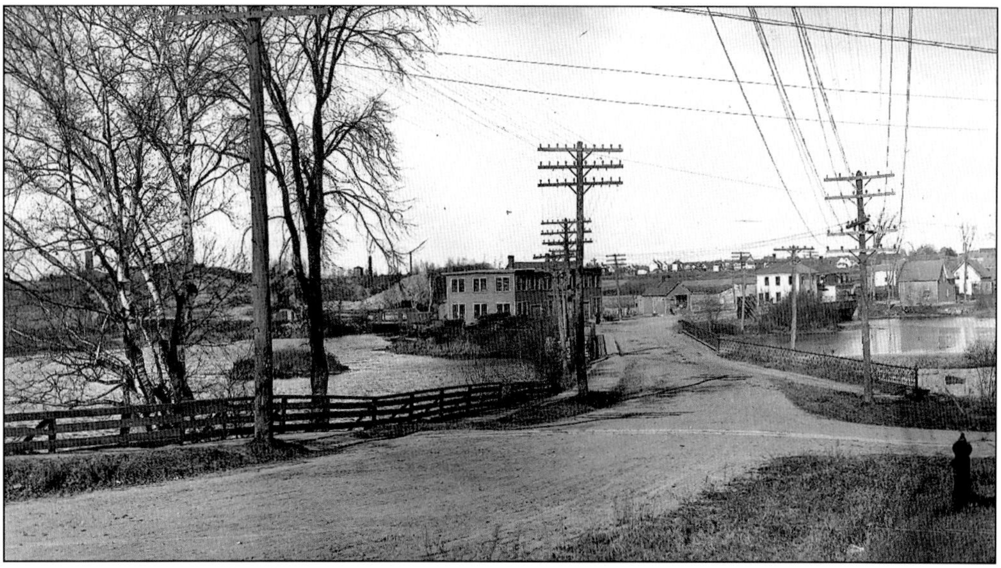

North Main Street still takes the same curve off the hill as it crosses the river, but that is about the only similarity between 1904 and 2004 in this scene.

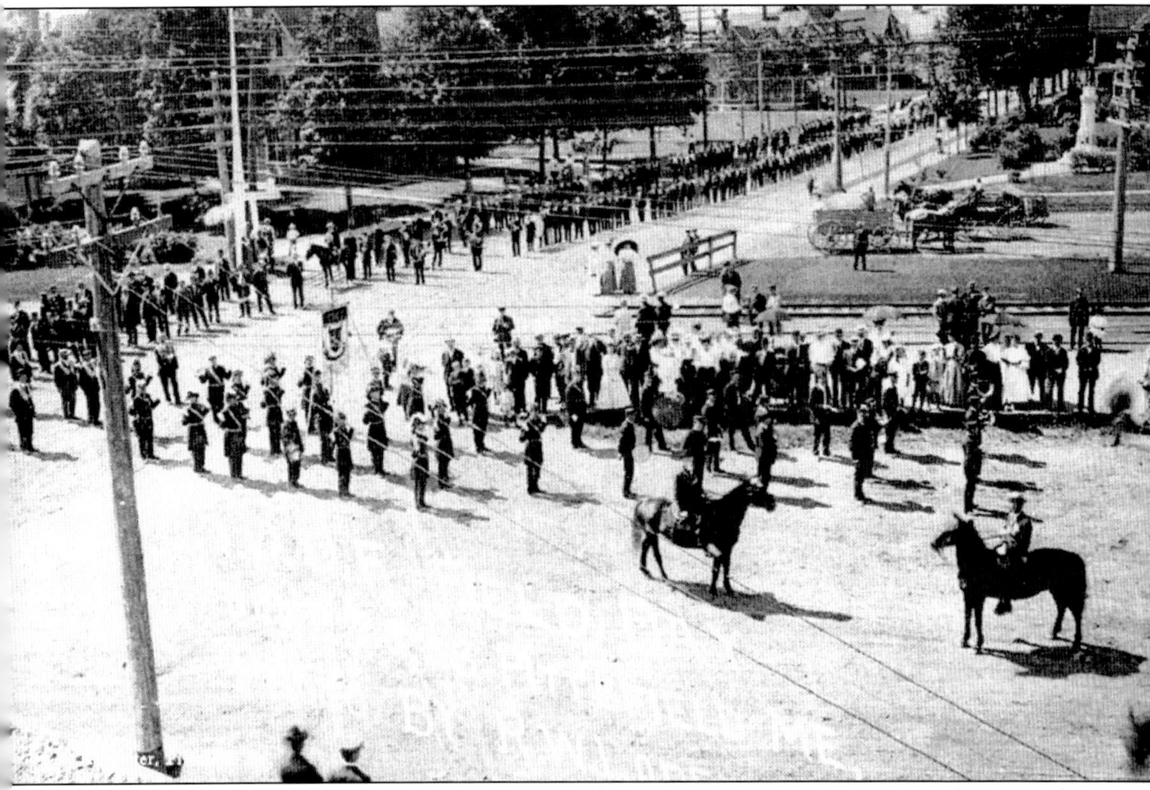

Pittsfield residents were loyal participants in their organizations, activities, politics, and patriotic events throughout the 1900s. This June 1908 field day event, sponsored by the International Order of Odd Fellows, demonstrates the level of participation in fraternal organizations, not only early in the century but also in the following years.

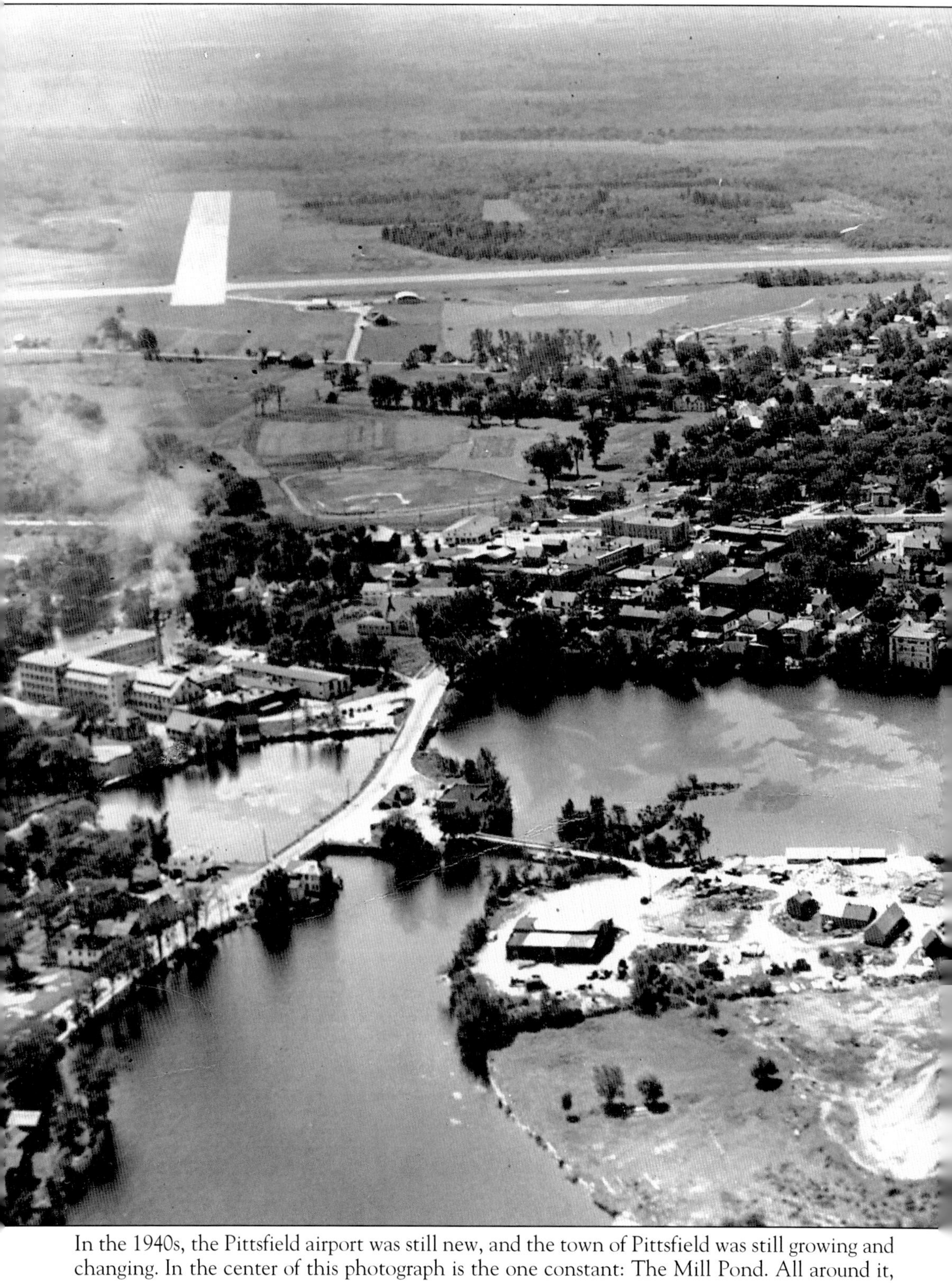

In the 1940s, the Pittsfield airport was still new, and the town of Pittsfield was still growing and changing. In the center of this photograph is the one constant: The Mill Pond. All around it,

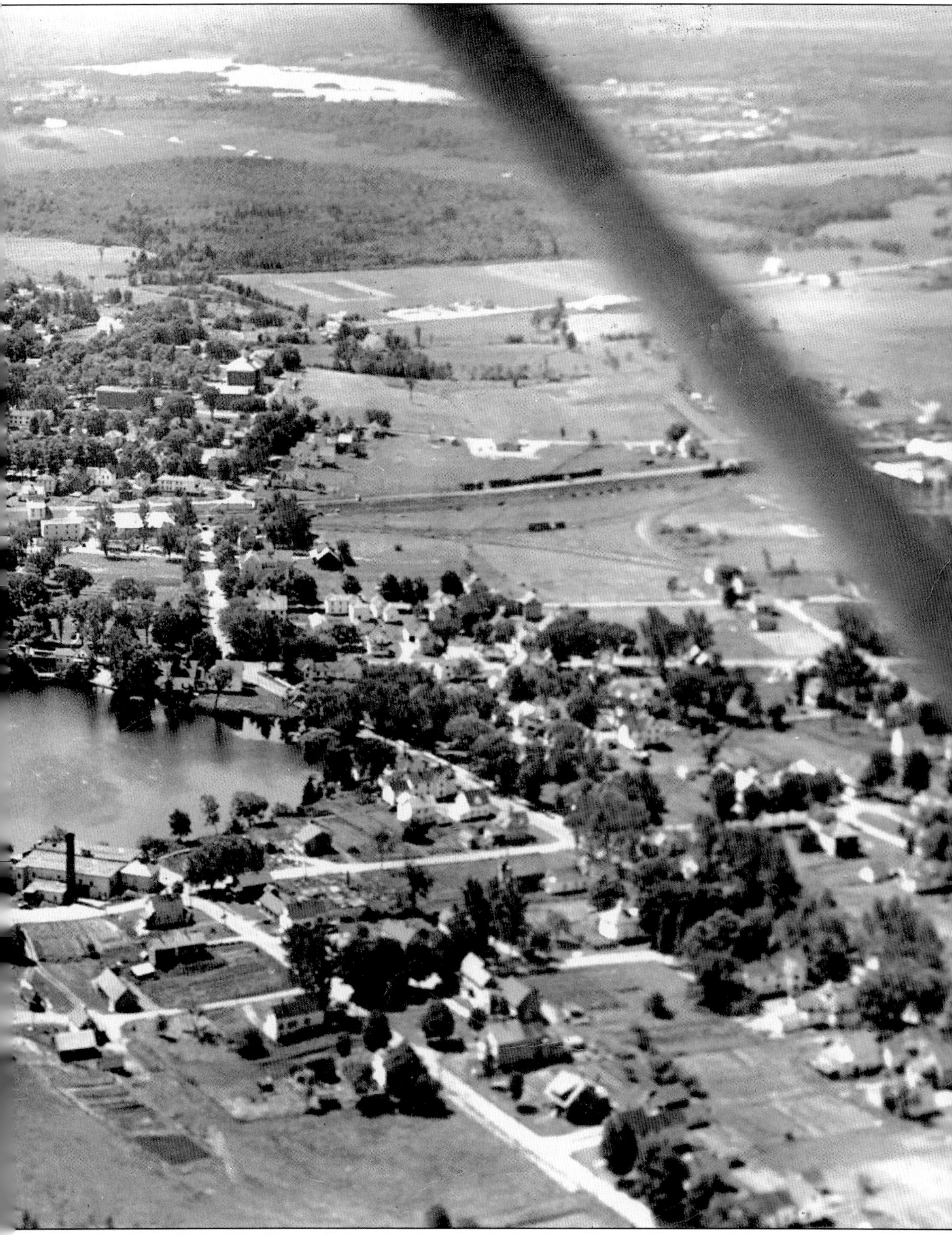

businesses and lifestyles have changed.

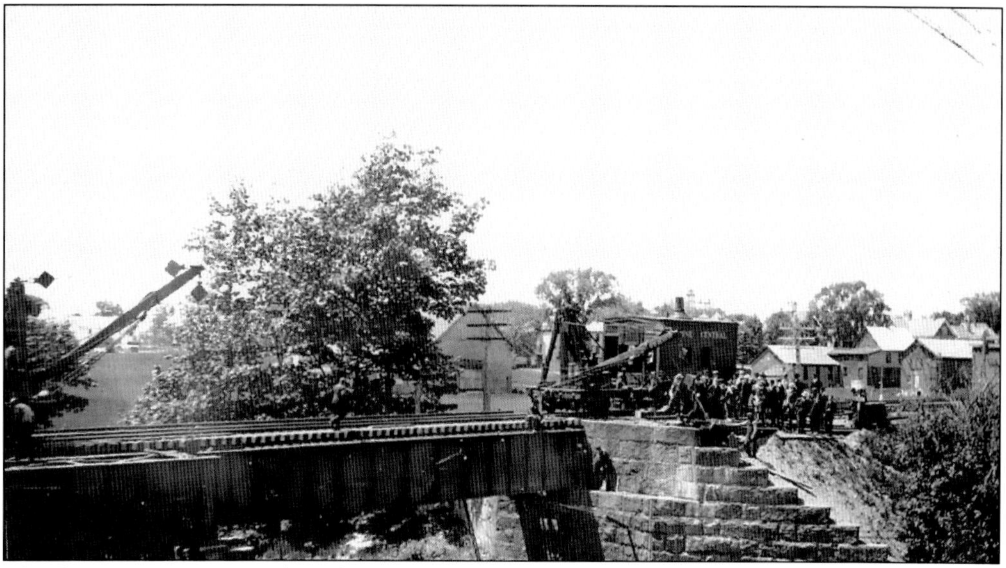

The former Maine Central Railroad has a long history in Pittsfield. Coming to town in the 1880s, the dual tracks still carry freight across Maine. Passenger service ended in the early 1960s, but the first half of the century saw a steady passenger business, bringing tourists, summer residents, salesmen, homebound and war-bound servicemen, and shoppers headed to Bangor or Waterville. The scene above is difficult to interpret because the date is unknown; whether it was trestle repair or replacement or cleanup from a spill or wreck, it was a popular attraction at the time.

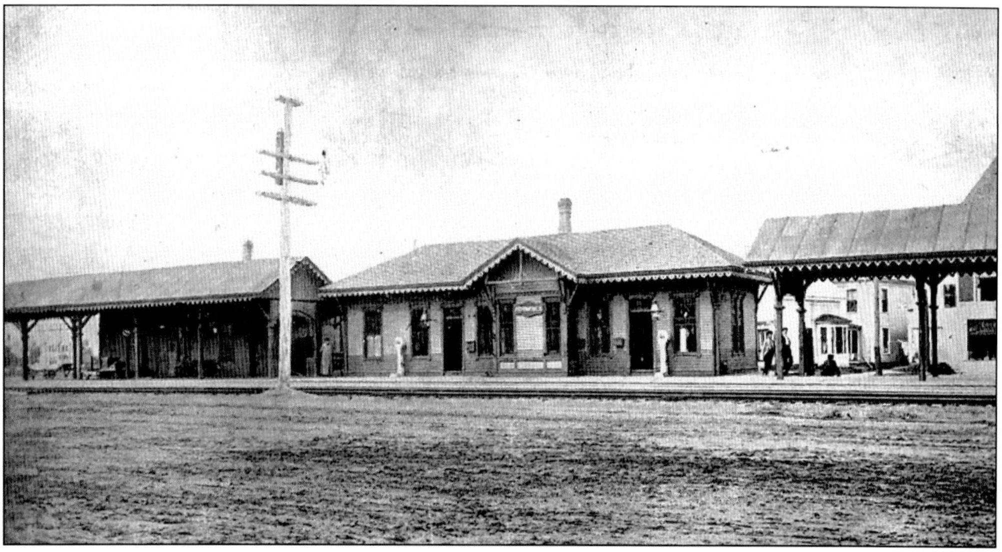

The Pittsfield depot is similar in design to most depots in rural Maine in the 1900s. When the canopies failed, they were removed, but the concrete and paved platforms remained long after passenger service ended. Today, however, only the main depot remains. It is now the Depot House Museum, owned by the town but operated and occupied by the Pittsfield Historical Society. Saving the depot was a community improvement project of the former Athenaeum Club, a young women's organization of the 1970s. In 1980, the depot was named to the National Register of Historic Places.

The Nelson family of West Pittsfield was typical of many rural families in the late 1800s. Augustus F. (father) and May (mother) Nelson dressed the small family in their Sunday best for a formal mid-1880s portrait. Augustus F. is holding Augustus S., the youngest member of the family at the time. The girls include Charlotte in front, Eva in the middle, and Etta May, the oldest, on the right. Etta became one of Pittsfield's earliest "liberated" women, although she may not have known or appreciated it.

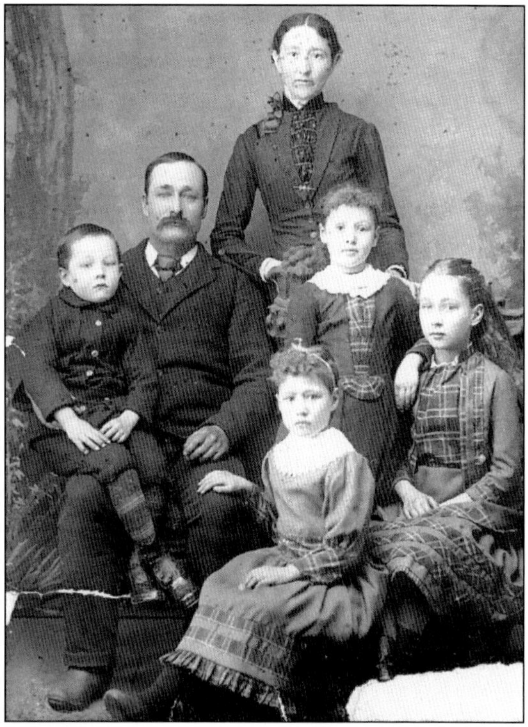

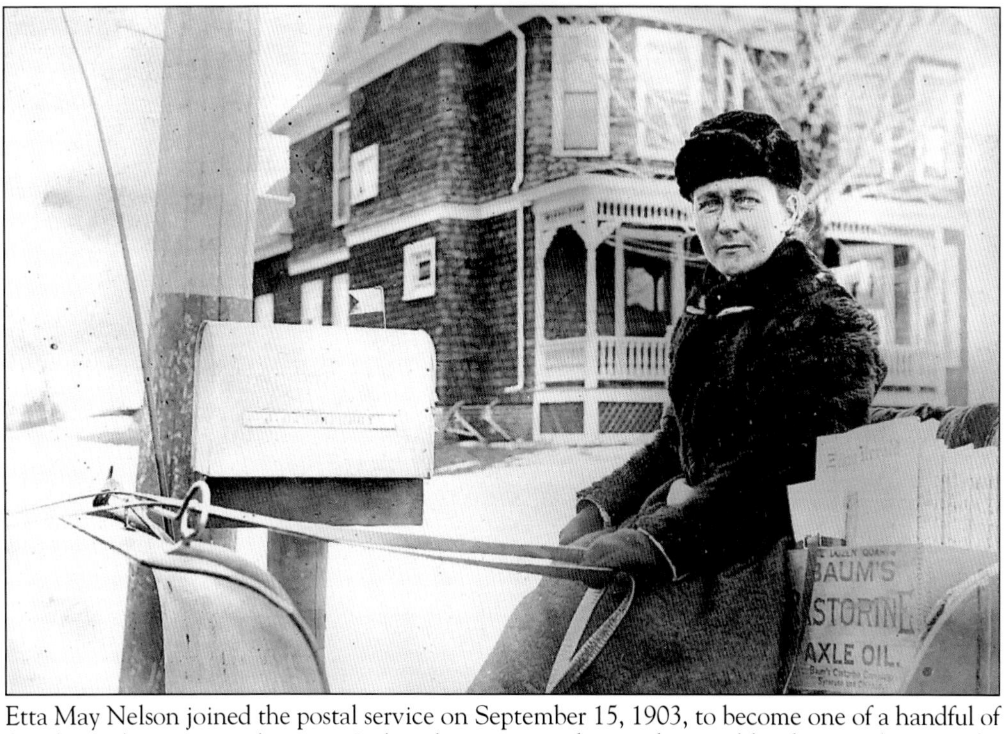

Etta May Nelson joined the postal service on September 15, 1903, to become one of a handful of female mail carriers in the state. In her short service she was honored by the postal service for never missing a day on her 17-mile delivery route. She completed her route by horse and buggy during three seasons and by sleigh in the winter. She kept the position until her marriage in 1906.

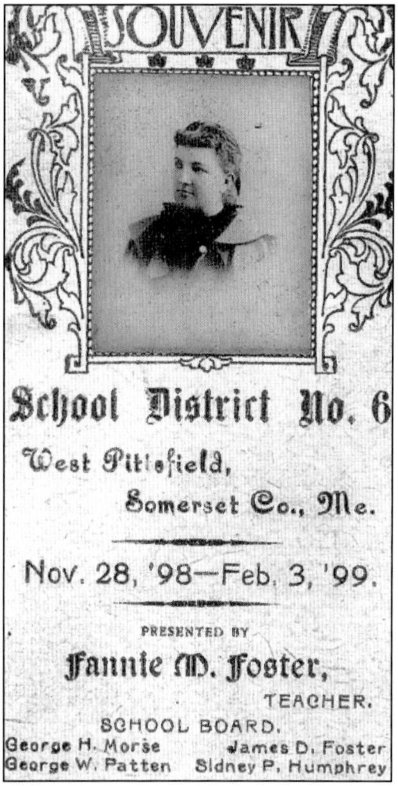

Before 1900, there were many one-room schools throughout Pittsfield, including one in West Pittsfield in School District No. 6. These two-card souvenirs were provided to the children as mementos of their attendance at specific sessions. (The second card listed the students in the session.) In this case, several of the Nelsons, as well as neighbors whose descendants still live in the area, attended school from November 28, 1898, to February 3, 1899, with Fannie M. Foster as their teacher.

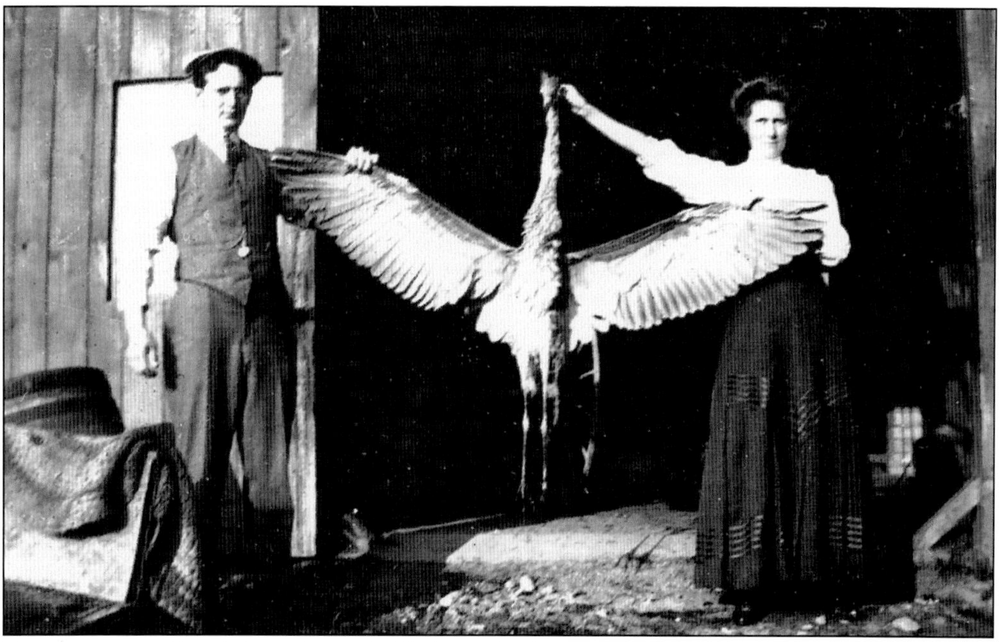

Hunting in rural Pittsfield in the early 1900s was both a necessity and a pastime, as is obvious from this photograph of George and Gwendolyn Nelson displaying a bird that he shot. Perhaps we have scenes such as this to thank for the many hunting laws enacted here and across the nation.

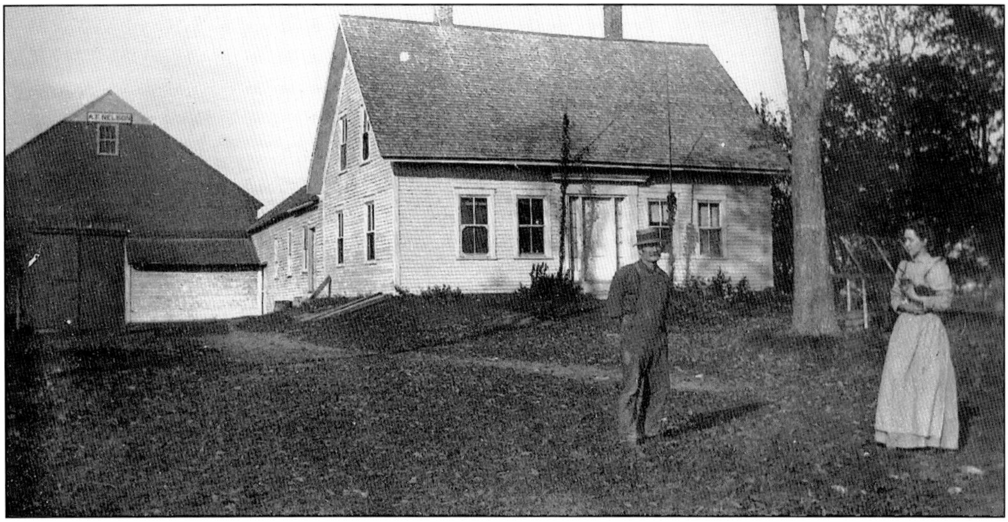

The Augustus F. Nelson family resided for many years on an old farm typical of the time period. It was off of a now-abandoned road off of the Higgins Road at the eastern edge of the Canaan bog. "Gus" Nelson is seen here with his eldest daughter, Etta, and a family cat.

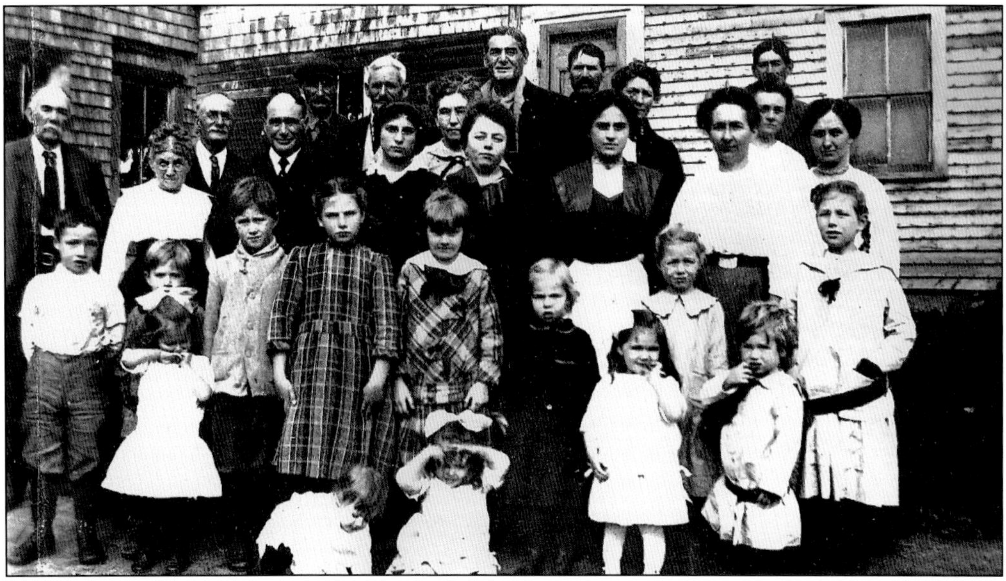

In 1916, the Nelson farm was the site of a family reunion, a gathering of Gus's brothers, children, and their families. The gathering included Gus's father, Sylvester, and his brothers, Fred, Frank, Van, and Ernest. Also part of this picture are Etta Nelson, second from the right in the white blouse, and her children, Florence, Marion, Stella, and Clement, in front. To Etta's right is Violet Nelson. Etta's husband, Aaron Libby, is in the back on the far right. Many of the descendants of the Nelson family still reside in the central Maine area. The format of the photograph and a handwritten identification to the side (not shown) indicates that the photograph may have been taken by a distant cousin of the Nelsons, Alice A. Manter of Oakland, a well-known and accomplished postcard photographer, artist, and music teacher of the time.

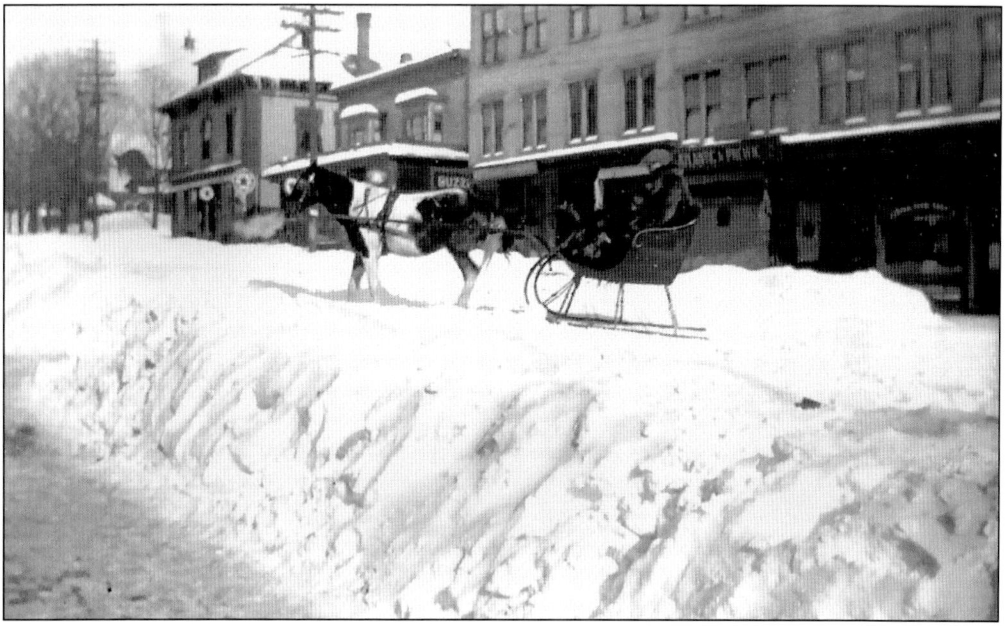

Traveling by sleigh was a necessity until cars dominated the streets. Rather than being plowed, streets and roads were routinely rolled in winter to allow the horses and runners better footing. Problems developed as spring approached and the snow softened. Travelers were often several feet above the actual roadbed or the sidewalks in the village, as this scene from Main Street shows.

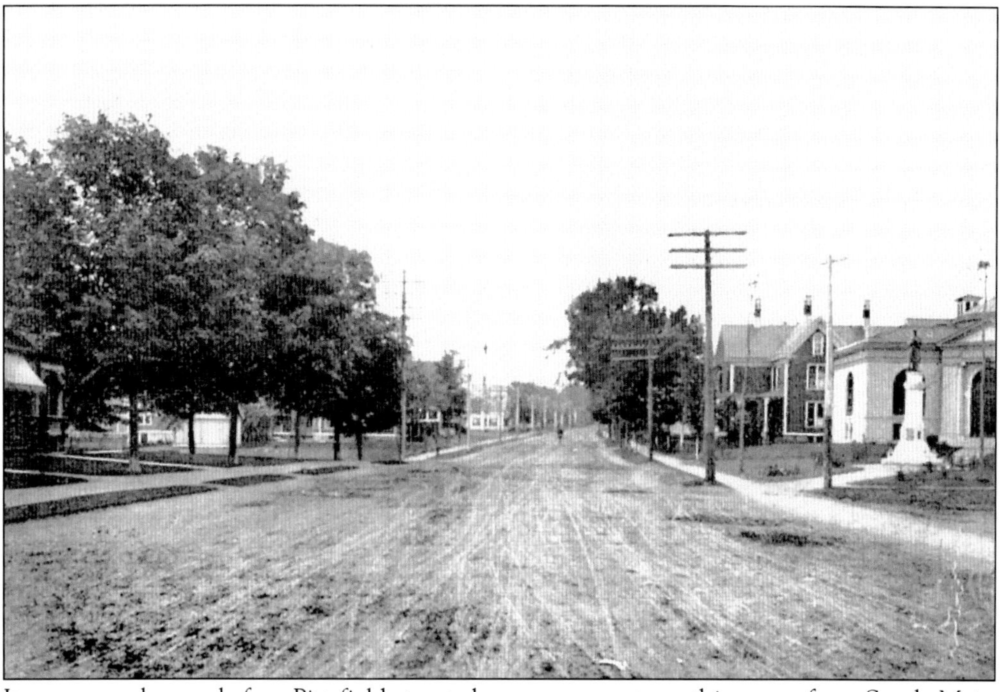

It was several years before Pittsfield streets knew pavement, as this scene from South Main Street in 1912 shows. The Pittsfield Public Library, a typical Carnegie library (shown to the right), was built and dedicated in 1904.

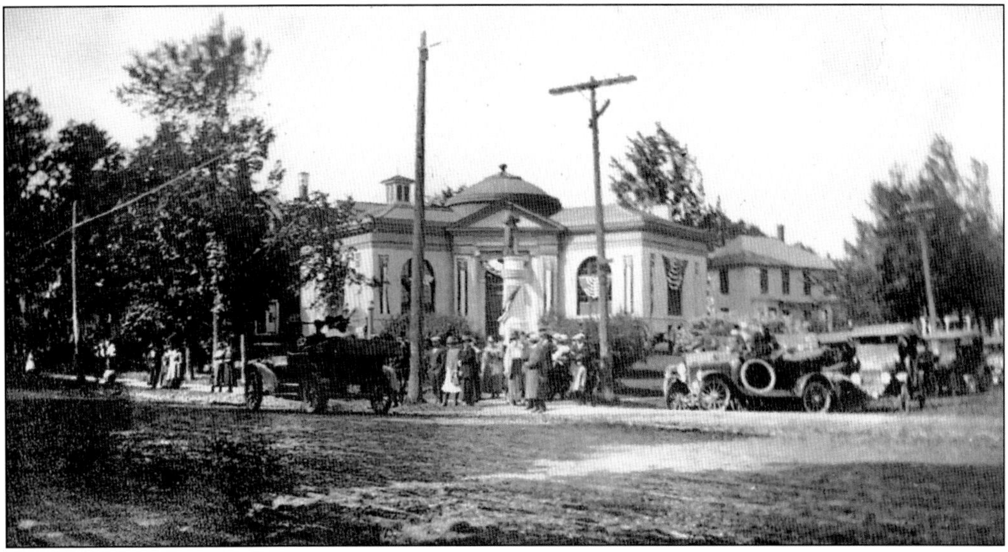

During the 1919 centennial celebration, the parade concluded at the Pittsfield Public Library with the dedication of a memorial tablet to the people who served in World War I. In 1983, the Pittsfield Public Library was named to the National Register of Historic Places. The basic structure has changed very little since 1904, with the exception of handicapped access that has been added to the rear. In conjunction with its 100th anniversary, the library has begun fund-raising and planning for a new addition on Library Street, shown to the right.

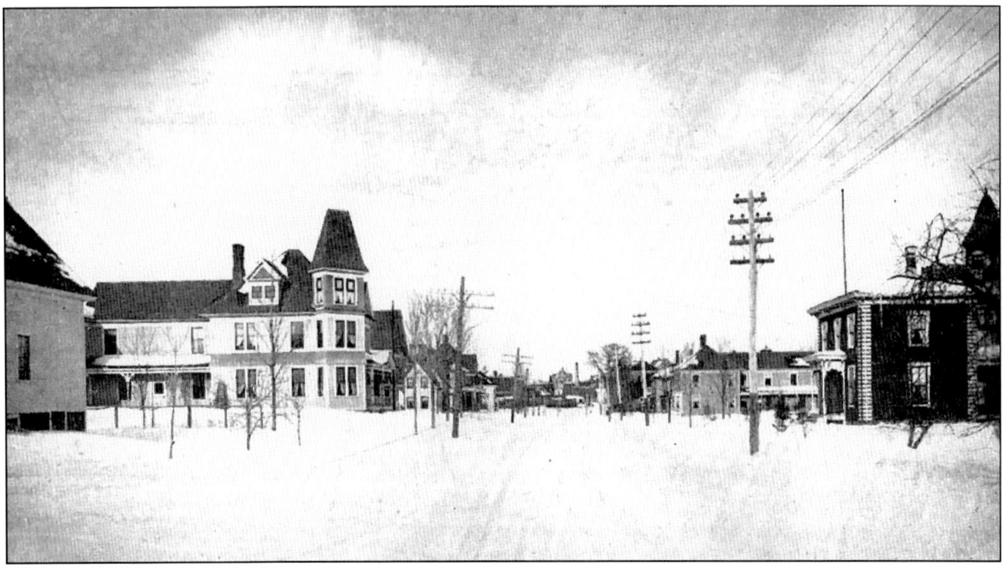

Many Pittsfield streets are still recognizable, even 100 years after they were first captured on film. Lancey Street is shown here, looking north towards the railroad and the village.

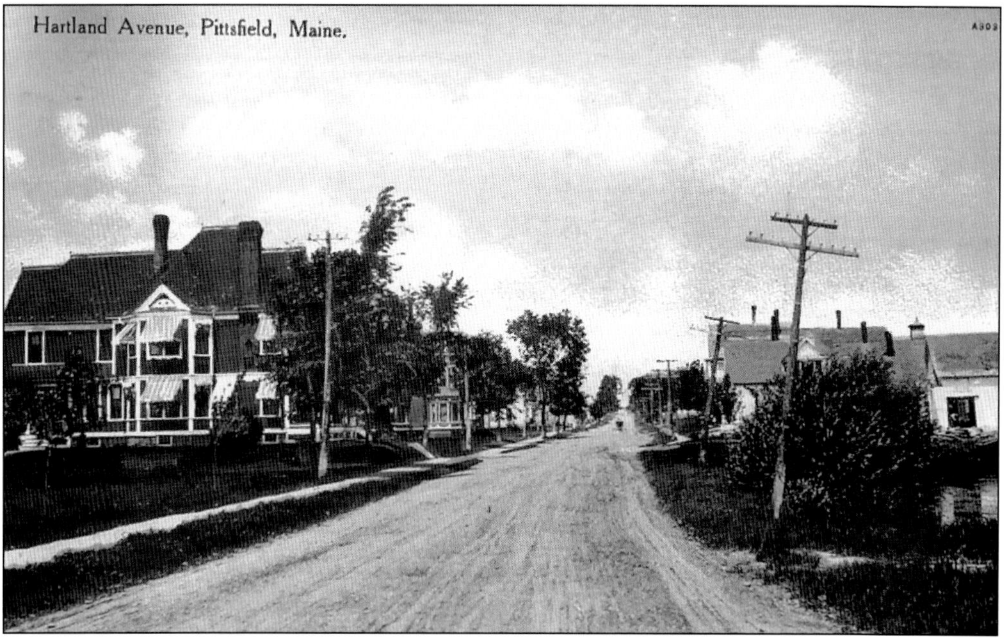

Most of the houses on Hartland Avenue, shown above, and Somerset Avenue, shown below, are still the same 100 years later, although pavement has been added to the streets. The additional traffic of 2004 demands wider roads. Even the Mill Pond on Hartland Avenue may be looking at a visionary makeover as local officials discuss the feasibility of creating a new park, swimming area, and picnic area on its perimeter.

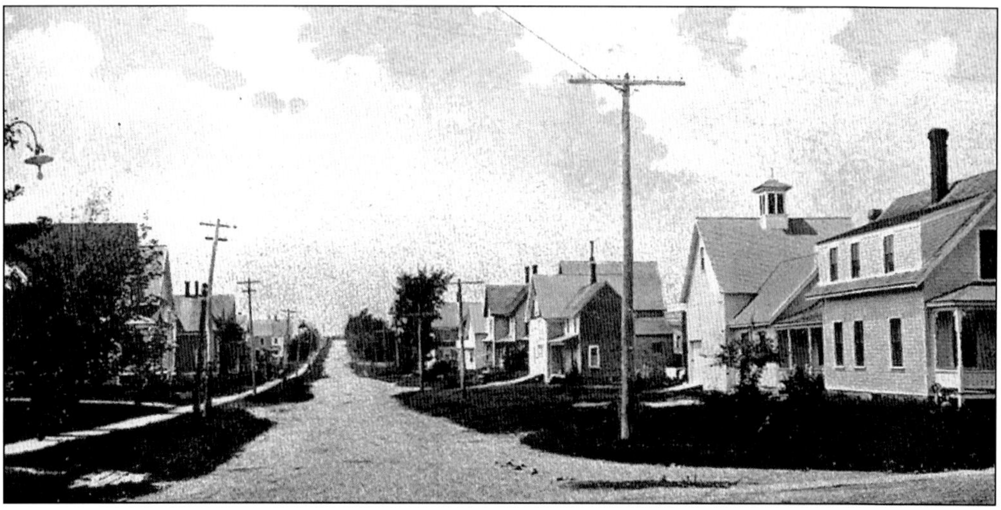

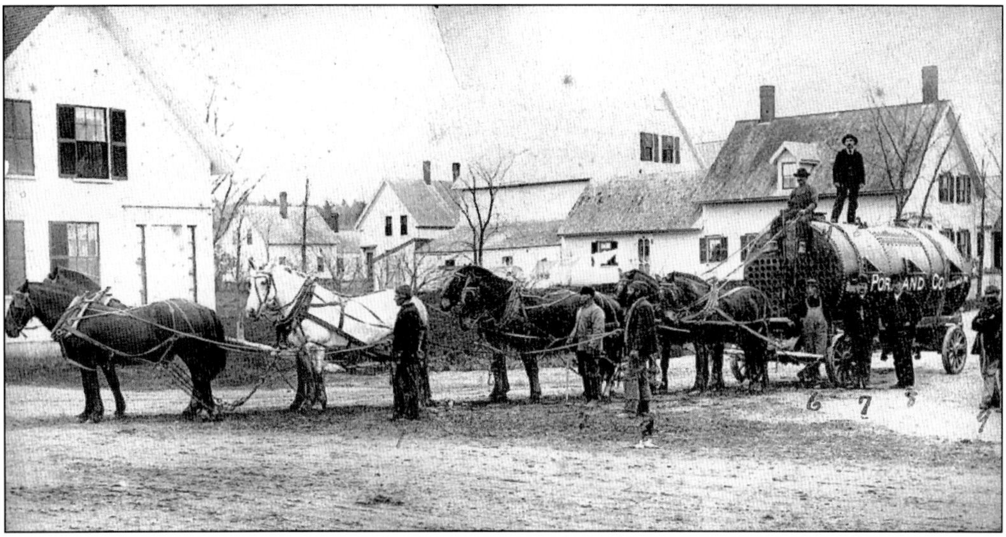

In 1891, the delivery of the new boiler for the Waverly Mill was a major undertaking, requiring an eight-horse hitch. At the corner of North Main Street and Detroit Avenue, this crew stopped to record the moment. Shown here are, from left to right, as follows: (on the ground) O. F. Parks, J. H. Mahoney, B. Burbank, Fred Emerson, H. W. Gardner, T. S. Dexter, and Eben Waldron; (on the tank) J. Glidden and the boss.

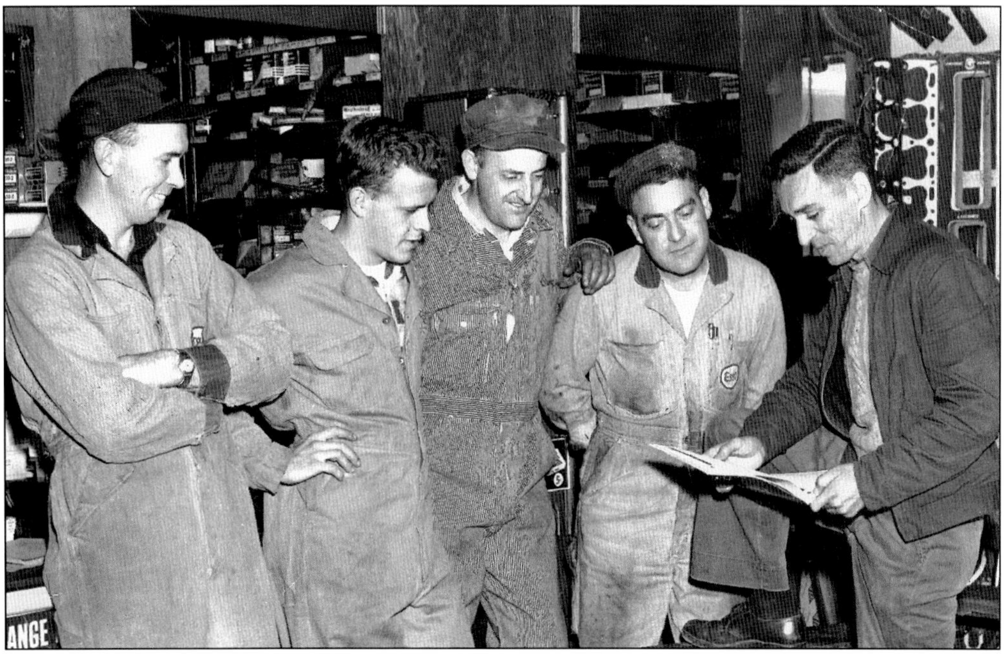

Hubbard's Oil and Esso gas station was located strategically "on the island" at the center of the Sebasticook River in Pittsfield. Bob Hubbard's business, a predecessor to Exxon gas stations, weathered more than one flood, including one that nearly caused the loss of Hubbard's own vehicle. In the 1950s, Hubbard's loyal crew included, from left to right, Tommy Tufts, Richard Peppard, George A. Hallenbeck, Buzz Belanger, and Hubbard himself.

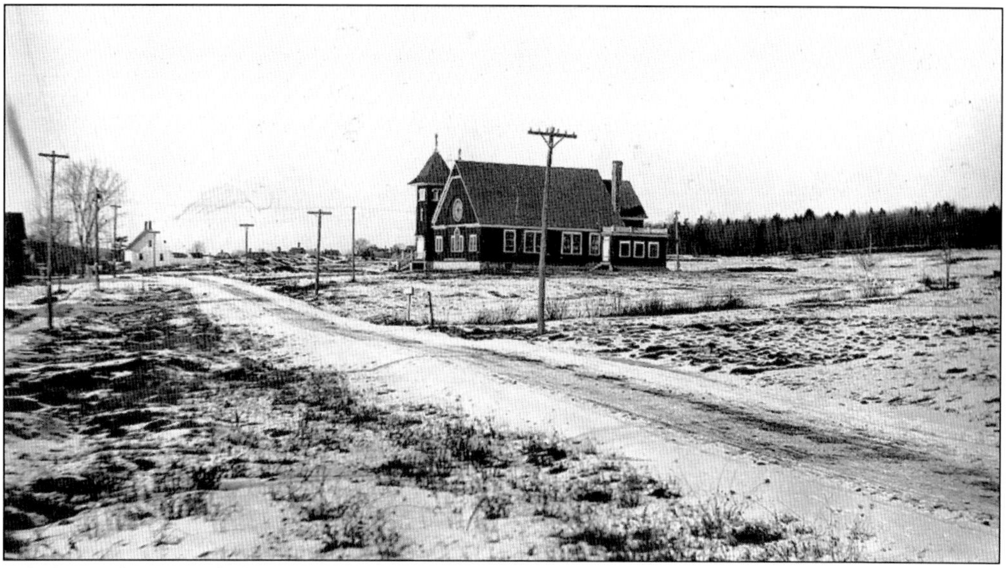

While much of Pittsfield has changed since the early 1900s, perhaps nothing is as telling of that change as the landscape around St. Agnes Catholic Church. Detroit Avenue appears to be little more than a country road and tells nothing of the large residential area that surrounds the church, its school, and the parking lot today.

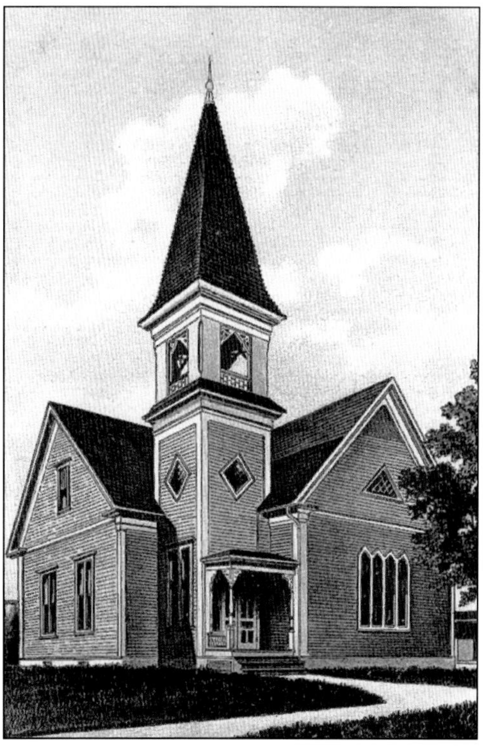

Pittsfield churches have changed since 1900, and at least one has been a church, a meeting hall, and then a church again. For a brief time in its history, the one-time Methodist Church, built on Manson Street in 1872, became a meeting hall for the Pittsfield American Legion. In 1964, the legion swapped properties with the Church of God on Waverly Avenue. The Manson Street church no longer has a steeple, but it is still home to the Church of God. The building on Waverly Avenue was used by the legion for several years before the organization moved to Middle Street, the site of the current Sebasticook Elks Lodge. The Waverly Avenue property became C. Jones Hardware and Flowers.

The First Baptist Church was organized in 1855 in conjunction with a union church. Early records, however, were lost, and it was not until the church reorganized at a meeting on January 2, 1867, that permanent records began. The church group sold its interest in the union church and moved to a new chapel at MCI in 1869. The present building appears to have been built sometime after 1889.

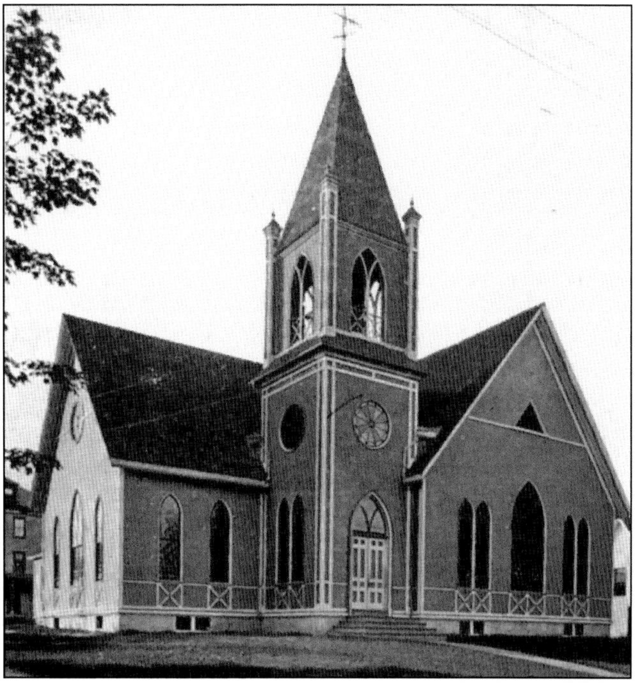

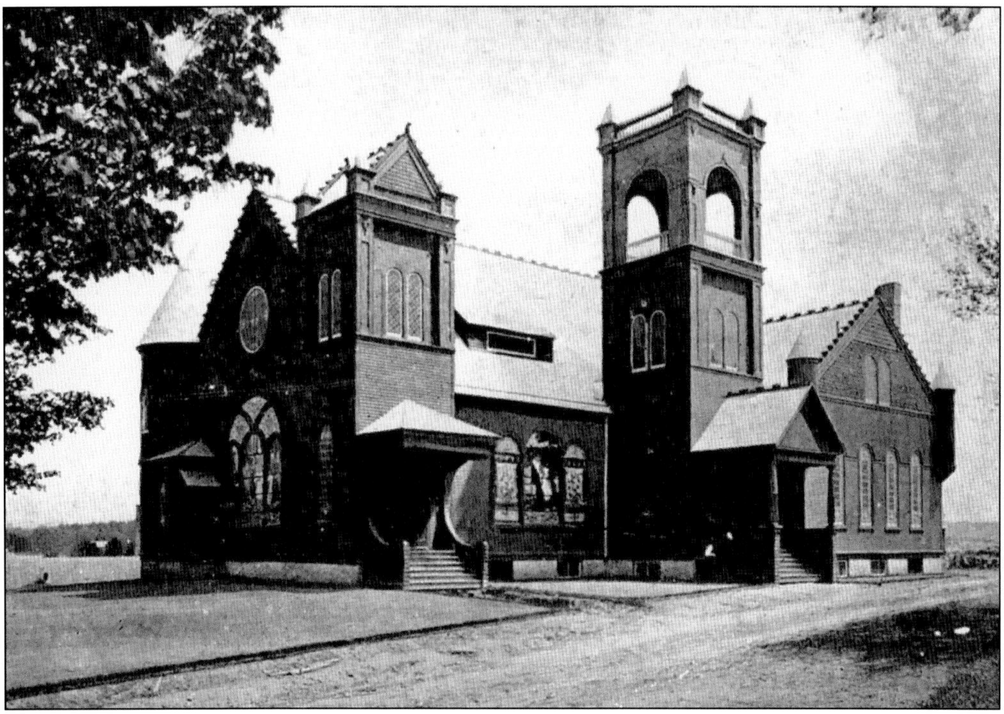

In 1898, plans for rebuilding the Universalist church began. The old church was moved to its current location, and it was made into the vestry of the new building. By October, the exterior of the building was nearly complete. Tiffany of New York crafted the large stained-glass windows. The unique design of the church and the rare treasure of its windows and murals caused the building to be listed on the National Register of Historic Places in 1983.

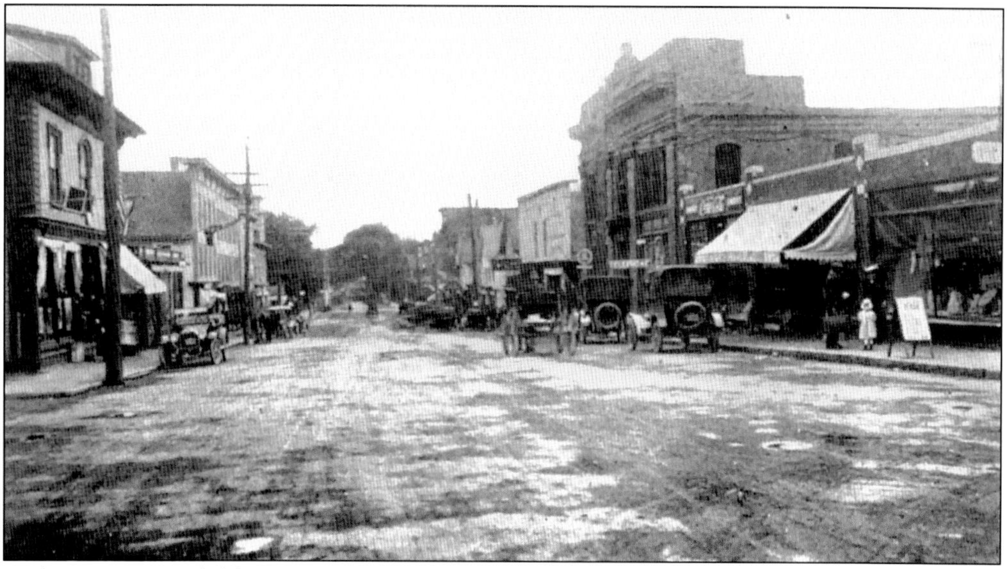

In the 1920s, Pittsfield streets were paved. Cars were the preferred mode of transportation, and most of the storefronts on Main Street were occupied and doing business. It was a number of years before the interstate highway west of town drew shoppers away to nearby cities for shopping. When the interstate was completed in the early 1960s, business began to decline. In the early 1970s, a shopping center on outer Somerset Avenue, closer to Interstate 95, was drawing business away from downtown, and there was virtually no business remaining on the east side of Main Street. The buildings were failing. A radical urban renewal proposal had already failed, and the town turned to federal grants to remove the dilapidated buildings and help build a new infrastructure in the downtown area. As part of the plan, overhead wiring was buried underground and utility poles were removed from the street corners.

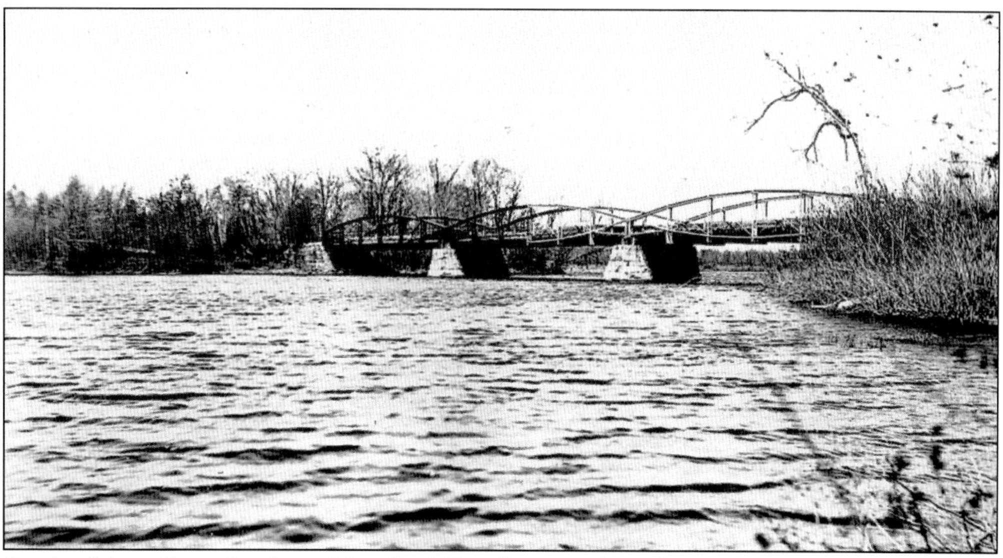

South of the village, the Outer Horseback Road crosses the Sebasticook towards Burnham and lower Detroit. The site is not far from the area originally settled by Moses Martin, Pittsfield's first permanent resident. For many years, travelers used the old iron bridge shown above. In the 1960s, it was replaced by the current concrete structure.

Two

NEWPORT

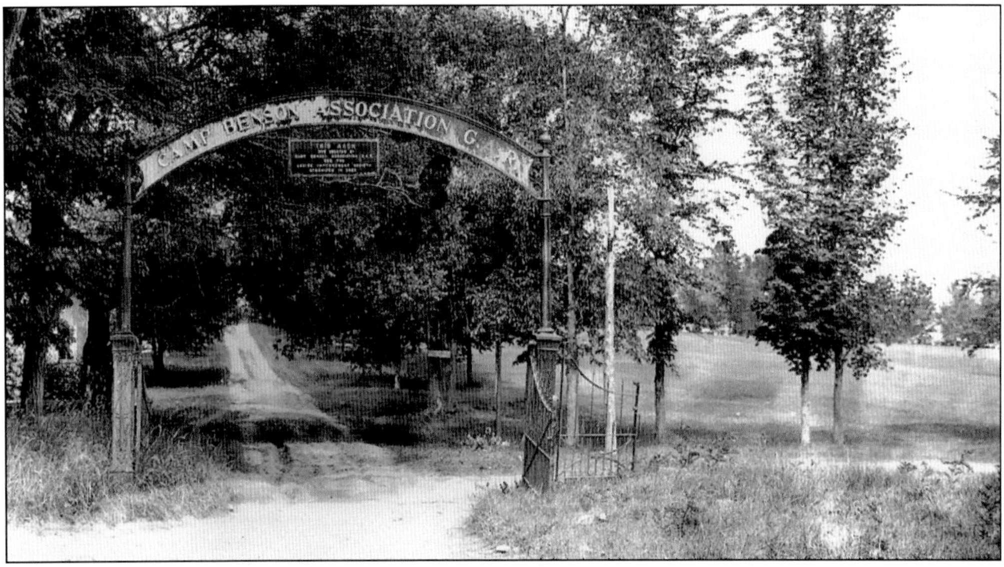

Few things are as identifiable or recognizable for their Newport connection as Camp Benson. Visitors to the grounds in the late 1800s were greeted by an archway marking the entrance to "Camp Benson Association, G. A. R." Founded in 1886, the unique compound on the shores of Sebasticook Lake was intended for the enjoyment of Civil War veterans under the banner of the Grand Army of the Republic. It was named for Civil War surgeon John Benson, who served with the 20th Maine Regiment. Each summer, the compound hosted two major events, a Fourth of July celebration and a reunion encampment of Maine regiments of the Union Army. Initial plans called for construction of a parade ground, a long wharf on the lake, and numerous cottages that would be owned by individual veterans. During the early years of the reunions, many veterans attended and tented on the grounds. The veterans were certain the camp would be "the most popular summer resort of central Maine." For much of its history, its popularity was undeniable. Veterans groups continued to vacation and summer at the compound, and Camp Benson was also known for its ability to host large gatherings, including military encampments and reunions, family reunions, and gatherings of other organizations.

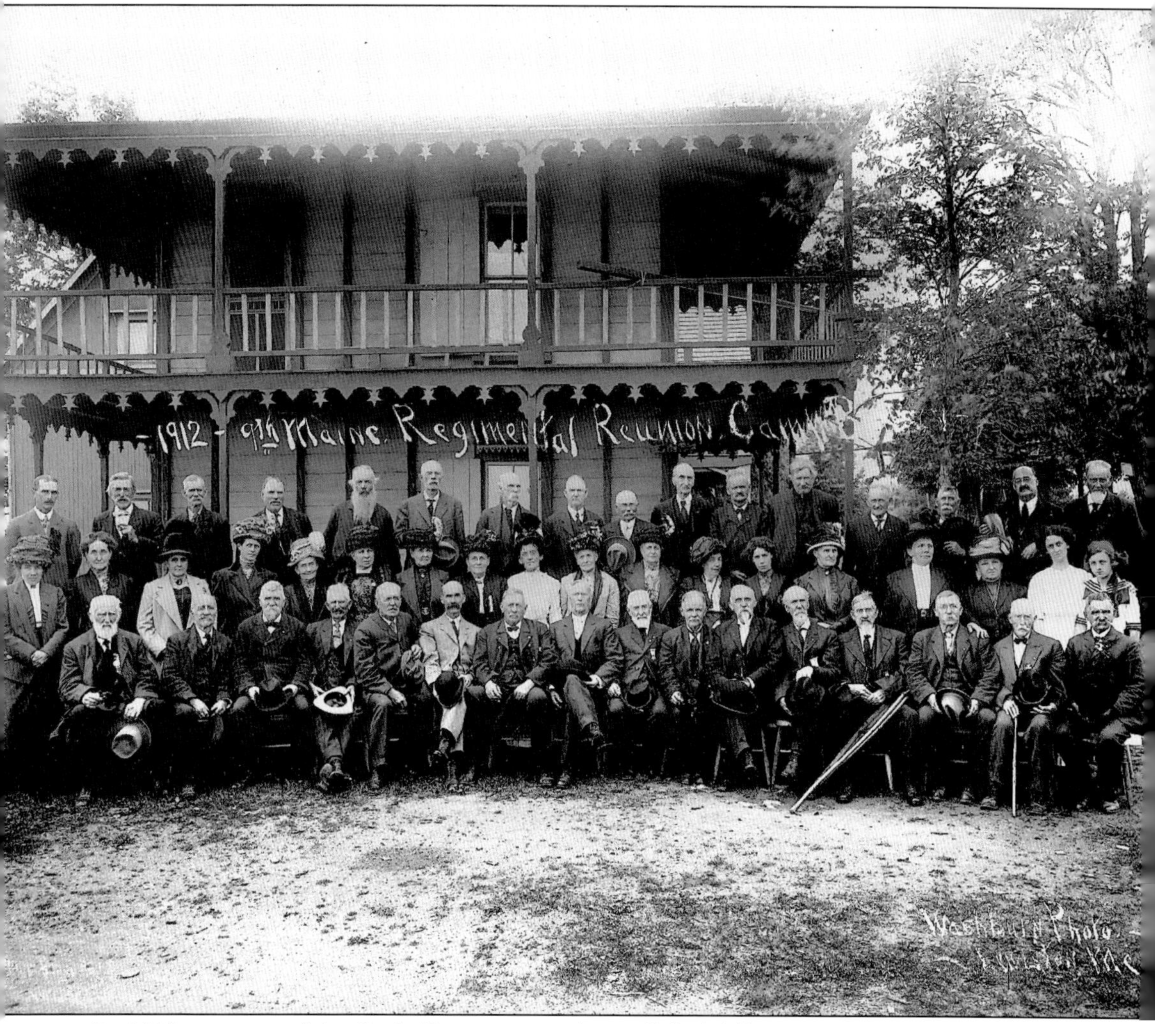

By 1912, veterans of the G. A. R. were aging but still faithfully returning to Camp Benson to renew friendships and their ties to military service. Unfortunately, although many of these reunion photographs still exist, several, such as this one, are unidentified. Owners of this particular photograph hope someone may recognize an ancestor among the group and may help to identify others.

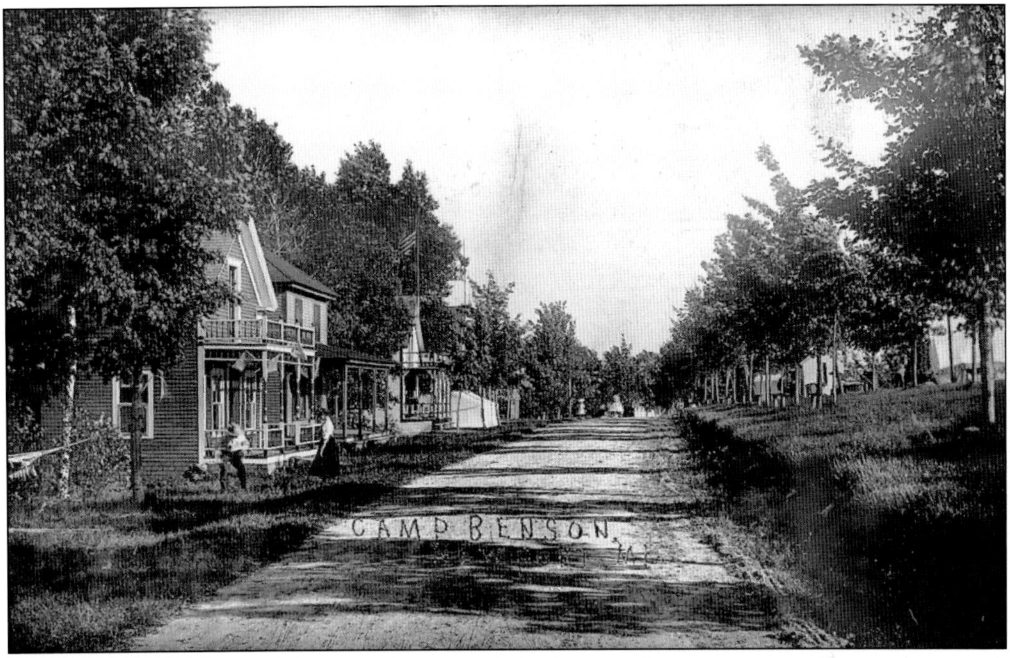

Camp Benson did, and still does, offer rows of closely spaced cottages around a parade ground. The grounds were used over the years for military reunion encampments, family reunions, children's activities, ball games, and socials.

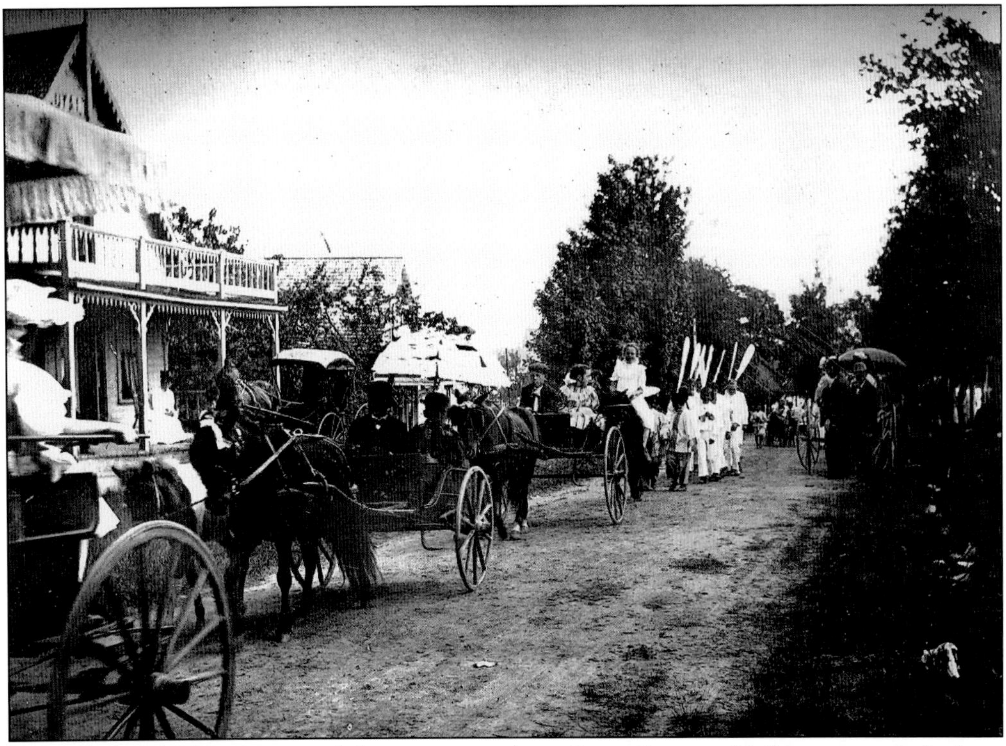

In 1907, the children presented their own parade at Camp Benson. Children were decked out in summer finery and drove pony carts around the parade ground.

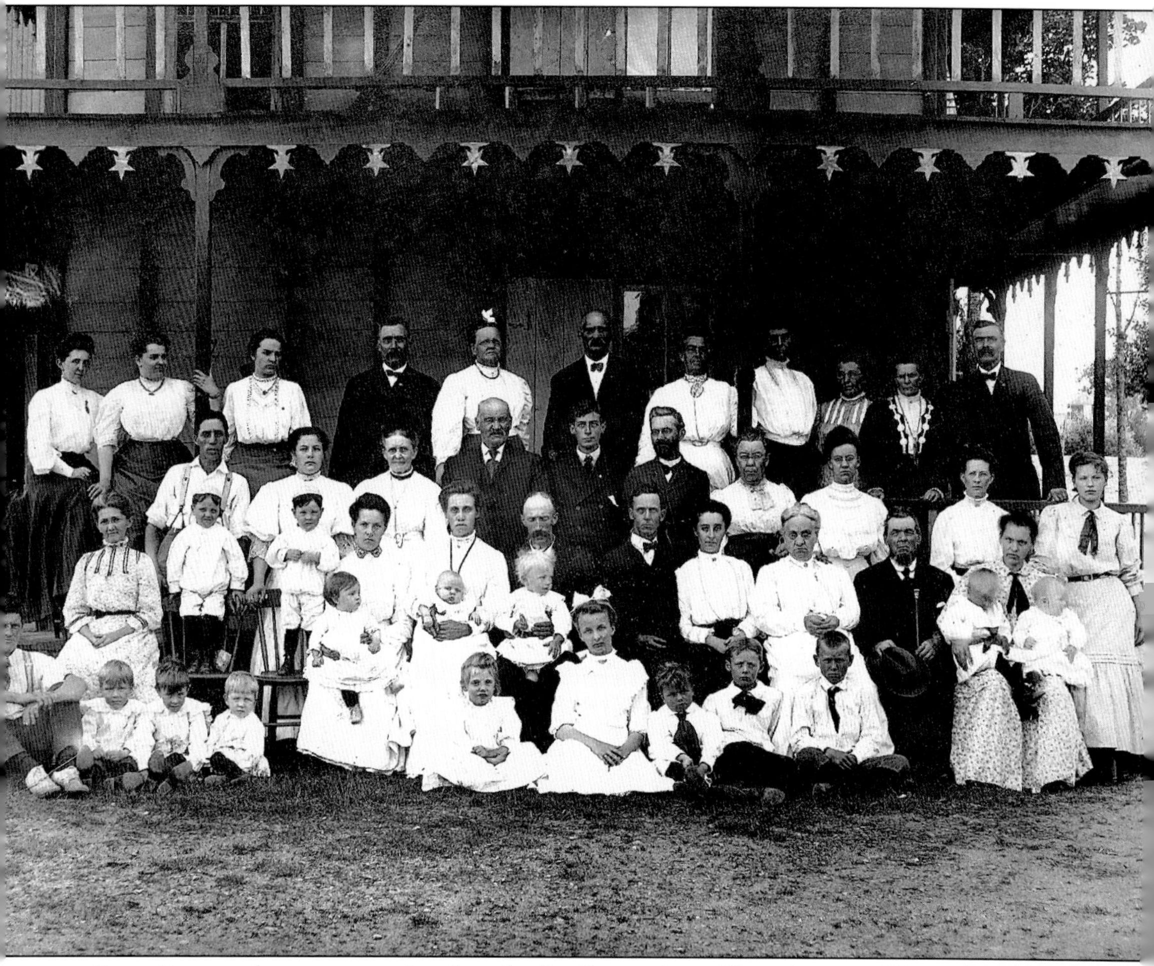

Camp Benson also was a popular place for family reunions. The relatives of Samuel and Sarah (Rowell) Brooks (seated, second and third from the right) gathered in 1909. Also identified in the photograph are Leona (center, with a large bow in her hair) and Leon Brooks (to the right of Leona). In the first row of seats are, from the left to right, as follows: four unidentified people, Bertha Heath, Frank Heath, Grant Brooks, Edith Brooks, Sarah Brooks, Samuel Brooks, and unidentified. In the second row (center) is Rev. Frank Brooks.

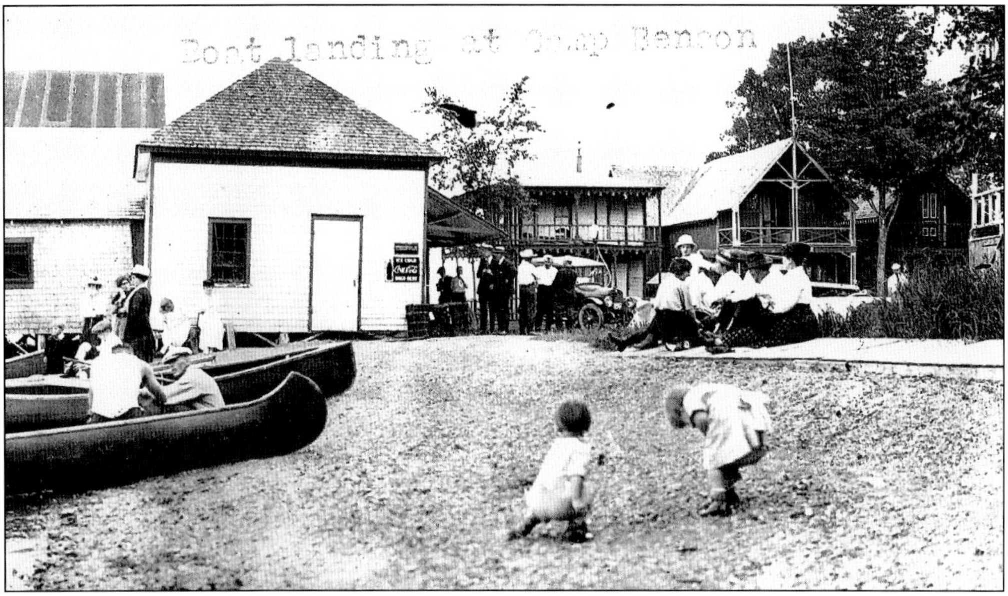

The boat landing and "swimfront" at Camp Benson offered lake access and summer recreation as well. The compound had a large pavilion and picnic grounds, a bandstand, and a dining hall. One of the churches in town would routinely load its stoves, food, and volunteers onto one of the many steamers on the lake and make the trip to Camp Benson to prepare meals for the various groups that used the facilities.

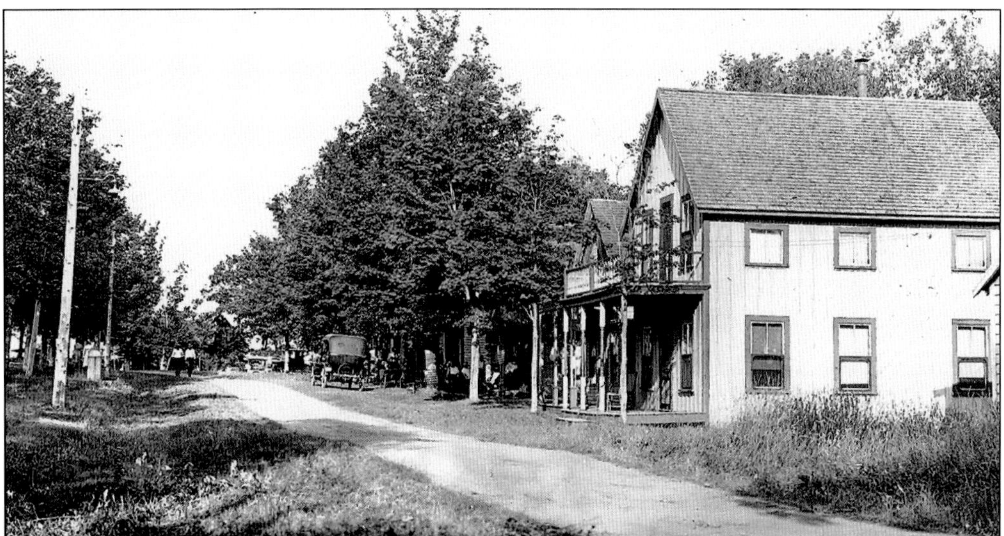

The appearance of the cottage structures has changed over the years out of necessity and preference. Many of the buildings were modernized and are used as year-round homes today.

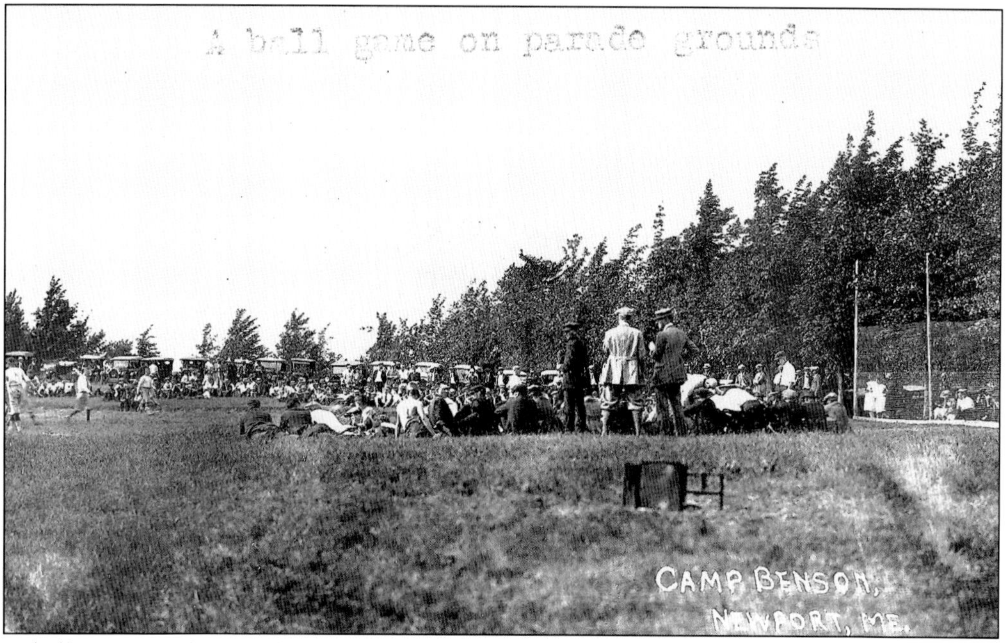

A ball game on the parade grounds could attract a large crowd and a long line of the latest automobiles (for more comfortable viewing).

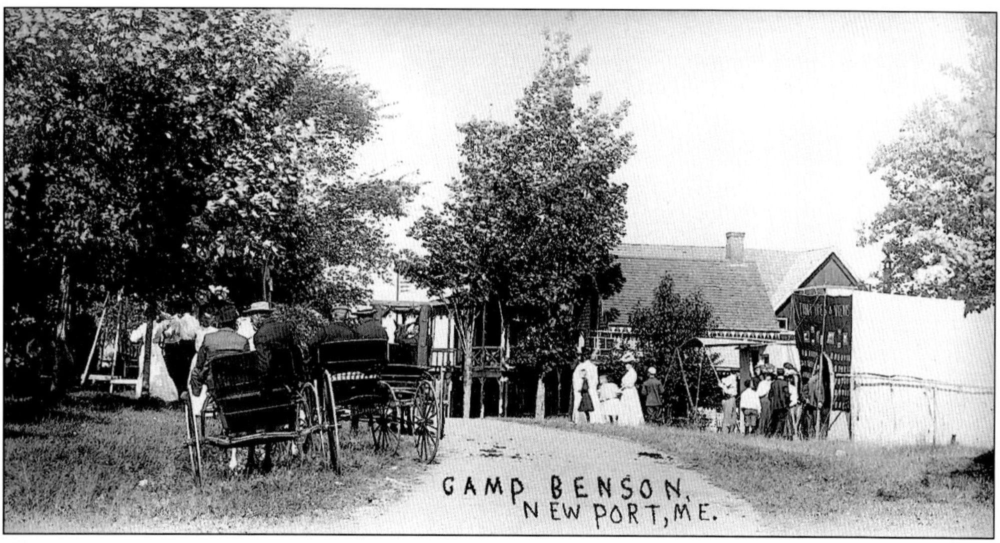

The Camp Benson Association also hosted fairs, as this scene depicts in 1906, when automobiles were not yet the standard mode of transportation.

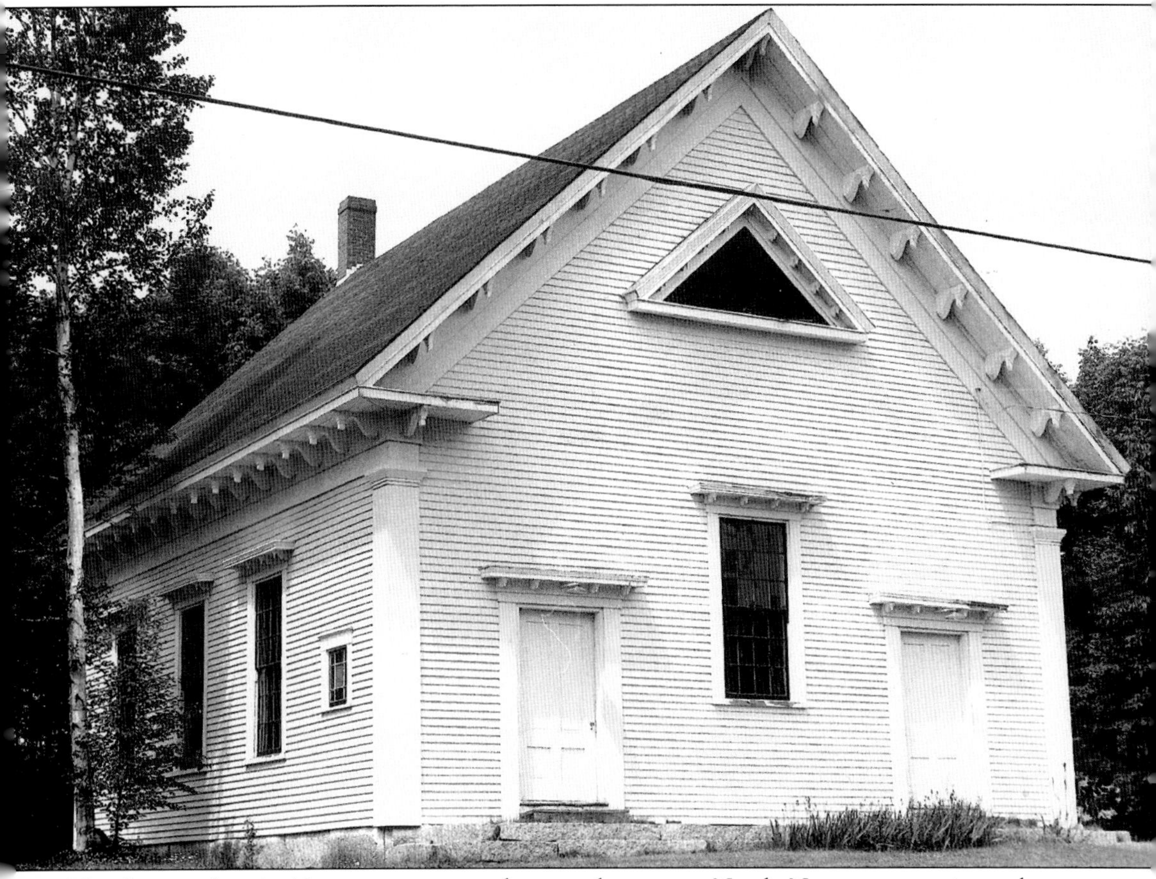

The first settlers in Newport came to the area known as North Newport, creating a busy settlement that lasted well into the 20th century. The North Newport Church, founded in 1857, was a major part of that area and is on the National Register of Historic Places. The church's interior currently appears much as it did when it was new. A church association still hosts annual gatherings at the church. On October 23, 1907, the church's congregation observed a semi-centennial celebration and posed for a picture that hangs in the church today.

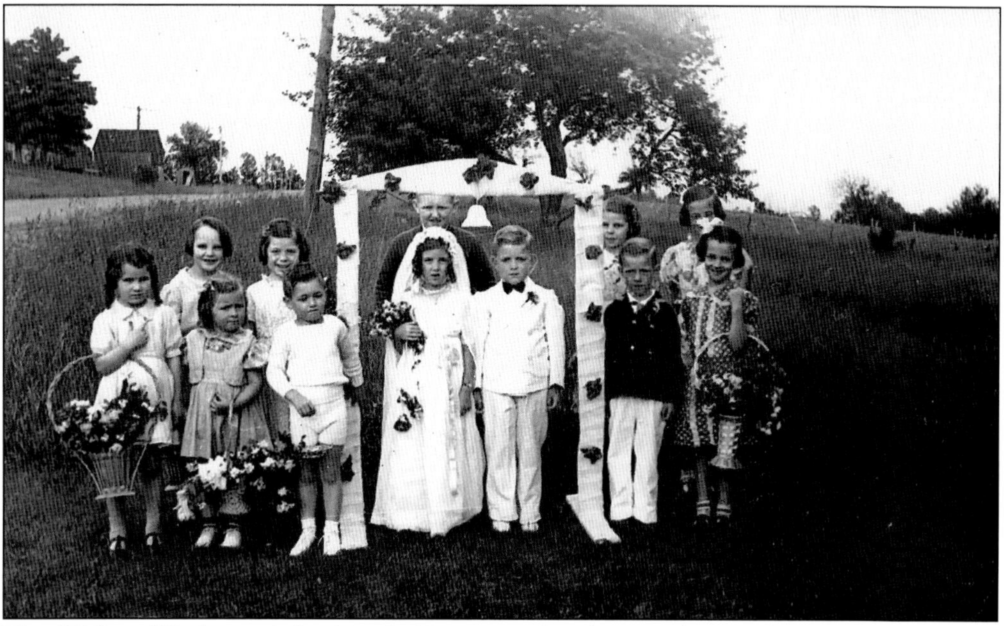

The Willing Workers of the North Newport Church were known for their fund-raising activities to benefit the church and its projects. In 1940, the group organized a Tom Thumb wedding as part of the annual Willing Workers fair. Shown in this photograph are, from left to right, as follows: (first row) Regina Gray, Donna Tasker, Stewart Smith, Marilyn Bryson, Carl Smith, Stanley Gray, and Joyce Gray; (second row) Dodie Wade, Polly Easley, Guy Mullen, Thelma Easley, and Gloria Gray.

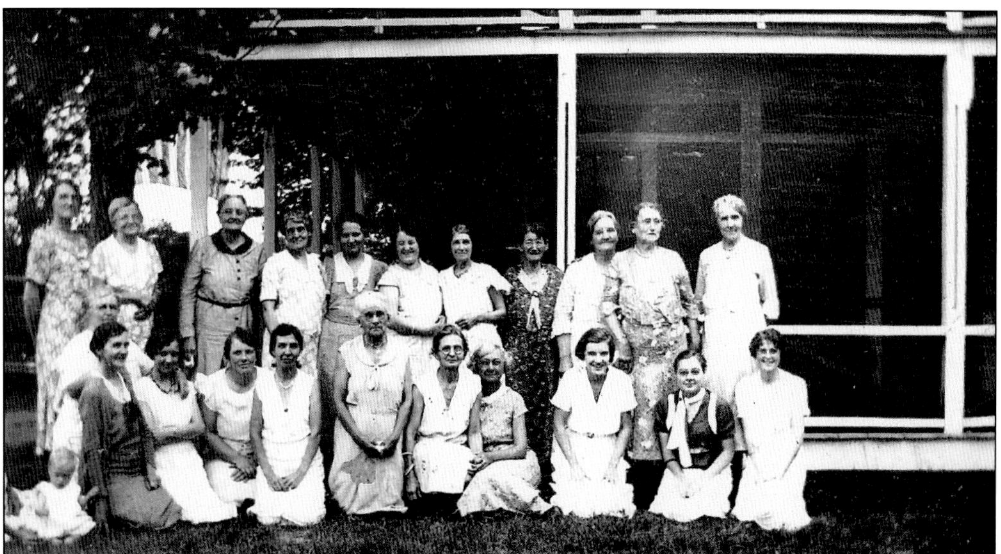

The Willing Workers treated themselves to an outing each summer. In 1933, they took their outing to Camp Benson; they are seen here posing in front of the cottages. In other years, the group took trips to members' cottages for summer fun. The members in this group are not identified.

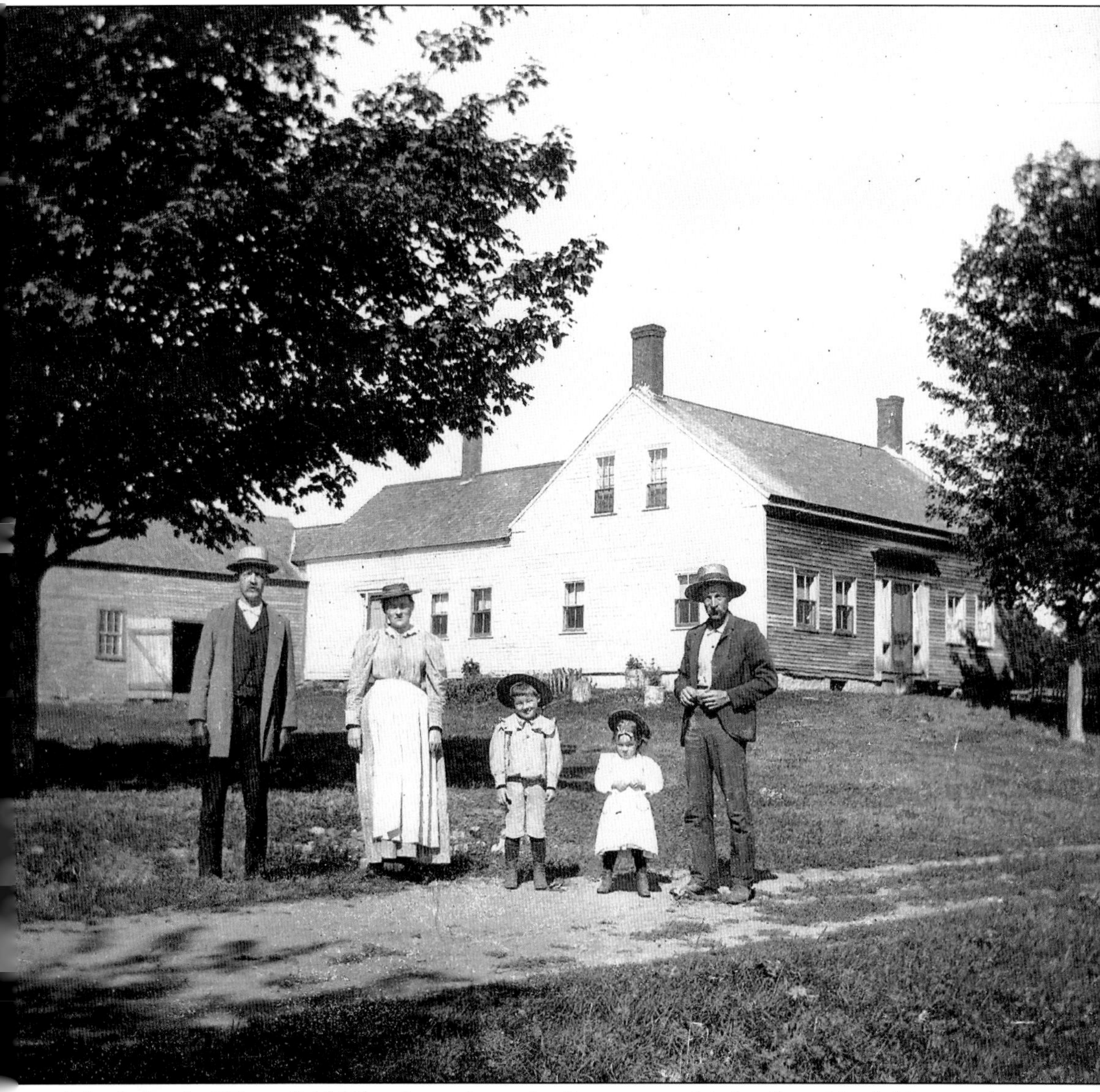

John Ireland of Bloomfield (Skowhegan) was the first to move his family to North Newport (or East Pond Plantation, as it was known in 1807), having explored the area the previous year. Bloomfield neighbors Elam Pratt and Nathaniel Burrill followed. It was another seven years before the town was incorporated as Newport. However, the first town meeting was held in 1812 to organize the settlers against a potential American Indian attack. A few days later, volunteers met a party of 150 Penobscot men near Stetson Stream. The Newport residents learned the American Indians were fleeing from a dispute with the St. John tribe and were headed to the Kennebec. The group remained in the area, hunting and trapping, for approximately 10 days before moving down the Sebasticook River. One of John Ireland's descendants still resides on Gray Road in North Newport at this home, built in 1828 by Horatio Patten. By 1893, it belonged to Calvin Gray, who left the home to his son Adelbert, pictured here to the far right. Also pictured here are, from left to right, John Gray, Lydia May (Ireland) Gray (Adelbert's wife), and their children, Wilbur and Gladys. Lydia was a descendant of John Ireland. Wilbur Gray's daughter Evangeline Matijczyk resides in the home today.

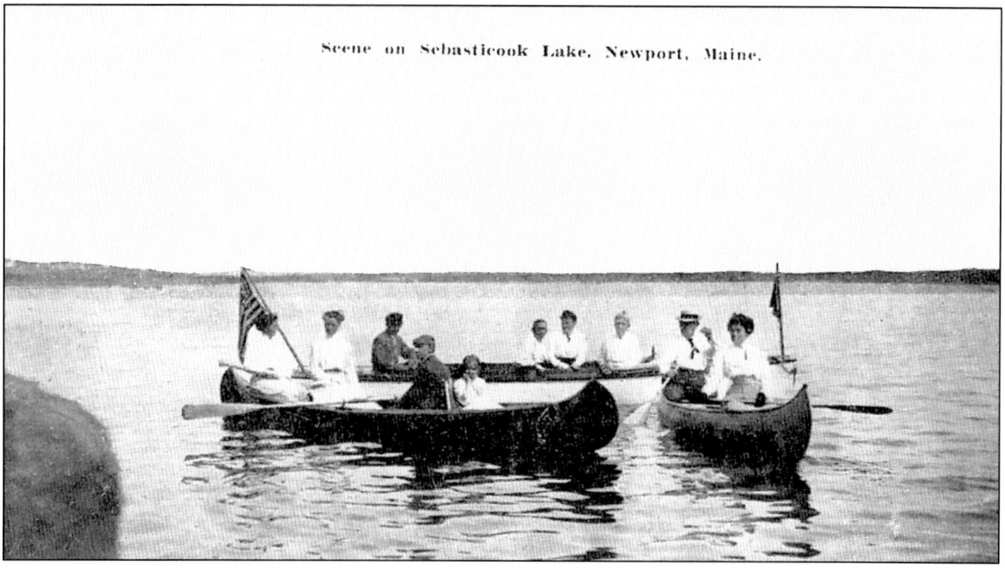

Canoes were a popular craft on Sebasticook Lake long before any white settlers arrived. Tribes from the Algonquin and Abenaki nations routinely crossed Sebasticook Lake after portaging from the Penobscot River to Stetson Pond and Stetson Stream, a tributary to the lake. It was a traditional route that the native people used between the great rivers, the Penobscot and the Kennebec, in search of hunting and fishing sites. In 1992, an 1,800-year-old fish weir was discovered in the shallows of the lake, confirming that the region was a gathering place for prehistoric travelers. The portage route ultimately gave Newport its name. The Maine Historic Preservation Commission lists 13 prehistoric archaeological sites along the shores of the lake. Future archaeological research is expected to reveal more about the early American Indian settlements at the lake.

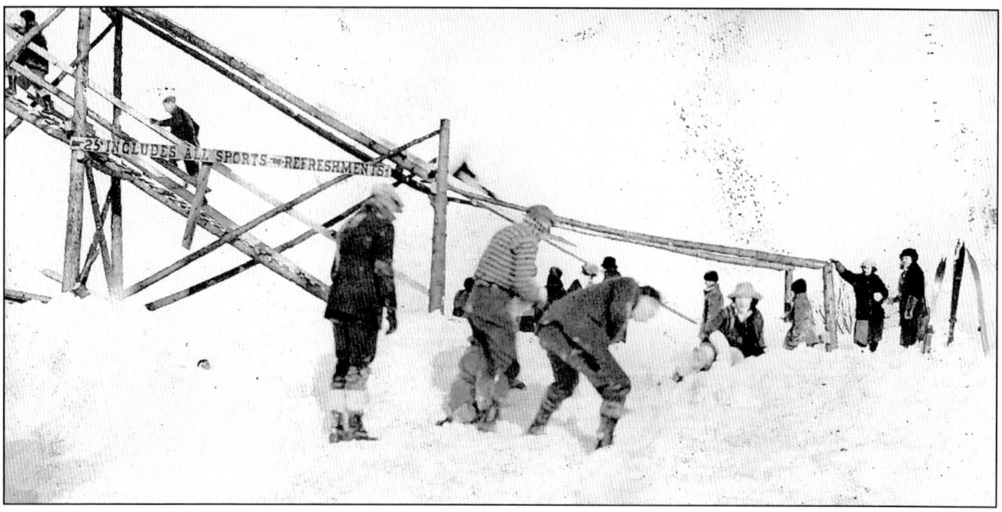

In the winter, Newport children and their neighbors from surrounding towns would head up TipTop, now known as Libby Hill, where an elaborate slide and toboggan run was constructed for winter fun. A fee of 25¢ was charged. Libby Hill, likely the highest point of land in Sebasticook Valley, is actually located in Palmyra. In the 1800s, it was briefly considered as a location for the University of Maine. Views from the top of the hill on a clear day include the White Mountains to the west and Mount Katahdin to the north.

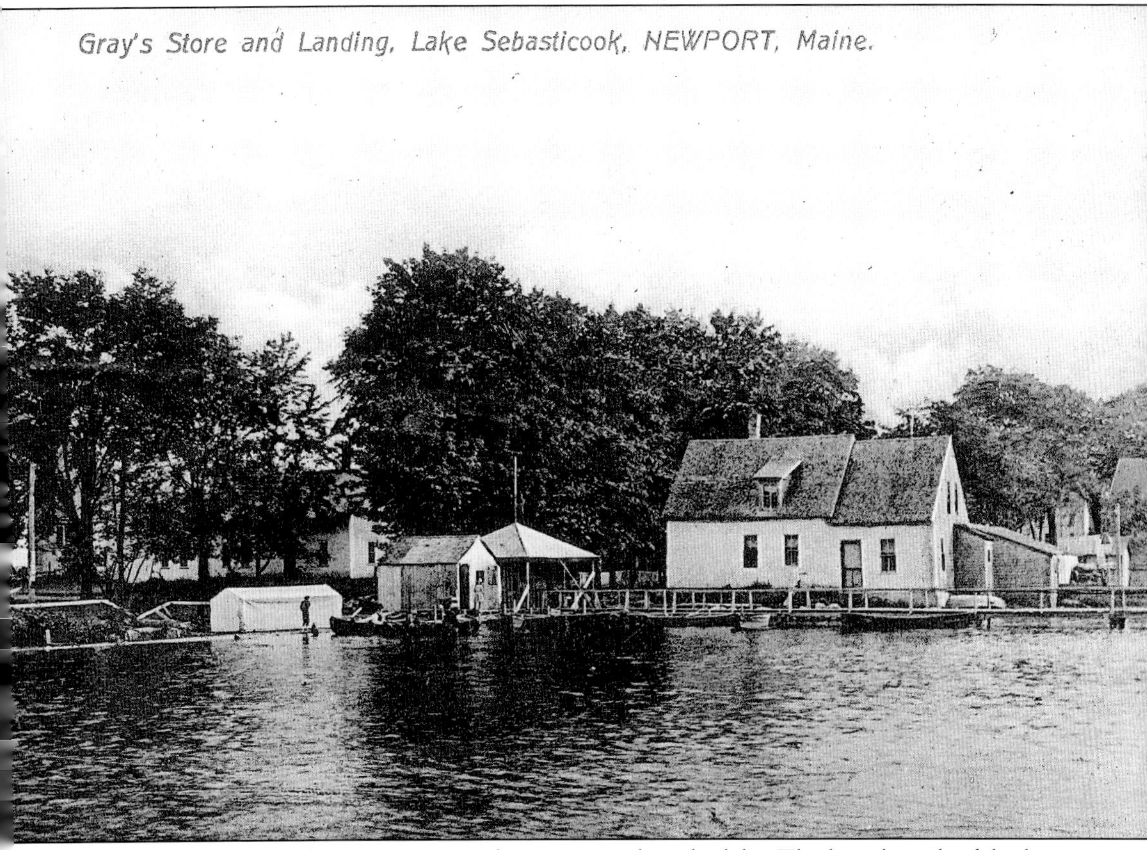

For much of Newport's history, activities have centered on the lake. The boat launch of the late 1800s and early 1900s was on the opposite side of the point from where it currently is. Capt. G. E. Wilson was the first to operate a steamer on Sebasticook Lake. The steamship *Norita* could transport up to 60 passengers to locations around the lake or simply out for a day of fishing. His success prompted up to 30 steamship operations around Sebasticook at a time when water travel was preferred over the primitive roadways to the lake's shore. The *Norita* was docked near the present-day American Legion hall, where Captain Wilson once operated a sheep farm and a summer boardinghouse. In the winter, the lake was used as an ice supply to cool the iceboxes in private homes and businesses throughout the community during the warmer months. In January 1910, ice harvesters were taking an average of 200 tons of ice a day out of the lake. The ice was stored in icehouses that lined the shoreline near the landing. The thick ice cover on the lake also provided a more direct route to the village in the winter. At the September 8, 1823, town meeting, it was voted "to bush out the road from Nathaniel Burrill's [in North Newport] to the outlet, set in a straight line by holes cut in the ice twenty rods apart." The job was sold to the lowest bidder, Jesse Prescott, at four shillings. The ice road trimmed nearly six miles off the journey from the North Newport settlement to the village, known then as the mill district. A trip that would have extended for nine miles by road could be done in three and a half miles on the ice.

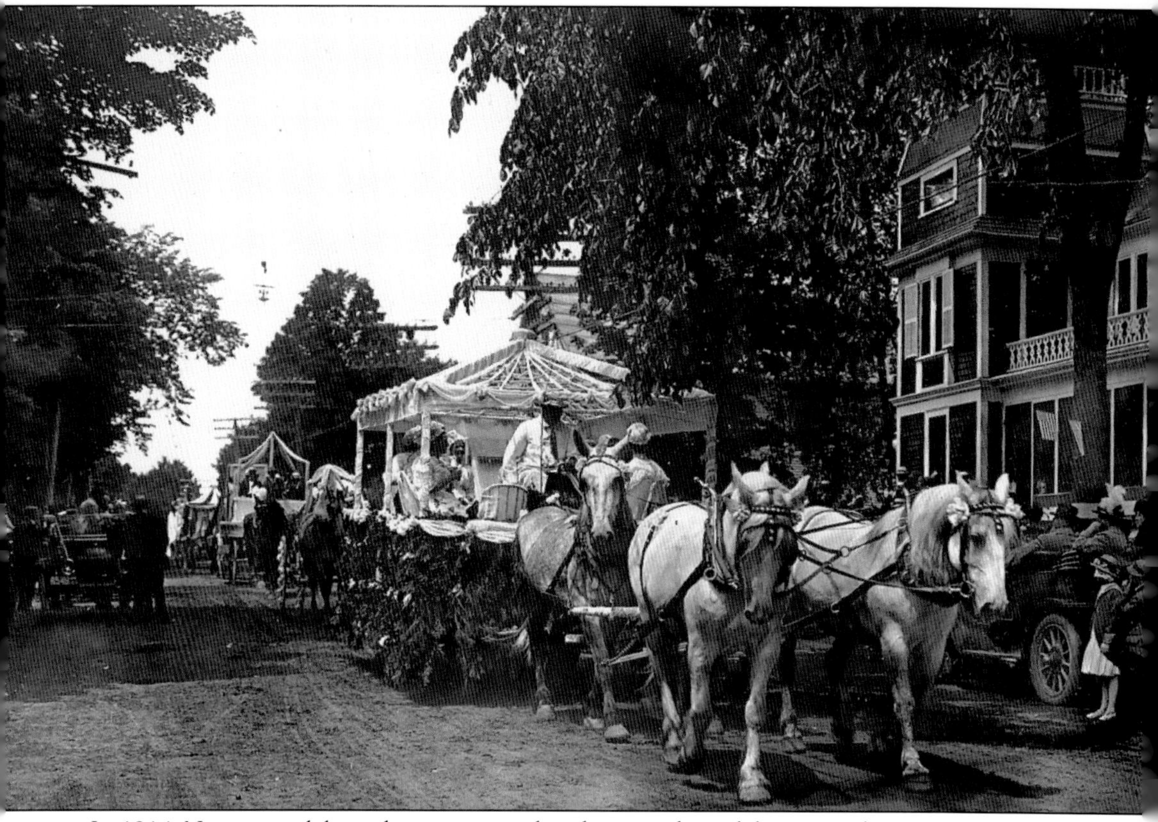

In 1914, Newport celebrated its centennial with a two-day celebration. The event included an early morning children's parade, followed by a business parade, a parade of automobiles, competitive footraces, a concert, a drill team presentation, ball games, and other competitions and field-day activities. A boat parade on the lake capped the day on Saturday. On Sunday, citizens gathered for the official celebration services at the school grounds. The program of activities and the individuals involved in the planning of the celebration were recorded in the centennial souvenir book, which includes a detailed history of the town's first 100 years. The Newport Historical Society has copies of the booklet.

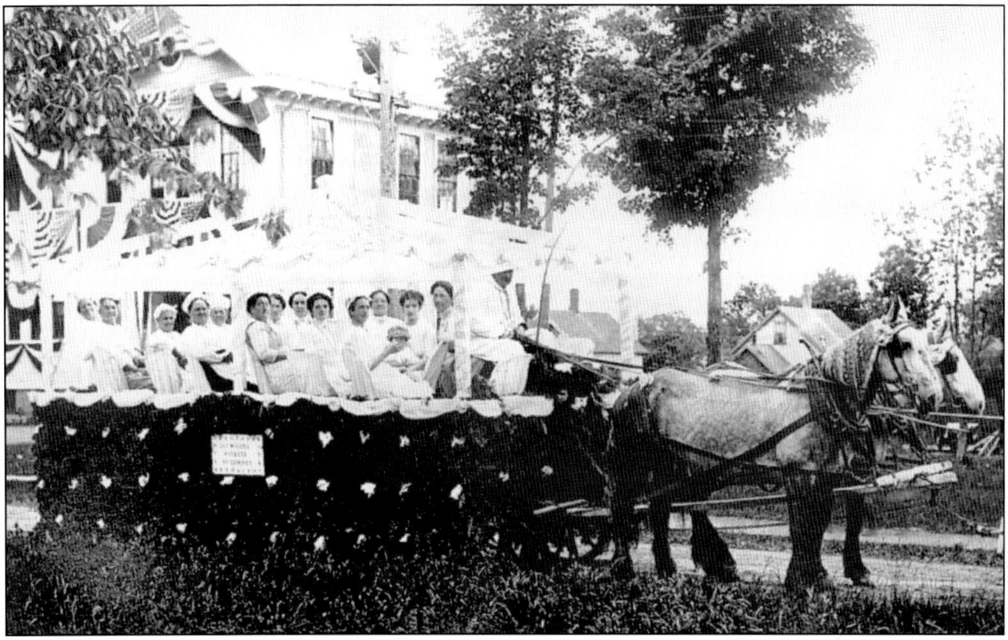

The Willing Workers of the North Newport Church also demonstrated their community spirit with a float in the centennial parade.

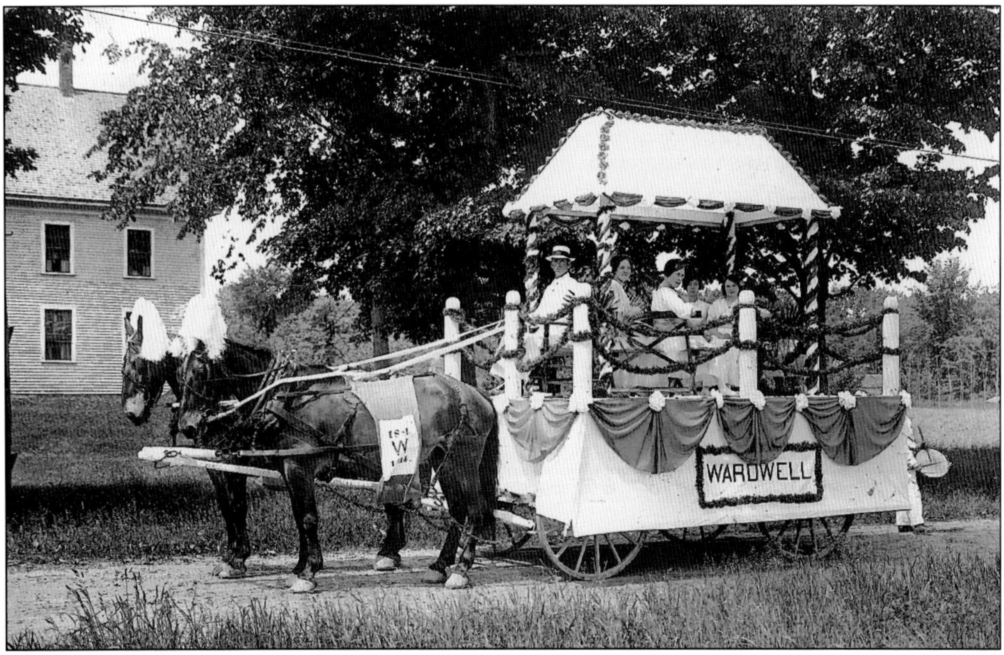

E. C. Wardwell Dry Goods participated in the centennial parade with this decorated float. Wardwell established its dry-goods store on Main Street in 1881.

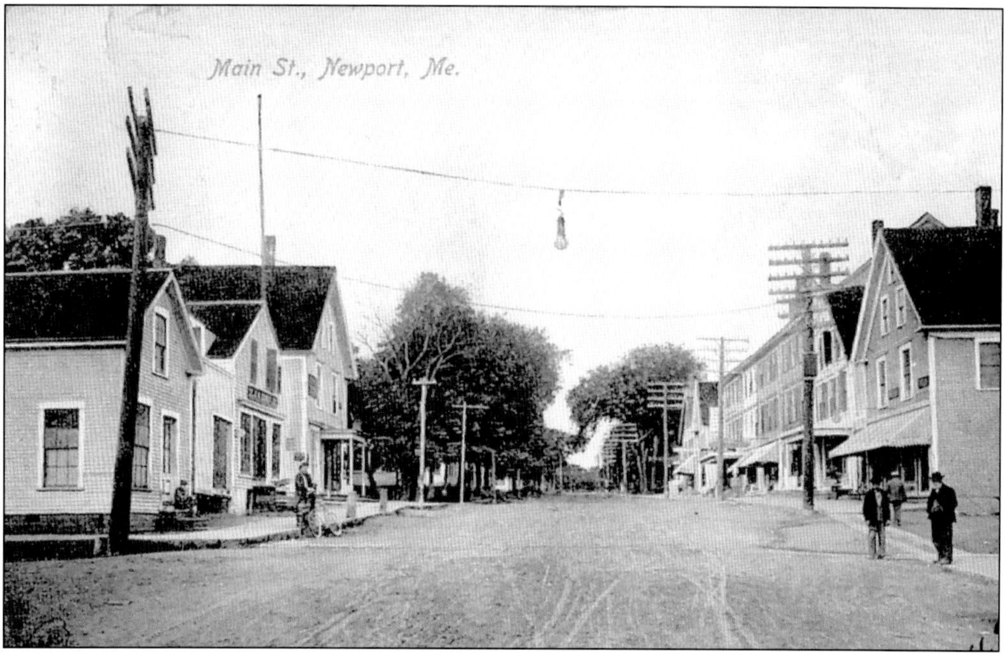

The Main Street of the early 1900s appears similar to Main Street today and to that of the 1960s (below), although several buildings have changed or have been lost to fire.

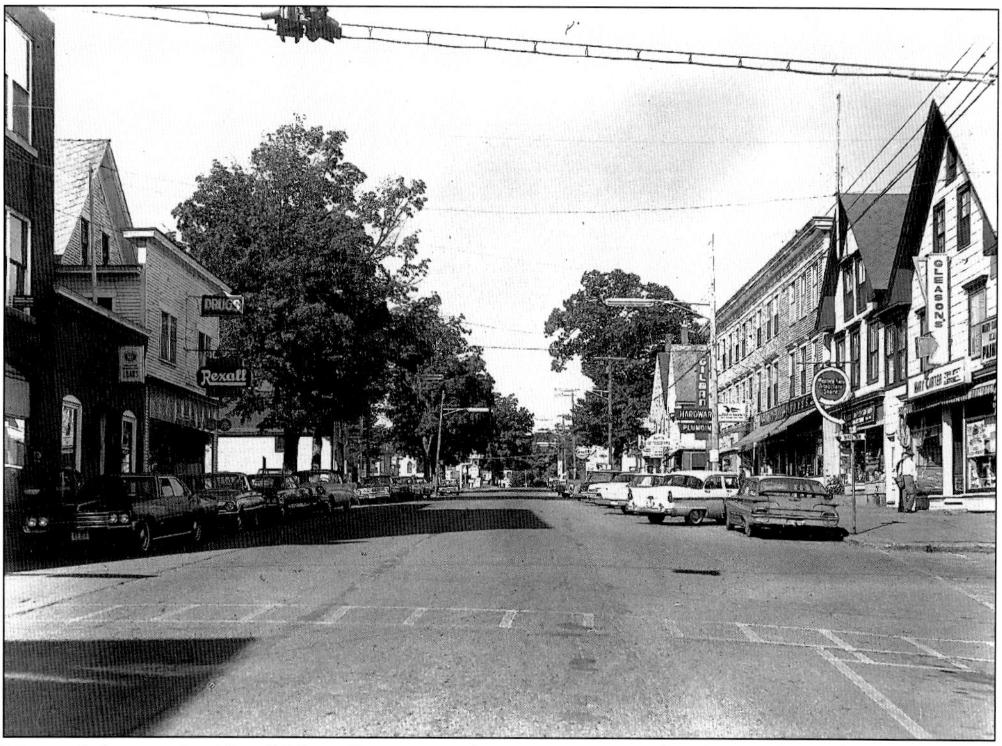

Most of the north side of Main Street was lost in a spectacular fire *c.* 1989, leaving a large vacant lot for more than 10 years. Current plans call for a new cultural center to fill the vacancy, housing the town's library and historical society.

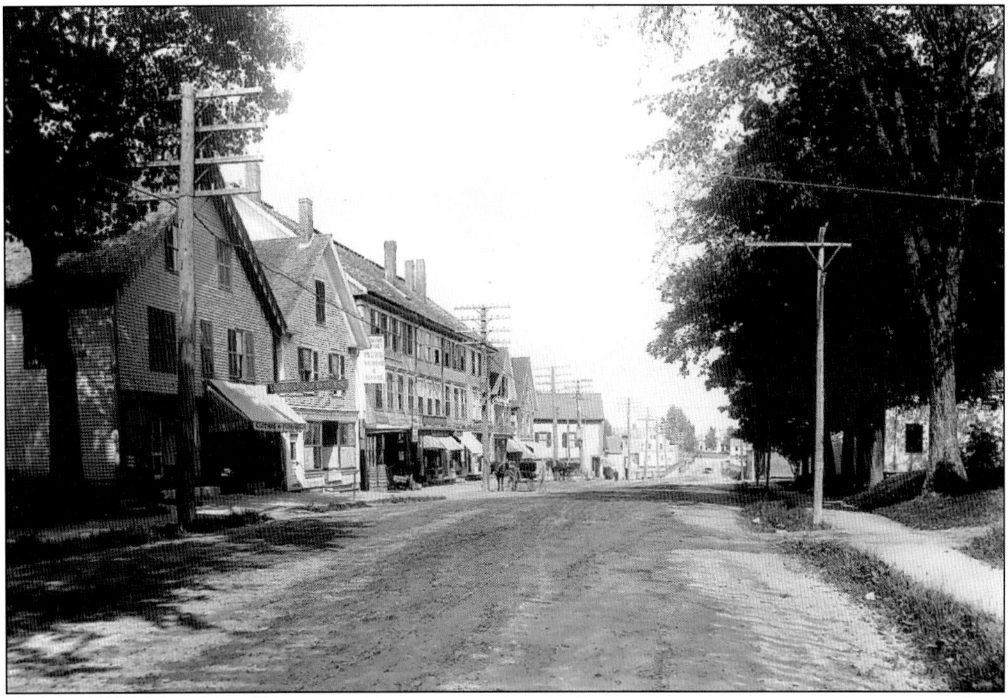

This view of Main Street looking east *c.* 1900 shows many of the buildings that were lost to fire, as well as the expansion of individual businesses and business changes. The arrival of the automobile eventually brought the need for pavement as well.

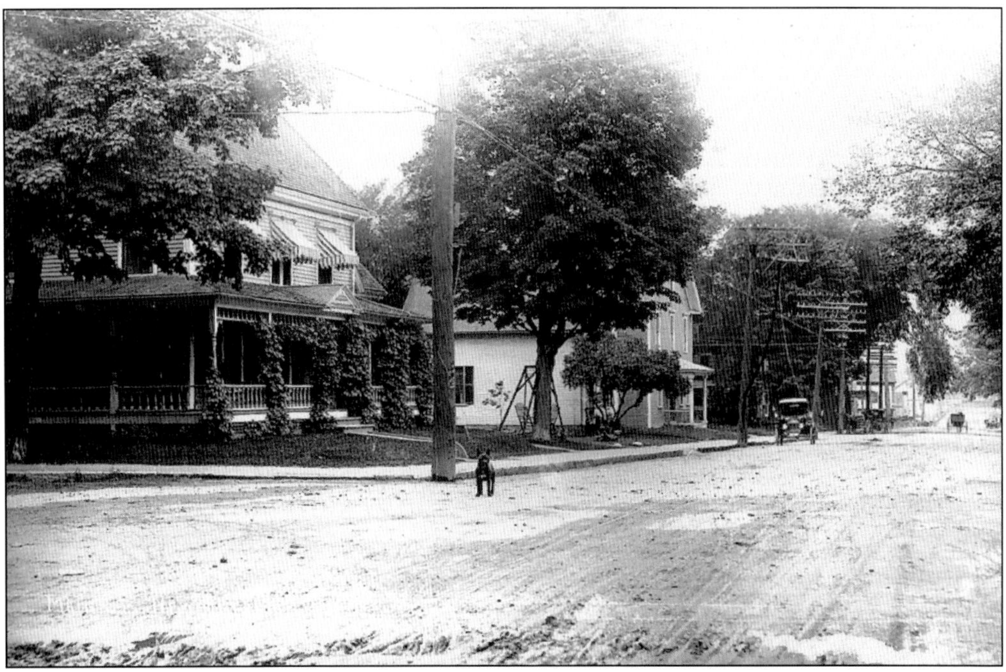

Another view of Main Street at the corner of Main and High demonstrates how many homes were lost to progress and development as the business district encroached on the residential district.

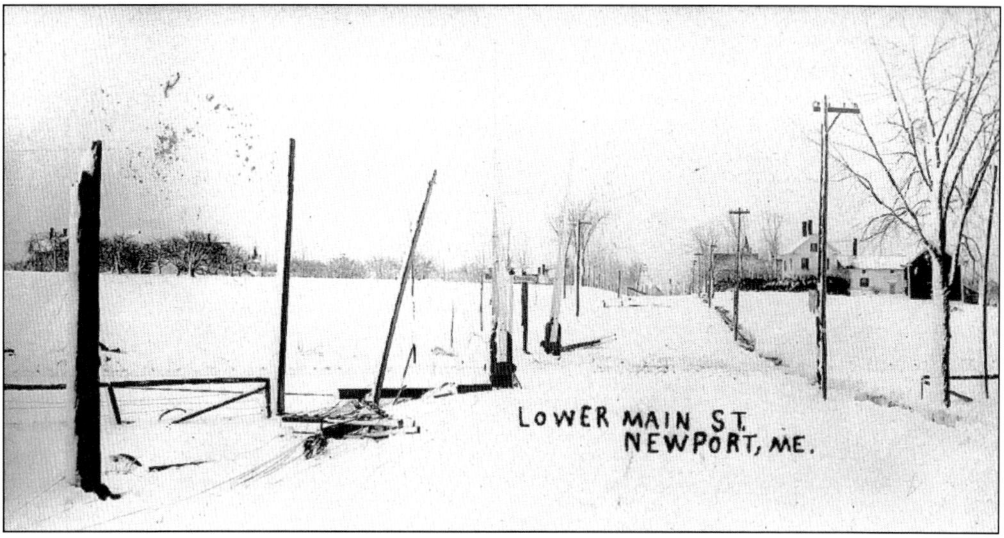

This scene from Lower Main Street *c.* 1906 shows a very different view than travelers in Newport's busy Triangle intersection see today. The view shows the now-abandoned railroad crossing at the bottom of the hill before the current Fleet Bank and U. S. post office. The opposite side of the street holds Peoples Heritage Bank and the former Lewis Brothers Tractor Sales.

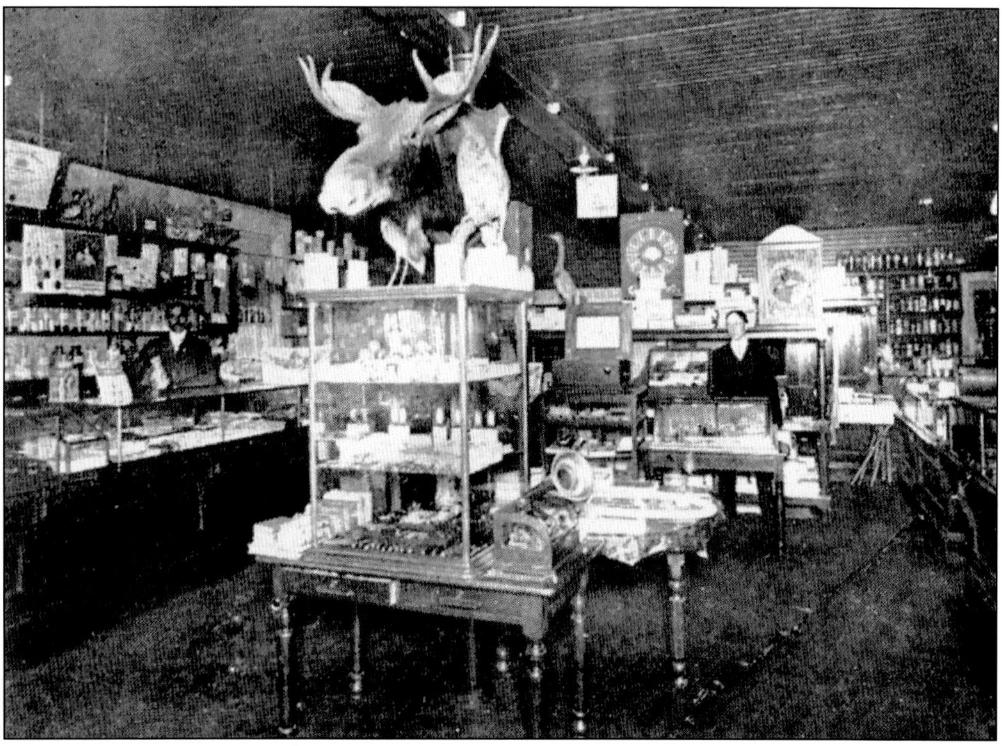

George M. Barrows operated Barrows Drugstore on Main Street in 1907. In 1917, he was joined by his son Lewis O. Barrows for a period of 22 years. The younger Barrows, however, had a greater destiny ahead of him in politics. In 1937, he was elected as Maine's 50th governor, and was reelected in 1939 for a second two-year term.

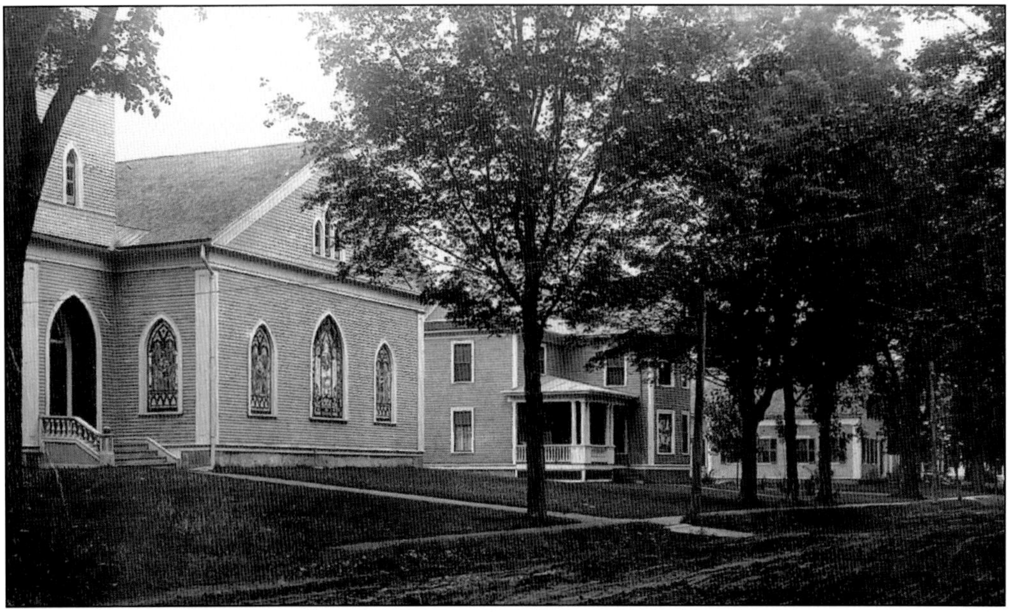

The Union Church on High Street was the first church in Newport, and was erected in 1837 in the "mill district," as the village area was originally known. Today, the Union Church is Newport's High Street Congregational Church. The original church was built by members of several denominations, including Baptists, Methodists, Congregationalists, and Universalists. It was the first church in town to have a steeple. The church was entirely rebuilt in 1902 at a cost of approximately $6,500. In 1914, the congregation made plans to build the parsonage, shown in this photograph. The parsonage was torn down in 2001.

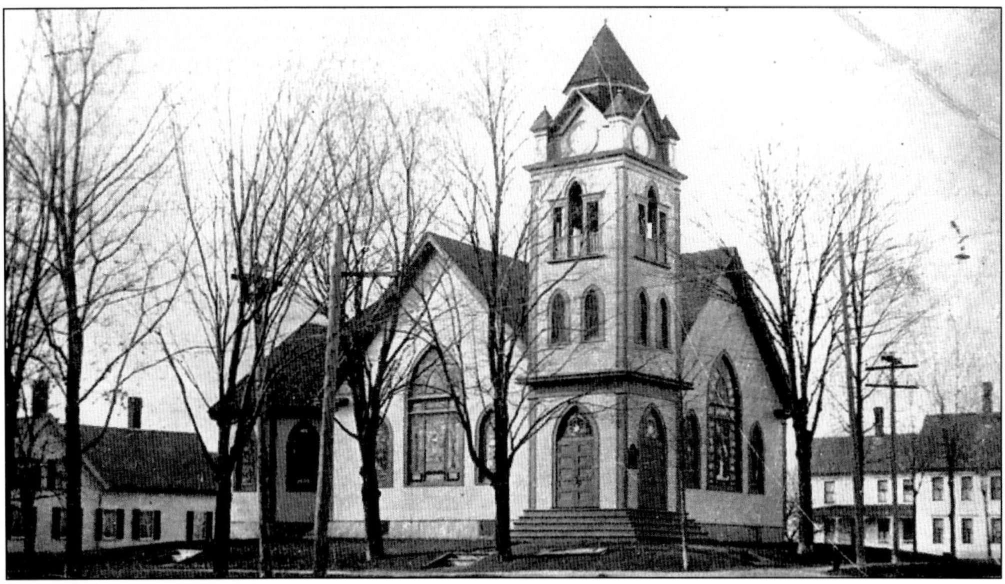

In 1901, the Methodists purchased land on Main Street after having operated a church on Shaw Street since 1859. The Main Street church was completed in 1902 and is still a Methodist church. At one time, it shared its minister with congregations in surrounding towns. The last church to do this was the Detroit Methodist Church, which was closed in the late 1900s and is now a community meeting house.

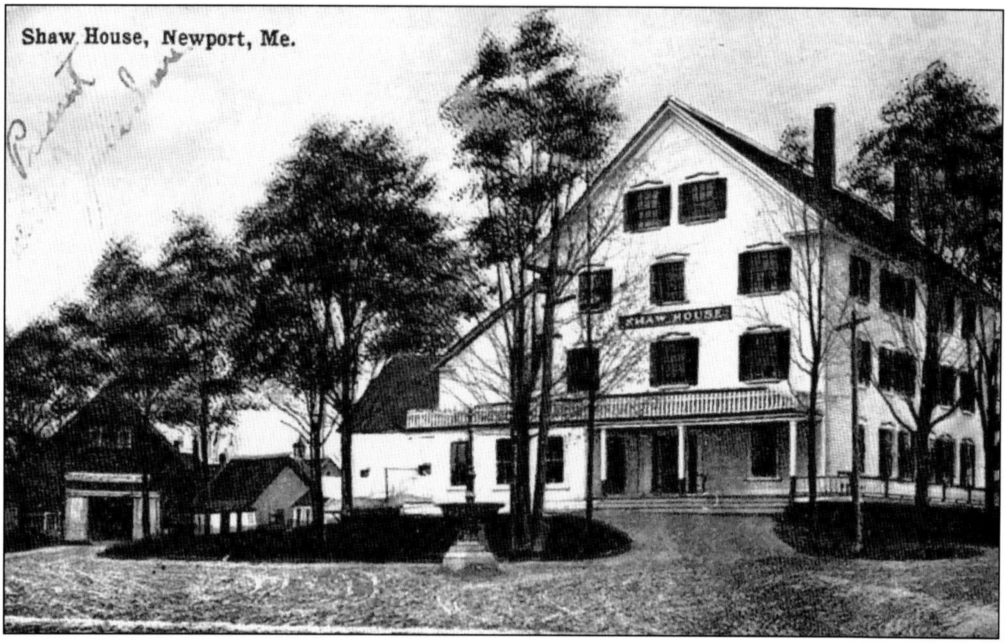

In the late 1880s, the Shaw House was a prominent structure at the corner of High and Main Streets, as it is today. The inn was built in 1860 by Benjamin Shaw and was operated as an inn for many years. Today, it houses senior citizen housing as the Newport Inn.

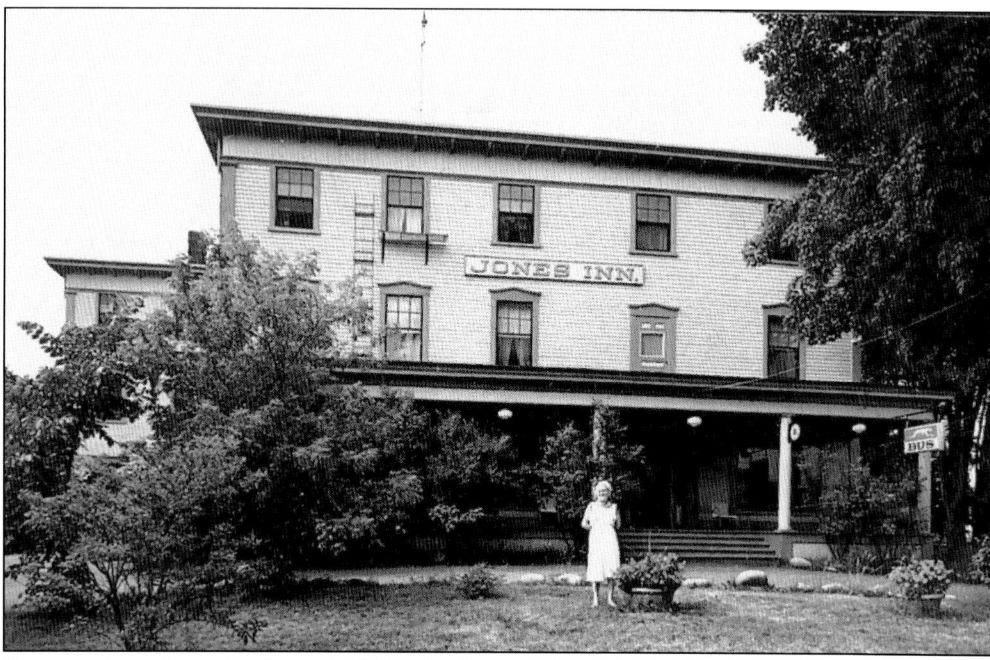

For a number of years in the mid-1900s, the former Shaw House operated as the Jones Inn, with Beulah Barrett acting as hostess. While the inn was known for its hospitality and dining, it also earned some notoriety for its inclusion in a fictional book of the time period.

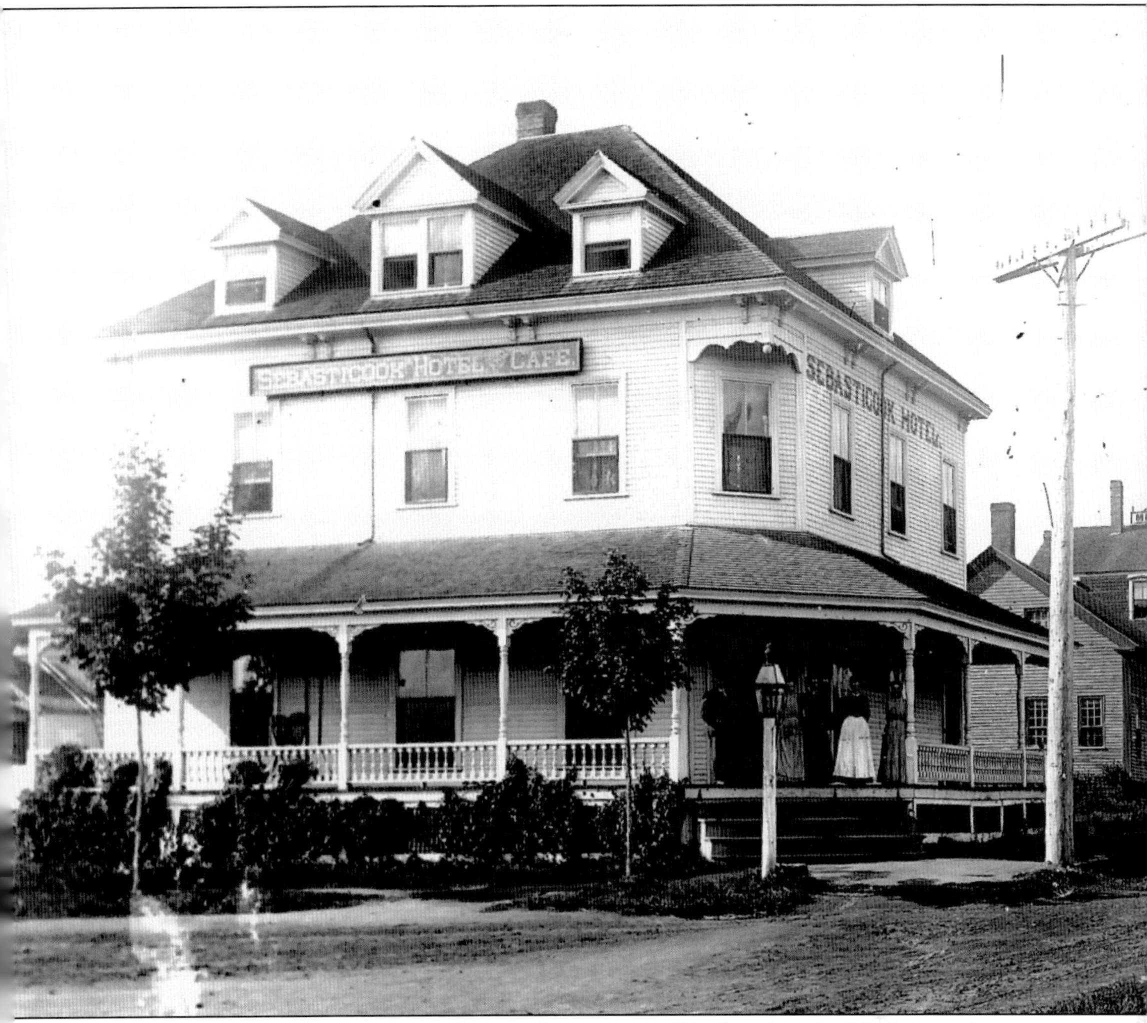

The Sebasticook Hotel housed travelers at the corner of Railroad and Mill Streets for many years. The location was convenient for train travelers on the main line of the Maine Central Railroad. It also was likely convenient for businessmen calling at the town's major woolen mills or the creamery.

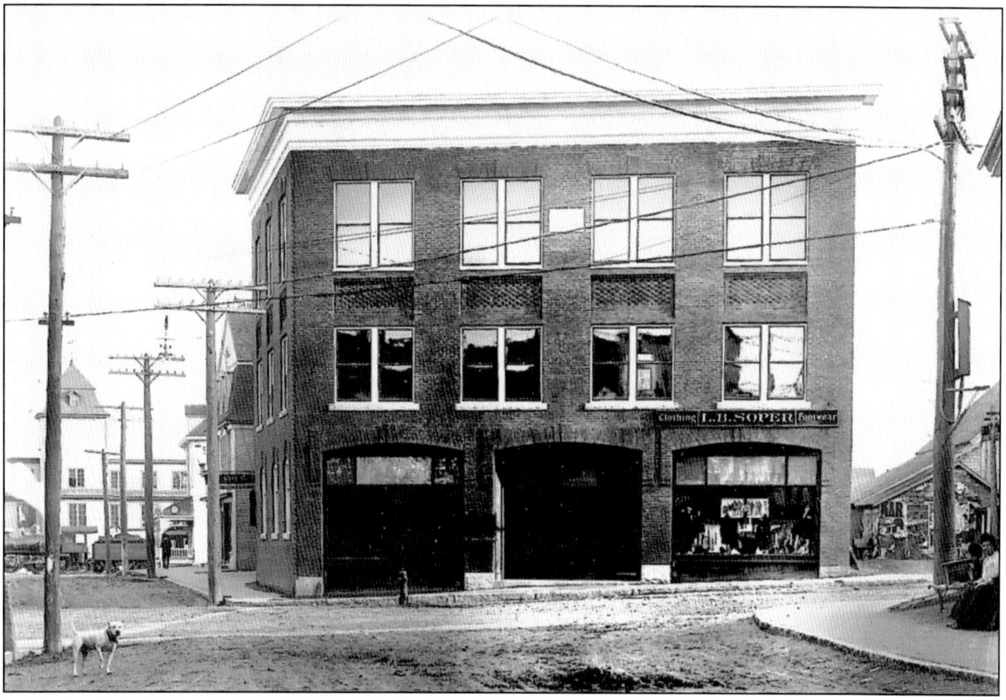

In 1908, a new brick block was erected on Newport's Main Street for the Waterville Trust Company. By 1914, the building was owned by the Kenduskeag Trust Company. Other banks to occupy the quarters included Depositors Trust and Key Bank. Soon after the building opened, the Victory Lodge Knights of Pythias took over the third floor. The floor is currently occupied by the Newport Historical Society, which is planning for new quarters in a library-museum complex on the opposite side of the street.

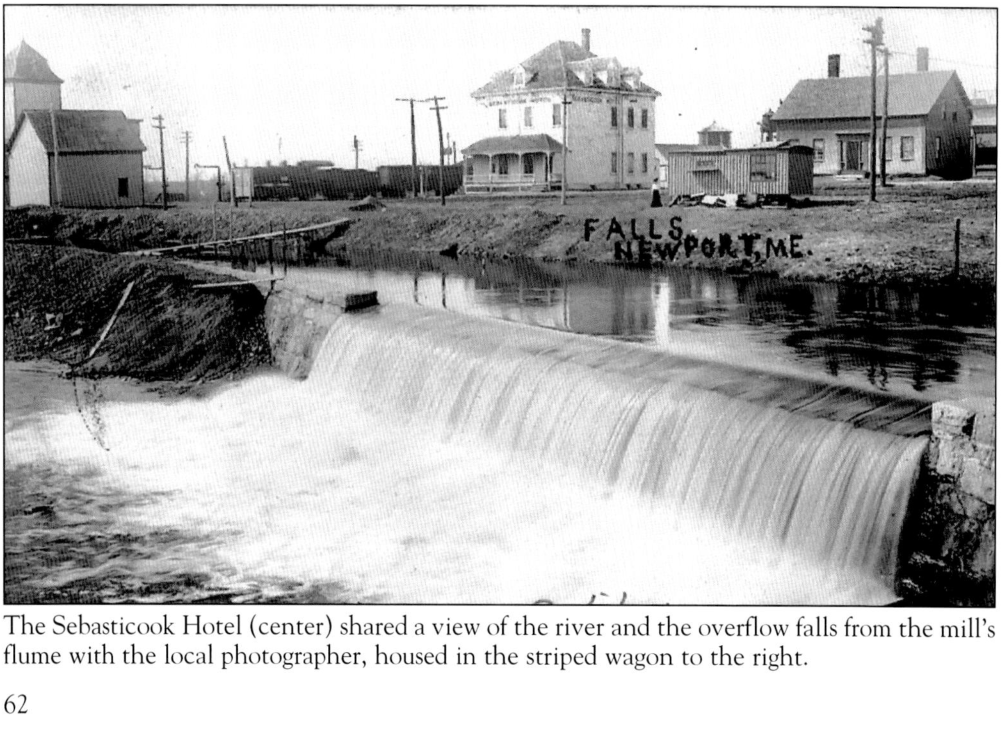

The Sebasticook Hotel (center) shared a view of the river and the overflow falls from the mill's flume with the local photographer, housed in the striped wagon to the right.

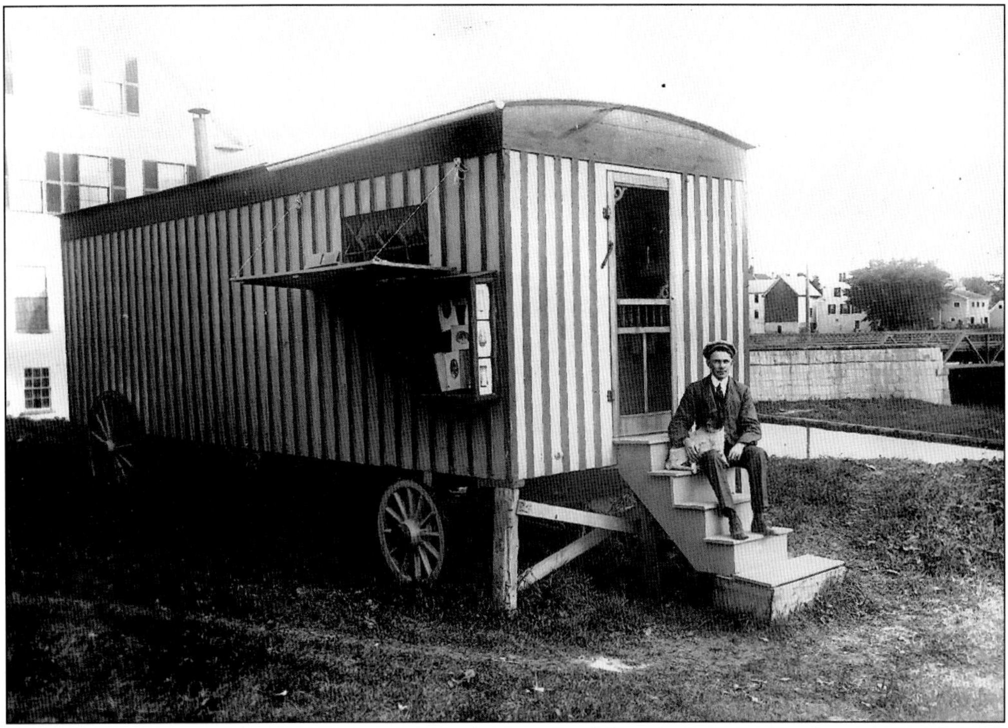

C. F. Huff's Photographic Saloon appears to be as colorful as the name of his business, although black and white photographs cannot tell the whole story. The mobile studio was located on Mill Street at the edge of the river until 1906, when it was sold and moved to Skowhegan.

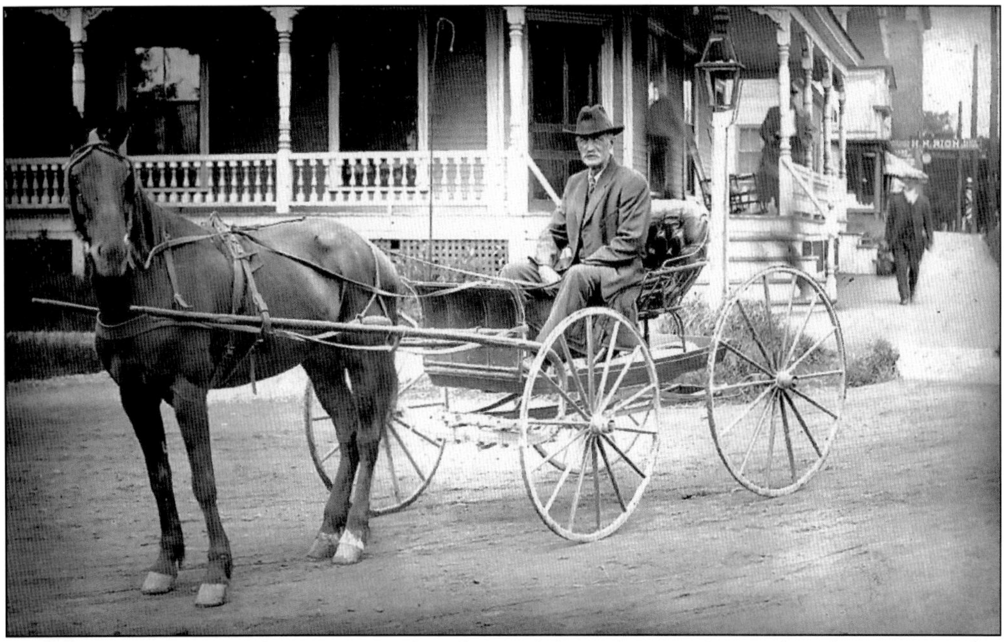

In 1913, this photograph was snapped in front of the Sebasticook Hotel and sent "to Nellie Parkman from Judson Willey," stating simply that it was taken in Newport and signed "Rose." Whether the man is Willey is undetermined.

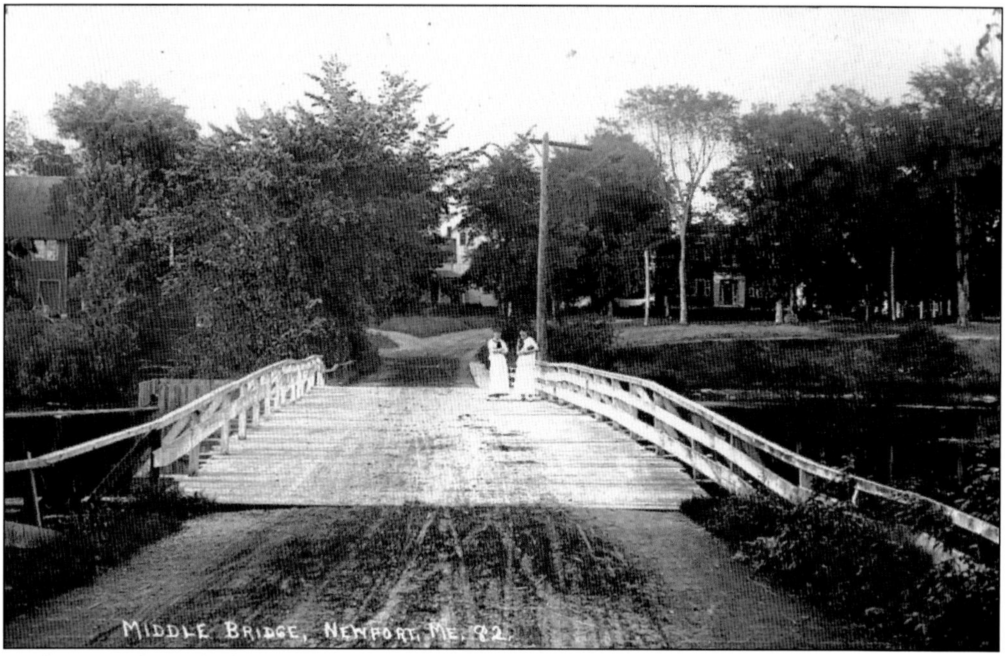

A photographer asked Donna and Marian, two local girls, to pose on the Middle Bridge over the river *c.* 1900. Reportedly, the girls' family was not pleased with this "forward" behavior. One grandmother of the duo apparently tried to buy all copies of the postcard to prevent her offspring's picture from "going all over everywhere."

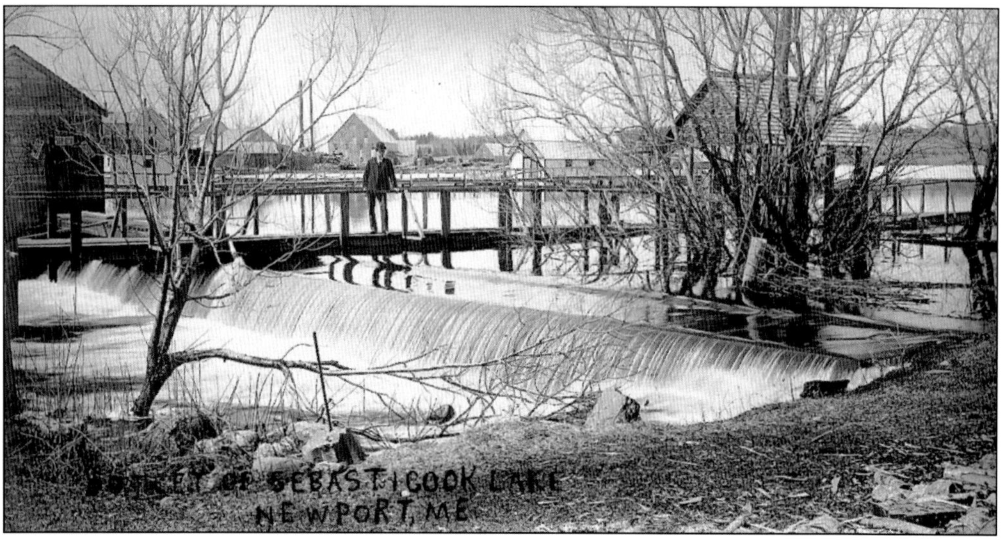

The outlet to Sebasticook Lake has had a dam for as long as anyone can remember, although it has been rebuilt many times. The most recent makeover included the addition of a fishway to allow sea-run (anadromous) fish access to the lake and the spawning grounds in its headwaters.

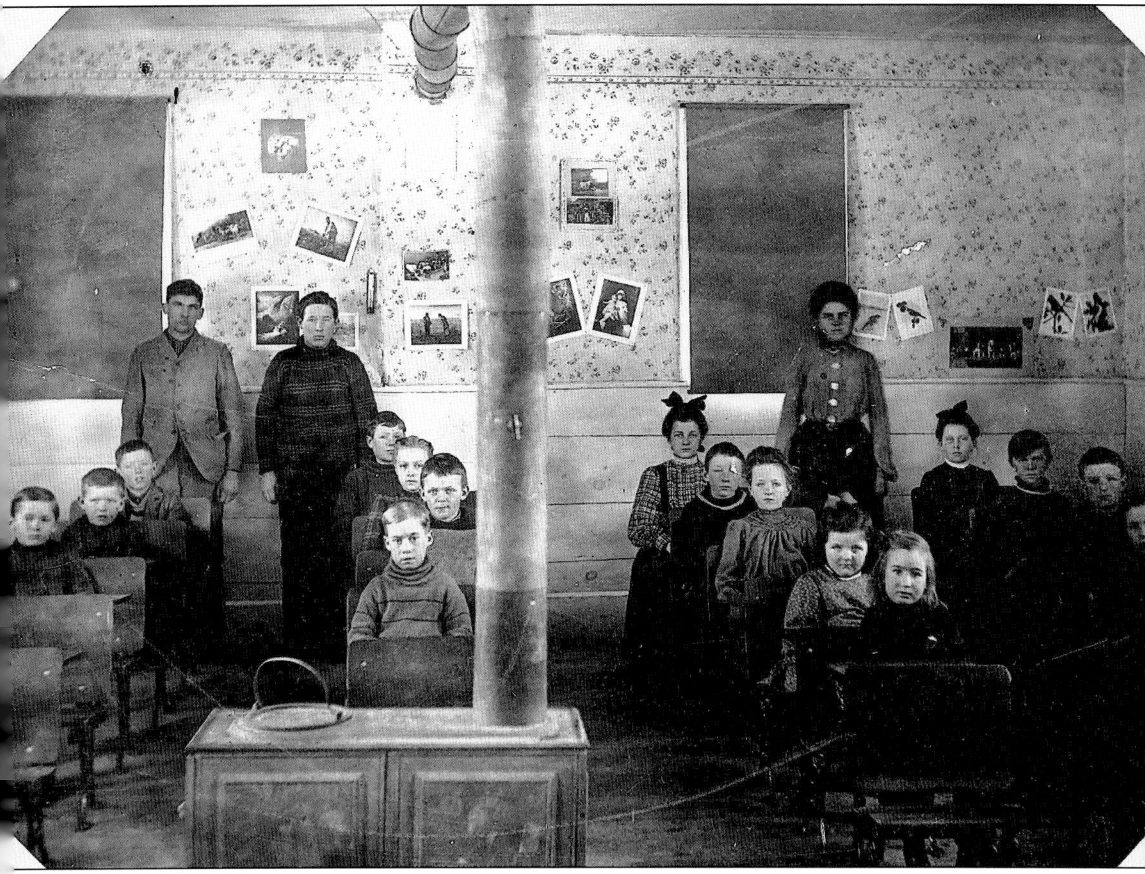

The Hubbard School and the Coburn Corner School were the two one-room schoolhouses in the North Newport school district before schools were consolidated in the village. Early church meetings of the North Newport Church were held at the schools before 1857, first at one and then at the other, so the church was built halfway between the two buildings. The Coburn Corner School burned in the 1940s or 1950s. The class shown above attended the Hubbard School in 1908. The children pictured are, from left to right, as follows: (first row) Ivan Gray, Harold Anderson, and Henry Riley; (second row) Edward Shepardson, Marshall Clark, Martha Rhodes, and unidentified; (third row) Minnie Shepardson, Emma Anderson, Annie Anderson, Ernest Gray, and Gladys Gray; (fourth row) Myrtle Clark, Willie Anderson, Errold Hilliker, and Hazel Patten; (standing) unidentified, Wilbur Gray, and teacher Myrtle Fitts Hilliker.

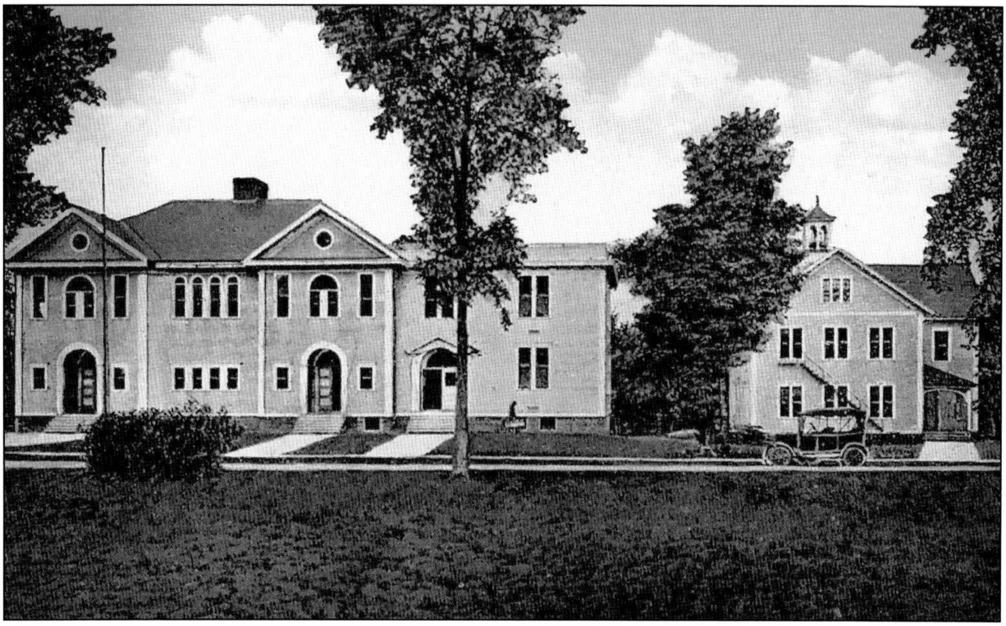

The building that housed Newport High School (right) was originally built in 1874 and was used as one of several district schools until 1910, when it was remodeled to house a high school on the upper floor and a grade school on the first floor. There were 36 high school students and 66 grammar school students in 1910. That was the same year that a lot was purchased along Shaw Street to build a new school (left) to house the primary and intermediate grades. Both buildings are now gone.

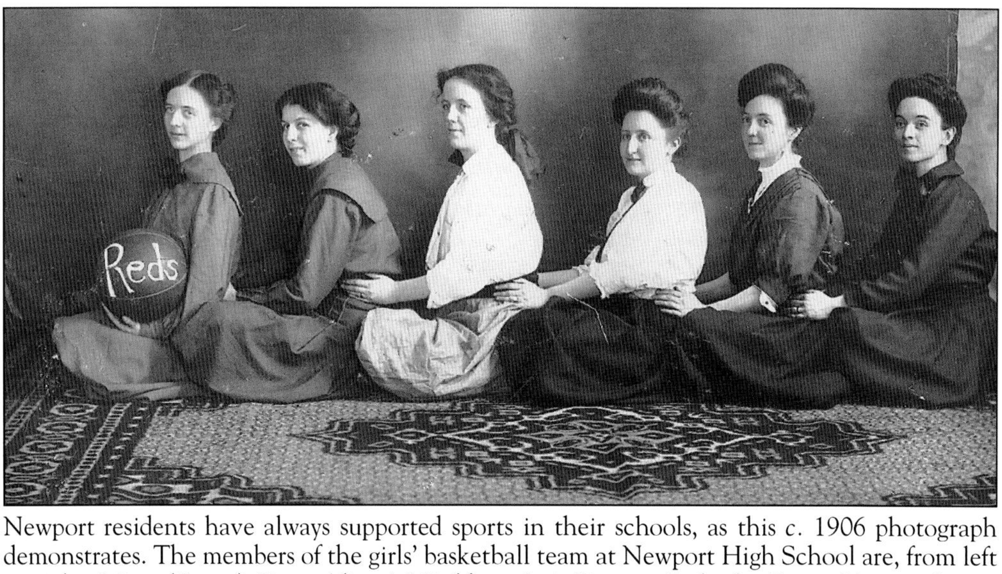

Newport residents have always supported sports in their schools, as this *c.* 1906 photograph demonstrates. The members of the girls' basketball team at Newport High School are, from left to right, Mina (Soper) Cary, Alice McFadden, Avis Benson Furbush, Carrie Norton Soper, Phyllis Benson, and Clara Redman.

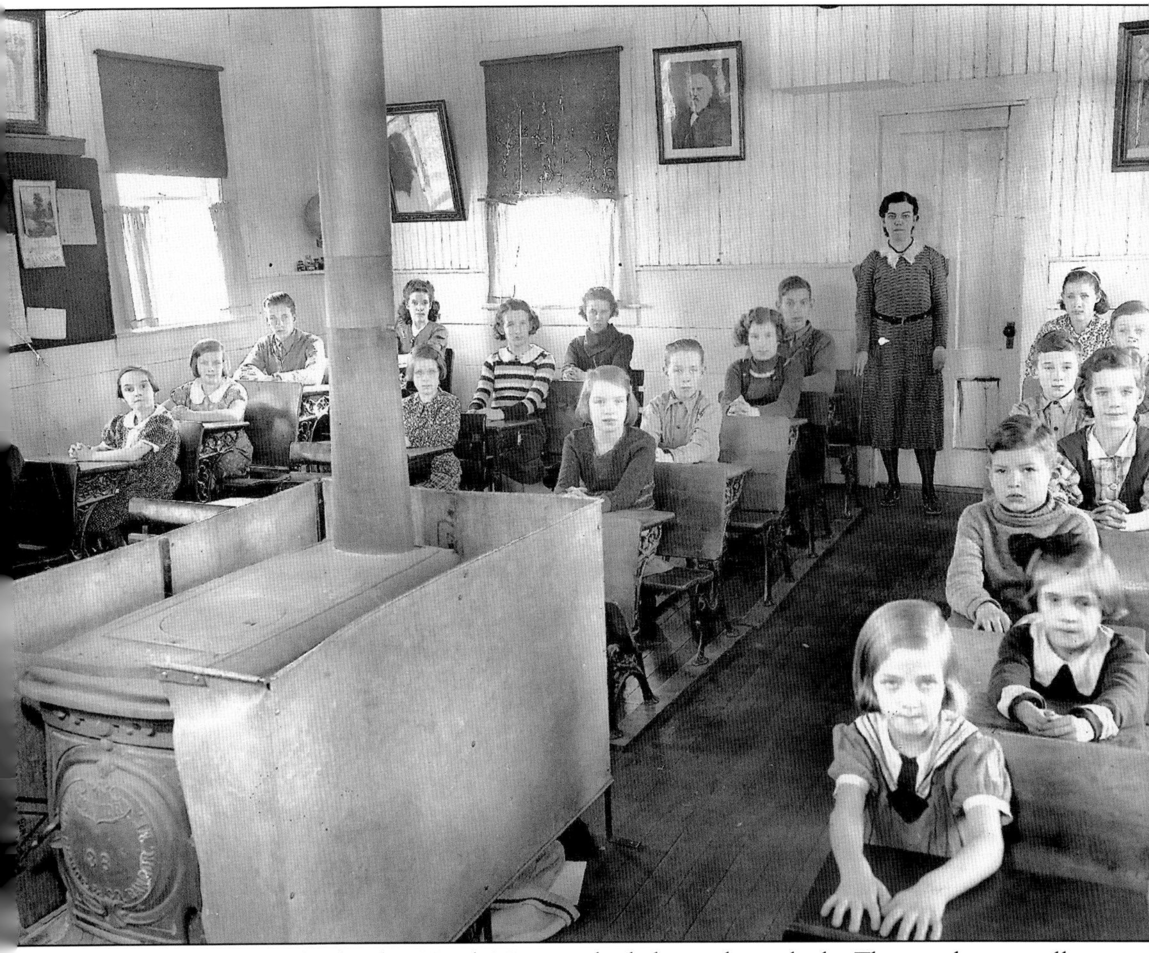

By 1938, the Hubbard School at North Newport had changed very little. The wood stove still provided heat for a second generation of students from some of the same families as the first. Some members of the class are, from left to right, as follows: (first row) Basil (Stearns) Ward, Rita Lancaster, Arlene Gray, Leon Gray, and Doris Russell; (second row) Winona Gray, Evangeline Gray, and Barbara Townsend; (third row) Beatrice Russell, Robert Gray, Elizabeth Jackson, and Silas Jackson; (fourth row) Gloria Gray, Helen Gray, Elmer Jackson, Bertha Russell, Howard Gray, Fred Townsend, and Barbara Gray. Their teacher was Geraldine Smith.

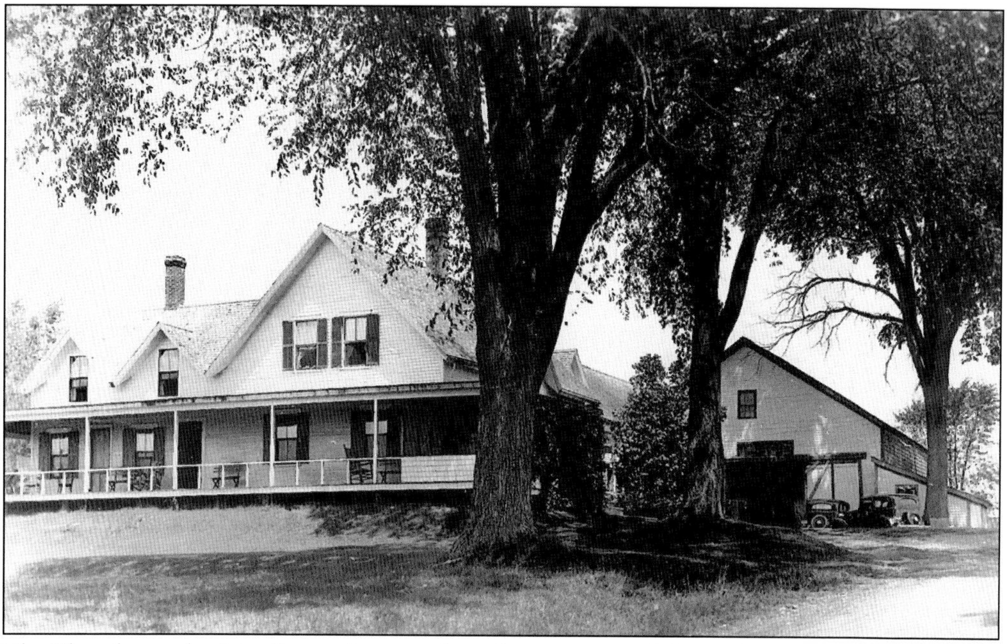

The Elms, located originally at what was then the terminus of Grove Street, was a summer inn for vacationers on the east shore of the lake. The inn was purchased in 1906 by J. W. Smart and was renovated, becoming a 14-room inn. The Elms was pictured in the 1914 Centennial Souvenir book, the writer of which noted that more and more visitors were coming to the lake each year to vacation.

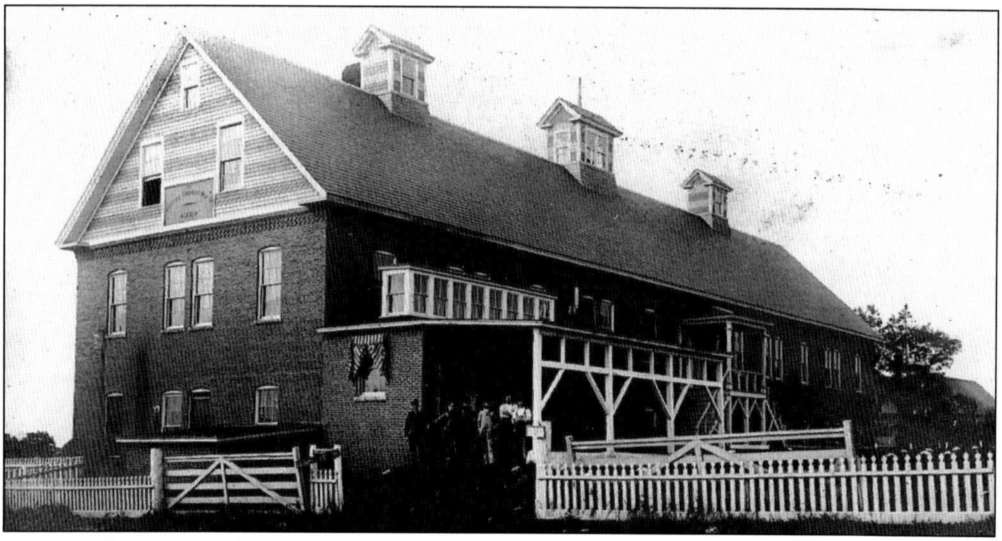

In 1891, the Aroostook Condensed Milk Company built a factory by the railroad, announcing it would need 4,000 cows to supply the plant. In 1902, Borden's Condensed Milk Company purchased "the creamery." In 1946, H. P. Hood and sons established a presence in Newport, renovating and expanding the former Borden's plant. The Hood plant at one time was the largest of its kind in New England. It closed in the 1980s.

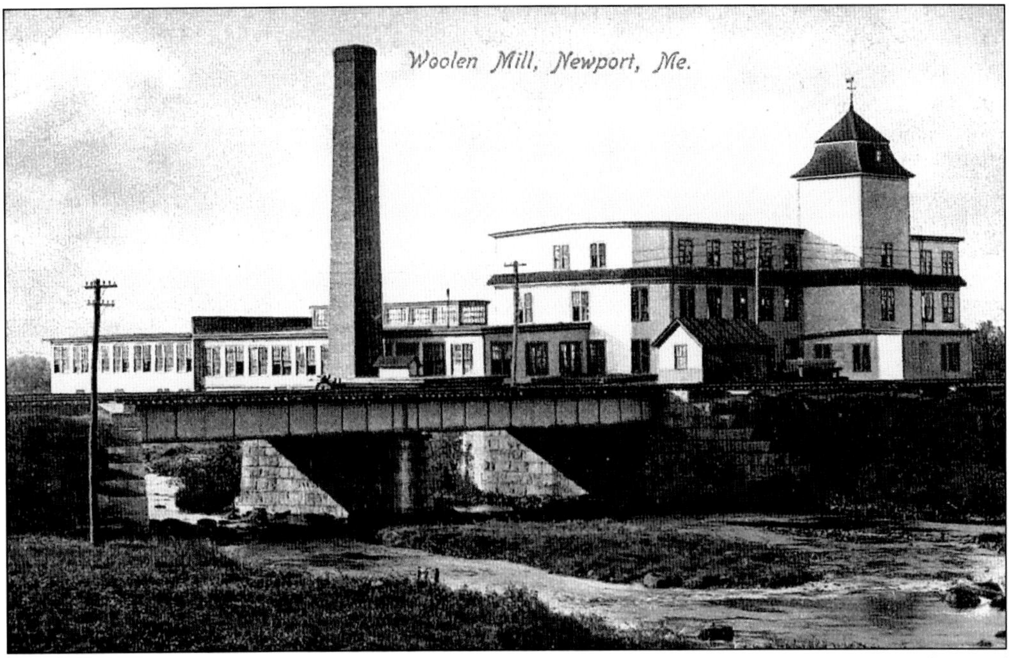

For many years, Newport had the good fortune to have two woolen mills: Newport Woolen and Weymouth Wool Company. Newport Woolen was constructed in 1891 and was operated by a local corporation. In 1896, it was purchased and run by a new corporation affiliated with similar manufacturing in nearby Pittsfield. It eventually became a division of Guilford Manufacturing. In the mid-1960s, the upper floors of the main building were lost to fire. The only reason the lower floor was saved was that firefighters flooded the building until water poured out the windows.

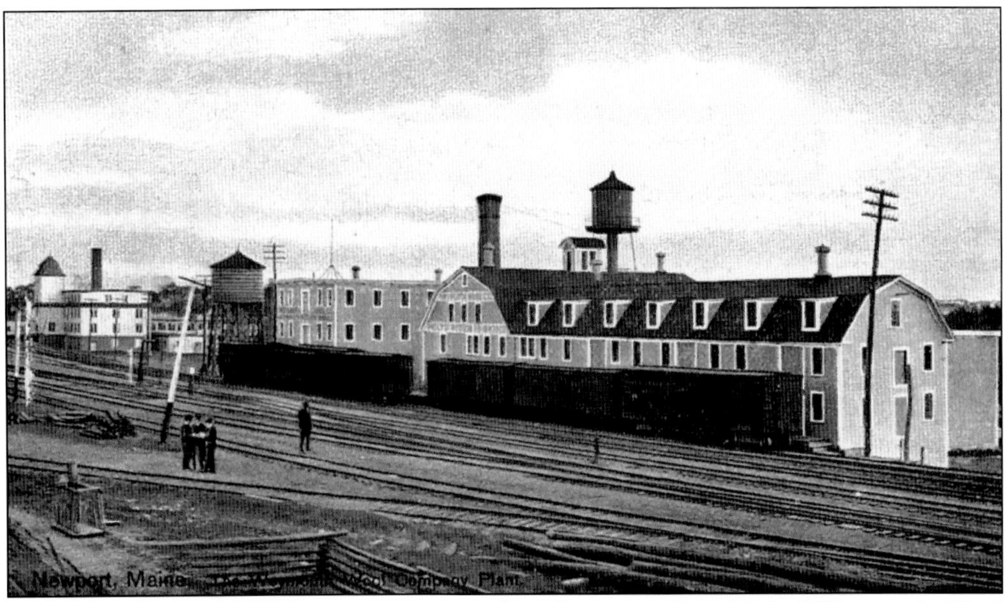

In 1902, J. H. Weymouth came to Newport from Bangor and established Weymouth Wool Company. Weymouth managed the mill until his death in 1912, when his son Carl took over the operation. It was still in operation during the Newport centennial of 1914.

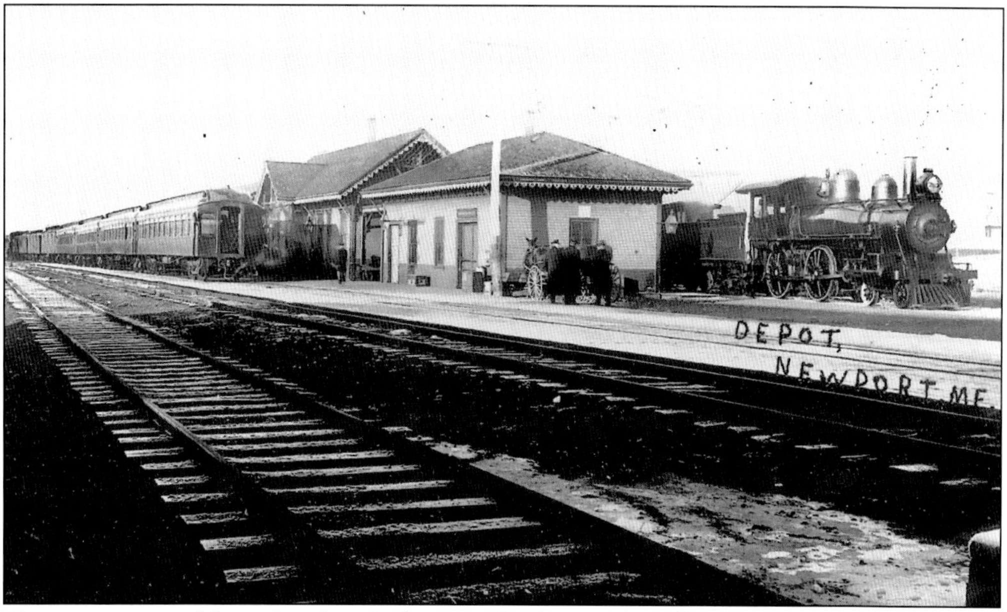

The importance of the railroad in the history of Sebasticook Valley cannot be underestimated. Without the main line of the Maine Central Railroad running through Newport and Pittsfield, it is doubtful either town would have grown as much or as quickly as each did. Several manufacturers were located along the main tracks in Newport, Detroit, and Pittsfield. Passenger travel by rail in Sebasticook Valley began in 1855, when the rails first opened between Pittsfield and Bangor. By 1862, that line was merged into what became known as the Maine Central Railroad, a line that dominated Maine rail service until 1981, when it was purchased by Guilford Transportation Industries. Spurs that ran from Newport to Dover-Foxcroft beginning in 1868 fostered further development, just as the Pittsfield to Hartland line, in 1886, did for Palmyra and Hartland. The Hartland line continued to Harmony in 1912.

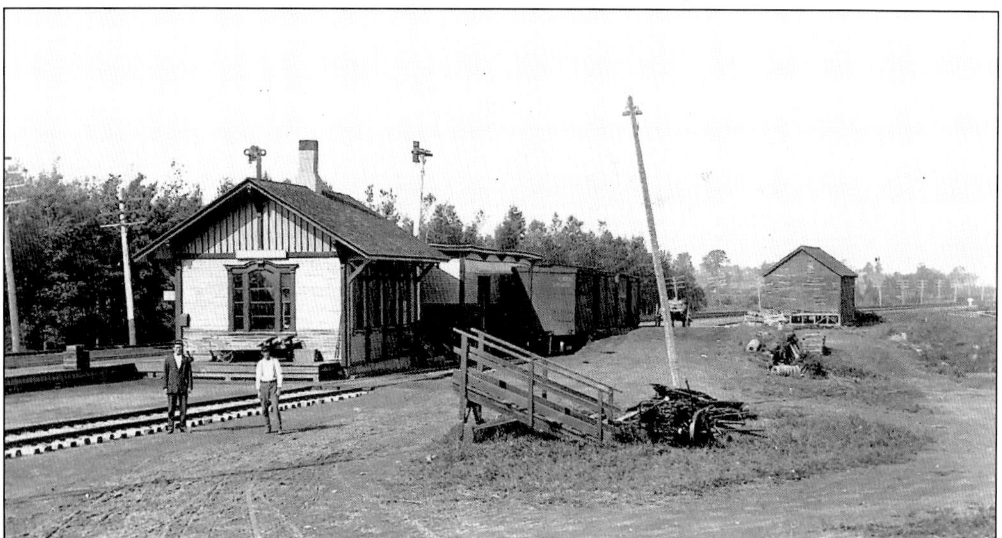

There were two depots in Newport, one in the village and one at East Newport. Today, the line is a freight line, and the picturesque depots in many communities such as Newport and East Newport have disappeared.

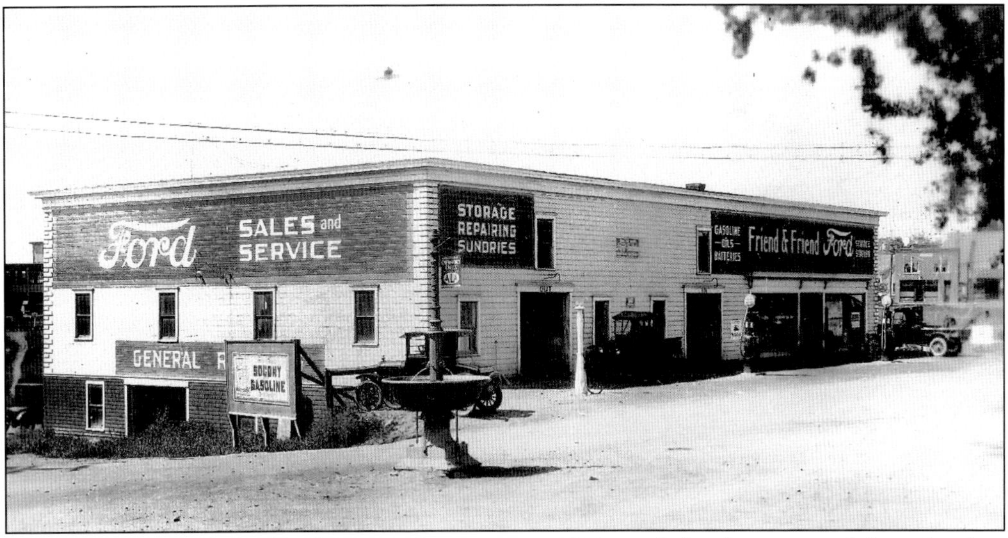

Henry Ford created the Ford Motor Company in 1903, and the first automobile sighted in Newport seems to have appeared two years later. Friend Ford Sales and Service was not far behind. The Friend family's Newport sales operation predated Earle Friend's Pittsfield Motor Sales, which opened in 1922. Both Ford dealerships eventually closed, although descendants still operate a Ford dealership in Skowhegan. The building that housed the Newport sales operation at the east end of the Main Street bridge burned *c.* 1990.

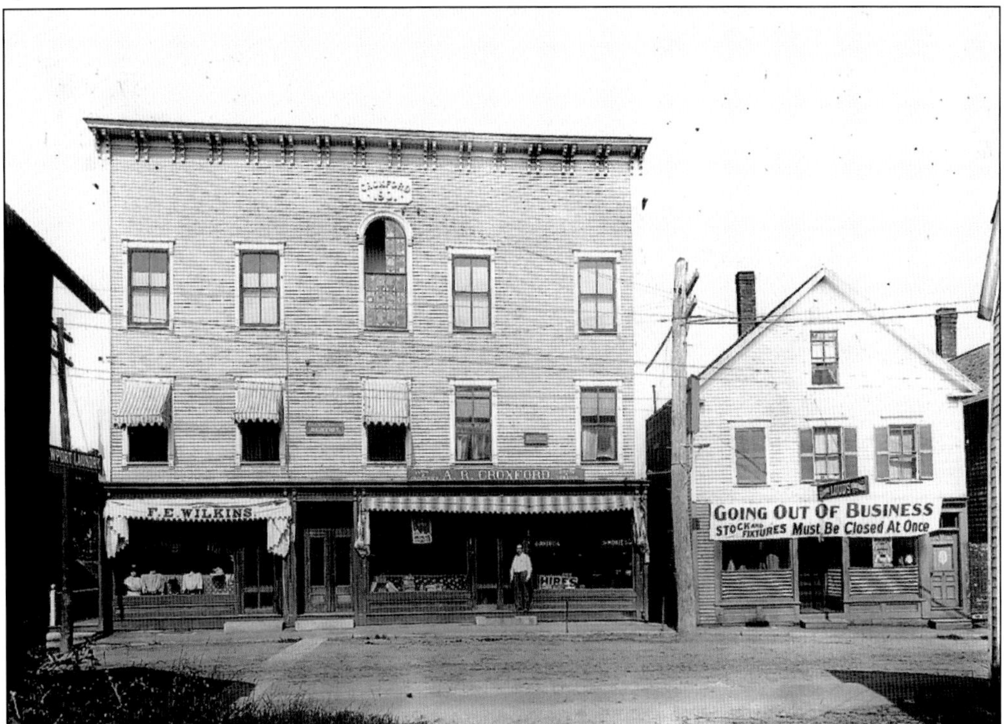

In the early 1900s, F. E. Wilkins ran a clothing store and A. R. Croxford ran a grocery in the Croxford Block, built in 1901 on Water Street. Loud's Clothing and Furnishings next door, however, was on its way out. A doctor's and dentist's offices were located on the second floor.

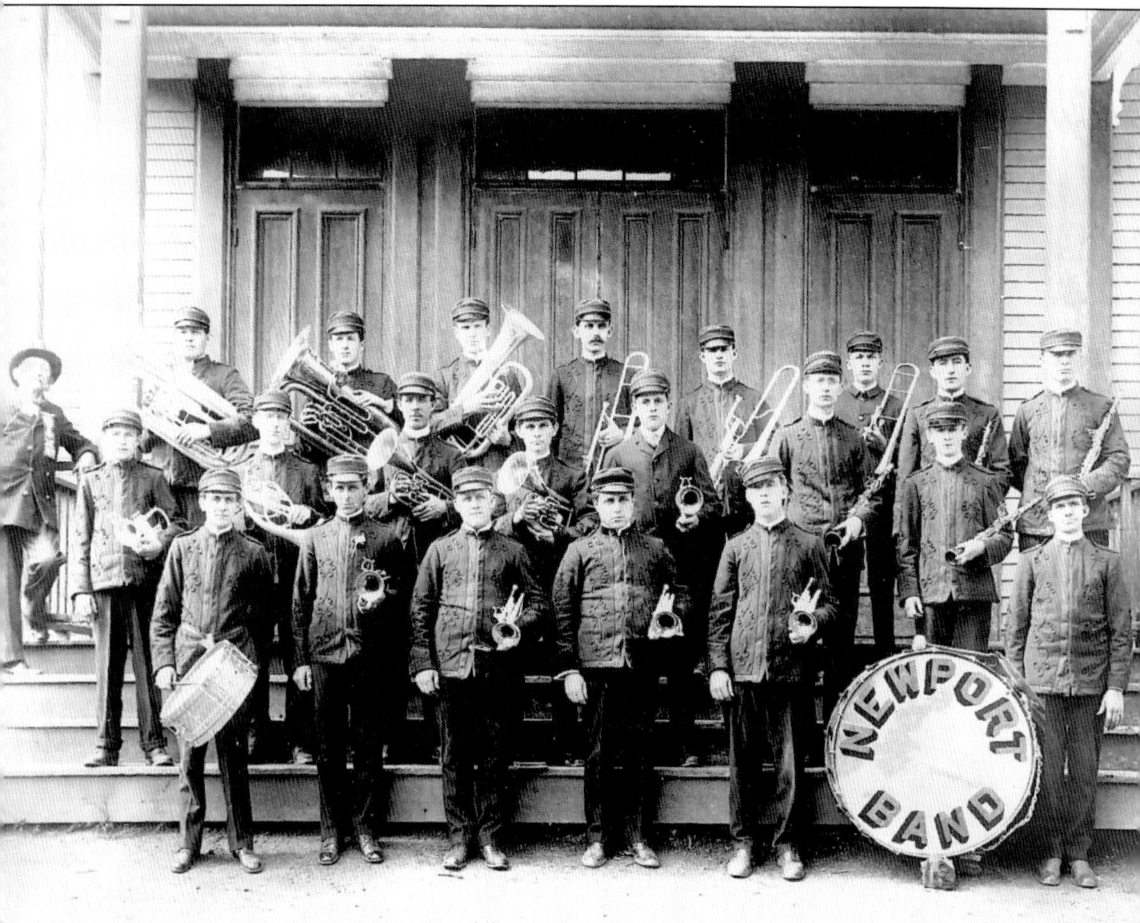

Newport had a community band to play for its many functions beginning in the late 1800s. This group is believed to have been organized by a Ralph Dyer. It was no doubt a prelude of things to come; the Nokomis Regional High School Warrior Band and its various units would take the region's musical expertise to parades and festivals across the country and even to Europe.

Three

DETROIT

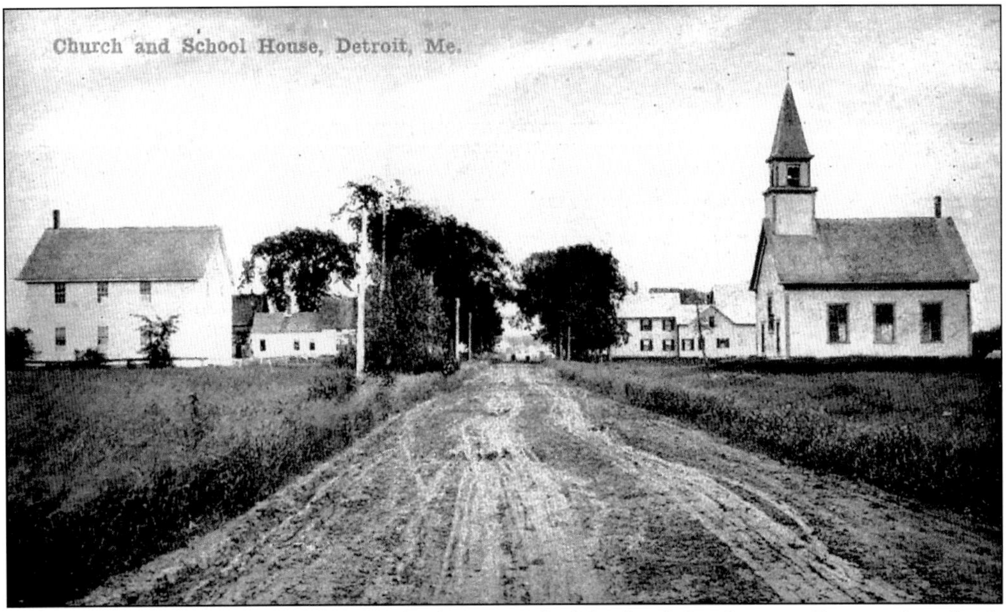

Similar to many neighboring towns, the first record of the land that became Detroit dates back to the 1792 survey created by Ephraim Ballard and Samuel Weston. Recorded first as "Township Number Five, Second Range, North of the Waldo Patent," the town knew many names, including Masts Town and Chandlerville, before becoming Detroit in 1841. The residents of the 19th century adopted a French name, D'etroit, to commemorate the rips in the Sebasticook River where the village center is located. The rips is a "body of water made rough by the meeting of currents or tides," and *d'etroit* is the French word for "straits" or "narrows." It was the attraction of the water flow that drew early settlers to harness it to generate power for a number of mills. Early photographs taken from a viewpoint north of the village show the former two-story schoolhouse on the left and the Union Church on the right. The church is now the Detroit Meetinghouse; it was purchased for the town when the Methodist conference decided to sell it.

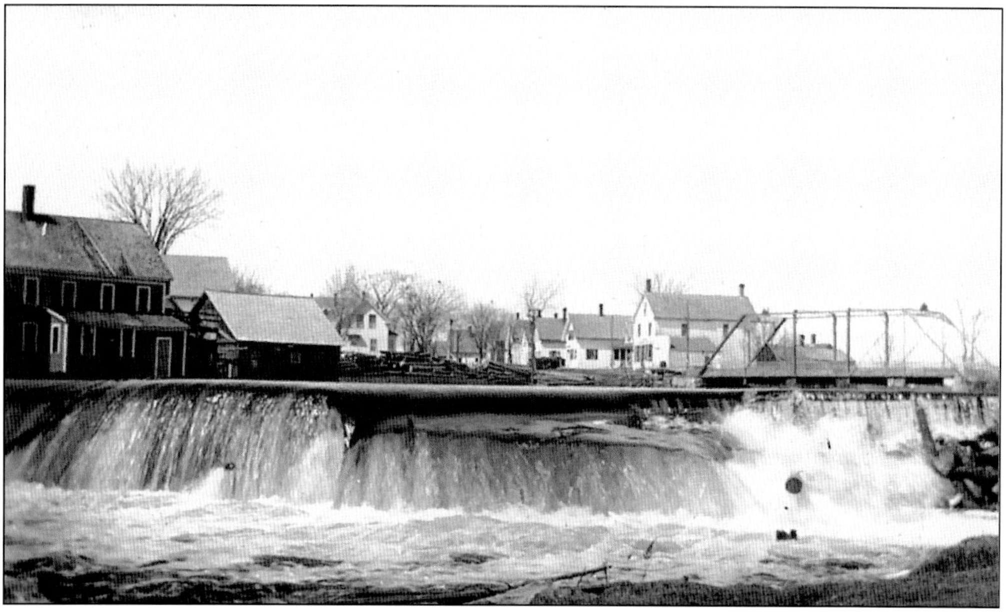

Business was booming around the village dam c. 1906. Lara and Whiting's Hub Factory is to the right of Crocker's Carriage Shop. Lewis Crocker and his crew manufactured and repaired all types of vehicles, including carts, sleighs, and carriages. In addition, the vehicles could be painted and decorated by the expert crew. A supply of fresh lumber is waiting on the banks for the variety of mills on the river.

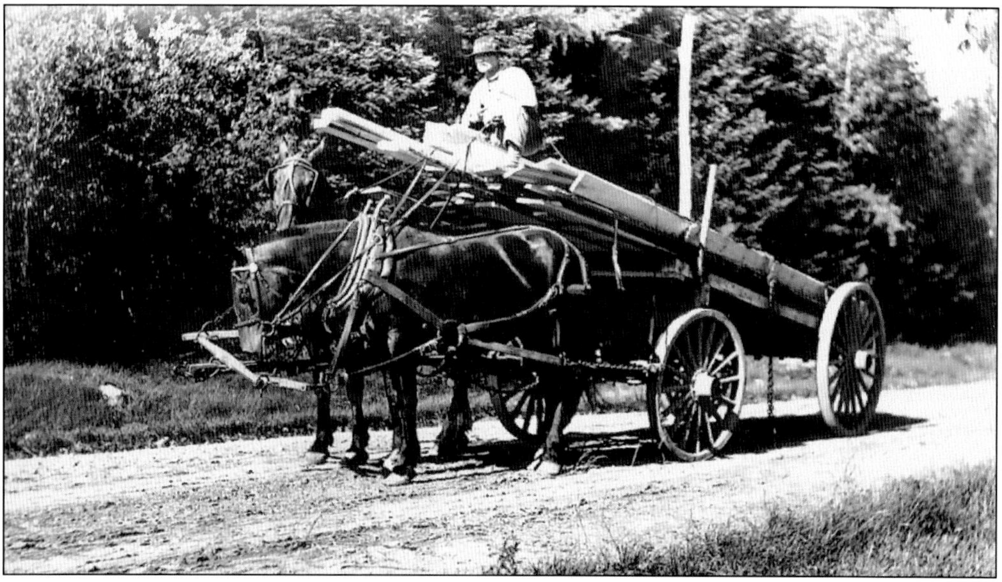

Hauling lumber in the late 1800s or early 1900s was physical toil for man and beast. Laden with a load of lumber, this driver was in for a lengthy ride to his destination (somewhere in Detroit), and it likely took a long time to unload and place the lumber when he arrived.

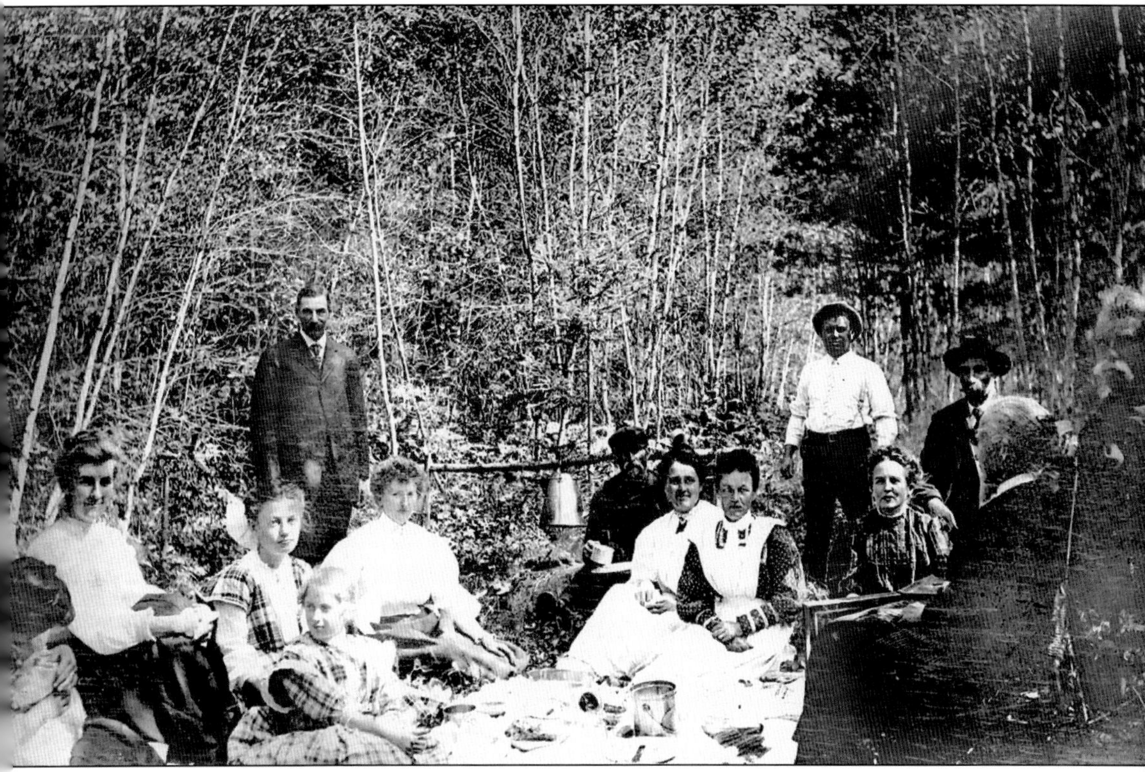

The Libby family came to Detroit *c.* 1842 and were large landowners in the area before the move. Several Libby descendants owned property on the Lower (River) Road for more than 100 years. A Libby picnic, possibly in 1908 or 1909, appears to have been held in the woods of one of the family farms. Aaron C. Libby is standing in the back, wearing a coat and tie. Emma T. Libby is seated in the center, and Nellie Sanborn Libby is at her left. Behind them appears to be George Libby. Marguerite Libby appears to be seated in plaid in front of Aaron. Orin Libby may be standing by a tree on the far right. The other people are unidentified.

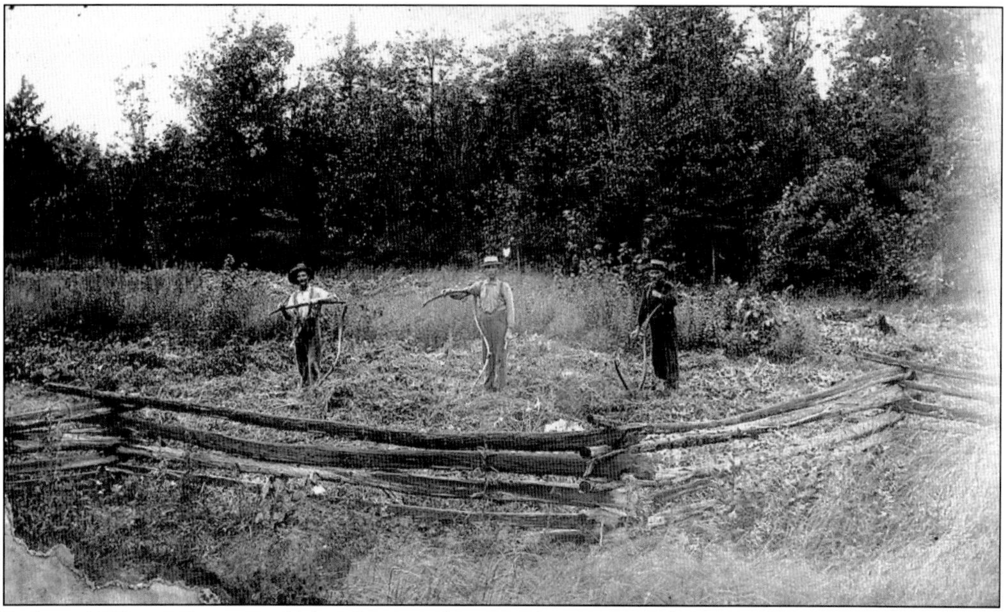

Before 1900, scything could be slow work, even for a crew of three. Shown in this *c.* 1890 photograph are, from left to right, Will Clark, Walter Harding, and Alvah Head, who were cutting fodder hay at Head Pitch on the banks of the Sebasticook River on Alvah and Abbie (Lord) Head's farm.

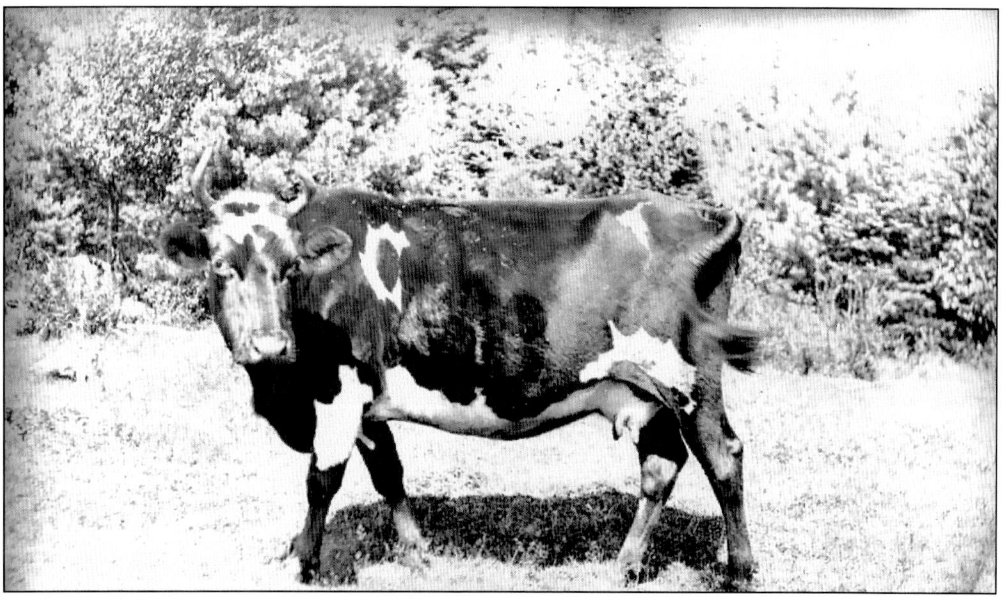

In the early 1900s, it was common for many rural families to have their own milk cow. However, the Aaron Libby family on the River Road did not think of their cow as common, for it was born with its own natural brand and was affectionately called "the G-cow," as the marking on her left shoulder noted.

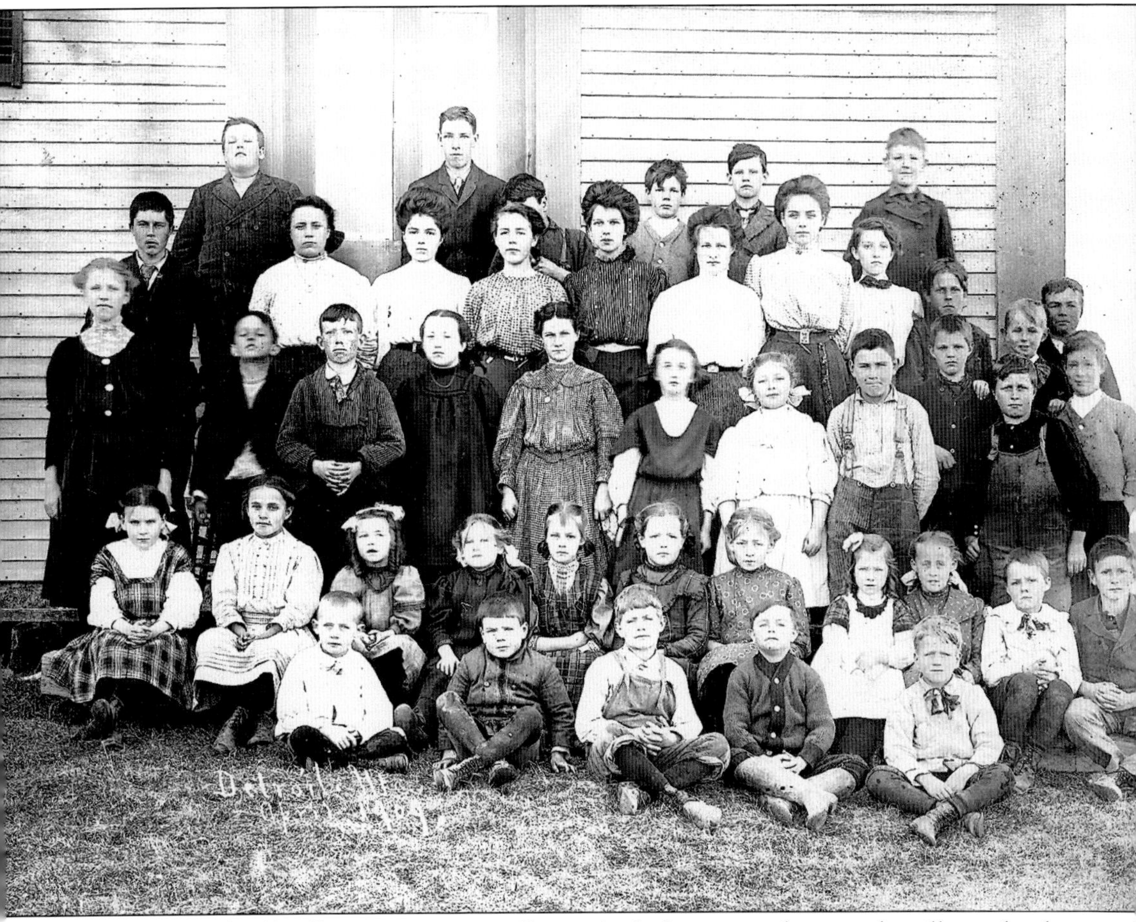

As a bustling and self-sufficient community, Detroit had a large attendance at the village school in 1909, when this class posed for a picture outside the church. Shown in this photograph are, from left to right, as follows: (first row) Frank Foley, Hallie Priest, unidentified, Bill Harding, and unidentified; (second row) unidentified, Evelynn Harding, two unidentified people, Elida Field, four unidentified people, Herbert Field, and unidentified; (third row) Olive Mayo, Bill ?, Arthur Bean, Achsa Bean, Min Giles, Hazel Springer, Rita Gifford, Vernon Priest, Augustus Field, Joe Davis, and unidentified; (fourth row) Arthur McFarland, Myrtle Raynes, Blanche Wyman, Florence Norris, Ethel Harding, Mae Giles, Esther Harris, Vaella Norton, ? Harding, Harold Gifford, and Leon Marcia; (fifth row) Lester Marcia, Winifred McPhee, Earl Harris, Everett Harding, Paul Field, and Eugene Field.

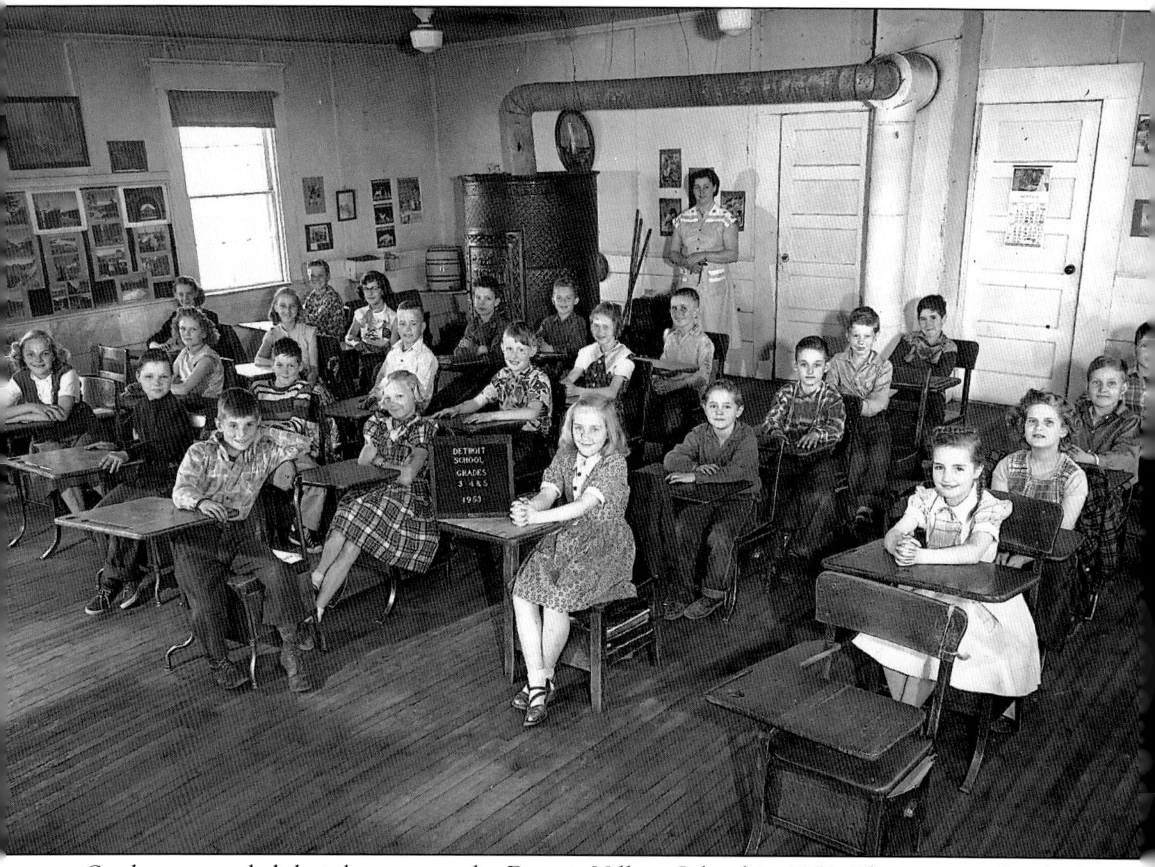

Students attended their last year at the Detroit Village School in 1953. The upstairs class had Anna Field Fernald (back) as a teacher. Students included in this photograph are, from left to right, as follows: (first row) Janis Withee and Ronnie Dodge; (second row) Judy Cookson, Joan Basford, Alma Garrett, and Jackie Jones; (third row) Maurice Dodge, Paul Ray, Donn Temple, Chris Krause, and David Starbird; (fourth row) Stanley Garnett, Donna Morton, David Rollins, Joyce Knight, and Ben Bickford; (fifth row) Barbara Davis, Howard Whitaker, Franklin Blanchard, Ronald Temple, and Dennis Raye; (sixth row) Colleen Withee, Patricia Basford, Ralph Hart, and Frank Raye. The old school was closed and a new one-floor school was opened at the lower junction of Routes 69 and 220. The school was eventually named in honor of longtime teacher Dorothy R. Cookson. When the school was given up by the school district in the 1980s, it became the Dorothy R. Cookson School Town Hall.

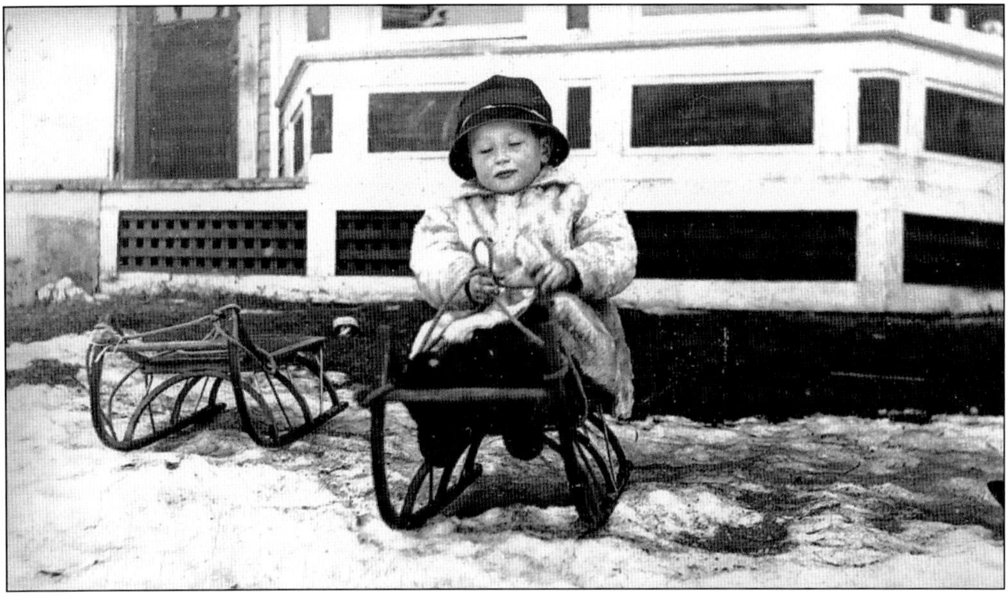

Clement O. Libby was just two and a half years old when his parents placed him on a wooden runner sled at the family home on the River Road.

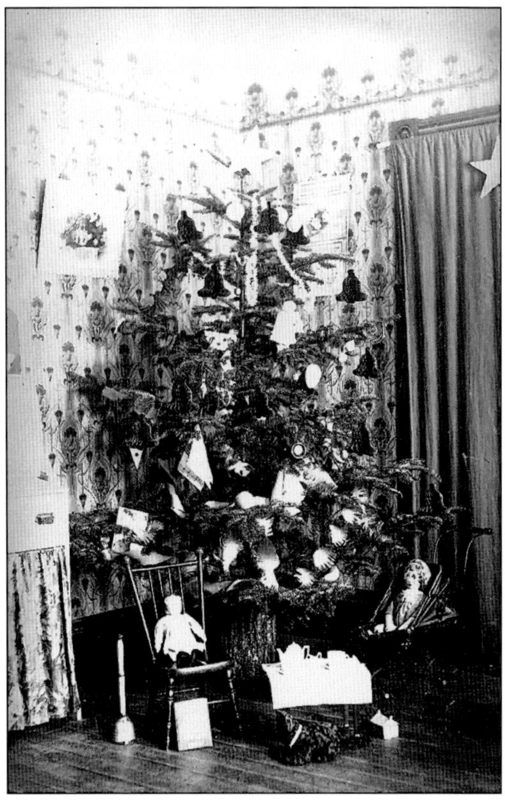

Christmas on the family farm in the early 1900s was much simpler than today's Christmas with artificial trees and plastic lights. The Libby family decorated its tree with paper bells and napkins and a paper star at the top, and the gifts consisted of stuffed dolls and animals, a wooden chair, a doll carriage, and a small tea set.

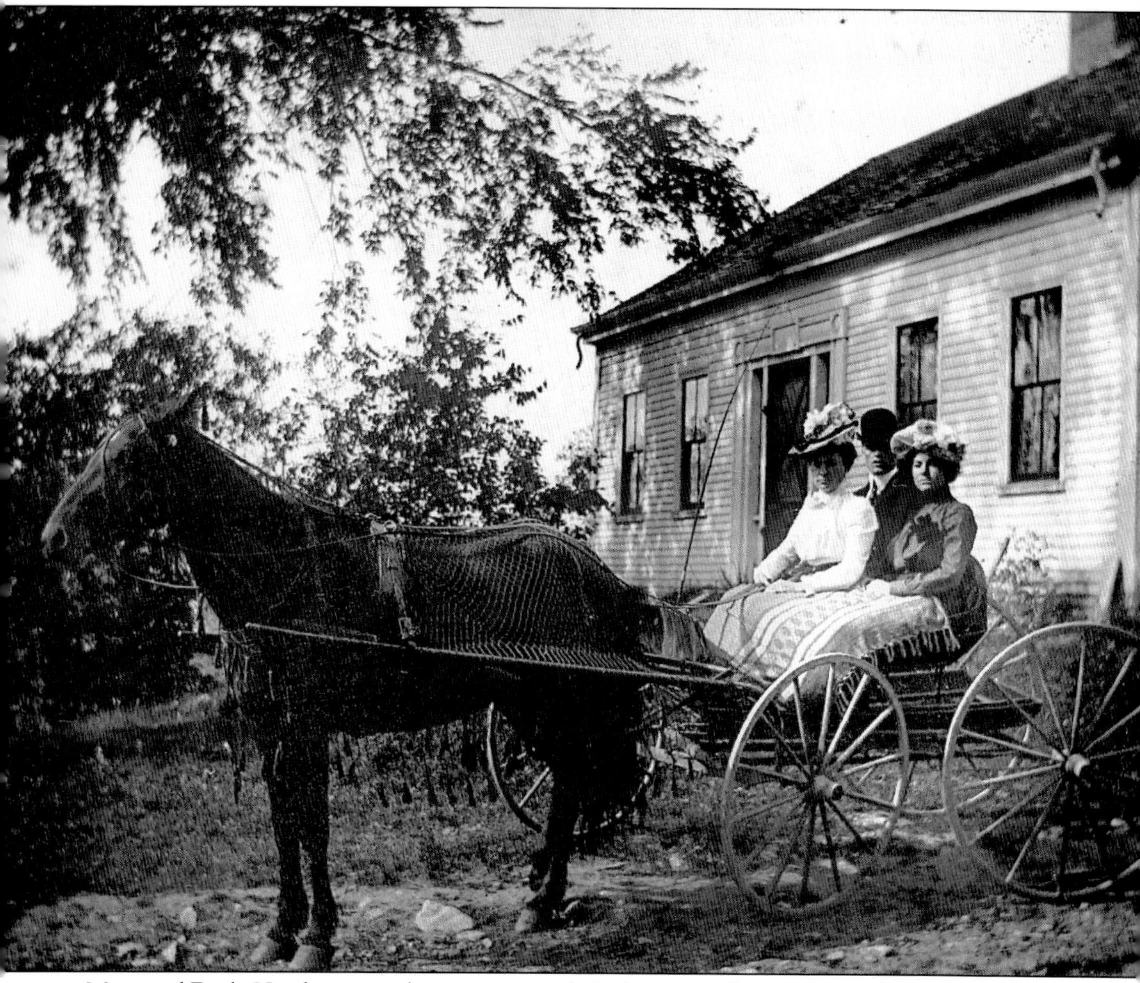

Mary and Freda Head apparently were accomplished carriage drivers. Here, they prepare to take Willis Rich for a ride through the village. The trio stopped in front of the Joseph Lord home.

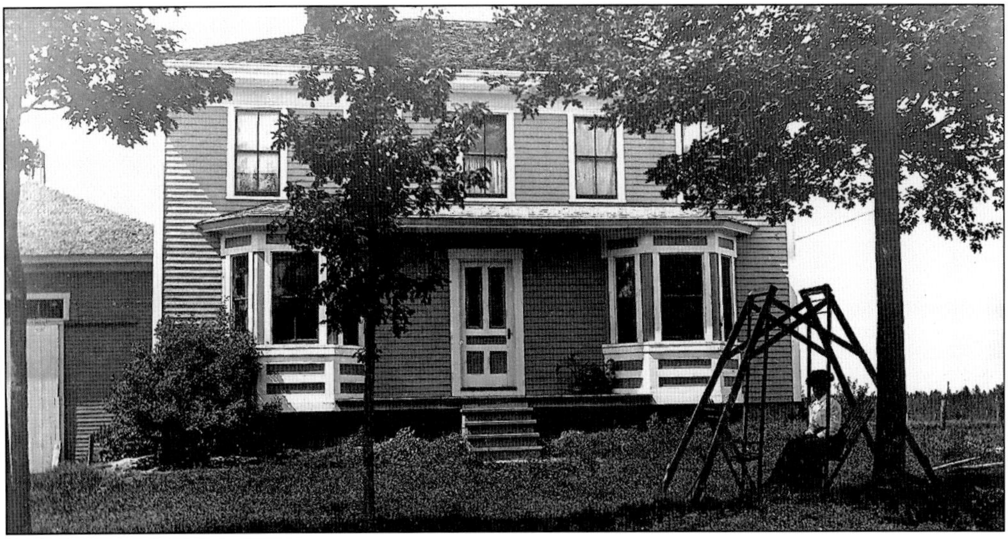

One of three Libby homes on the River Road in the 1900s was the Ed Libby house, known locally as the "pink house" for many years. It was eventually destroyed by fire. Emma Libby is seen here in the lawn swing.

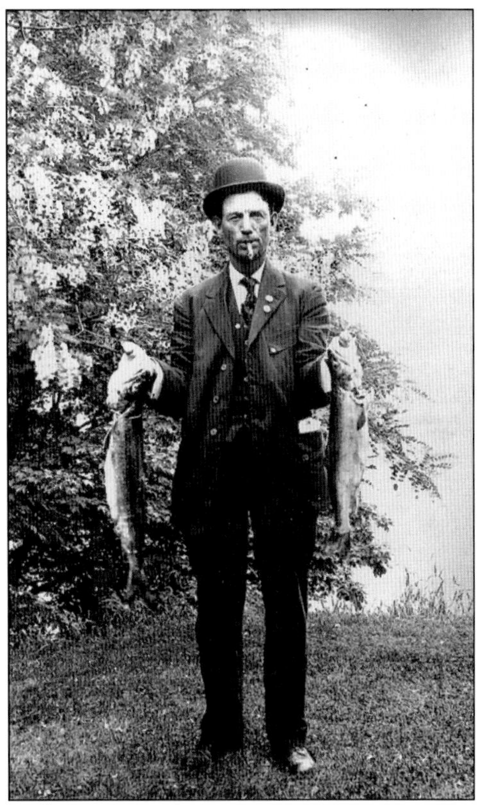

Ed Libby enjoyed fishing, apparently while dressed in style. It would appear that the Sebasticook River could still yield a nice catch in the early 1900s. The pollution of later years took its toll on the water quality, but cleanup efforts up and down the river have restored the water, and sea-run fish are again making their way past the many dams between the Sebasticook and the Kennebec.

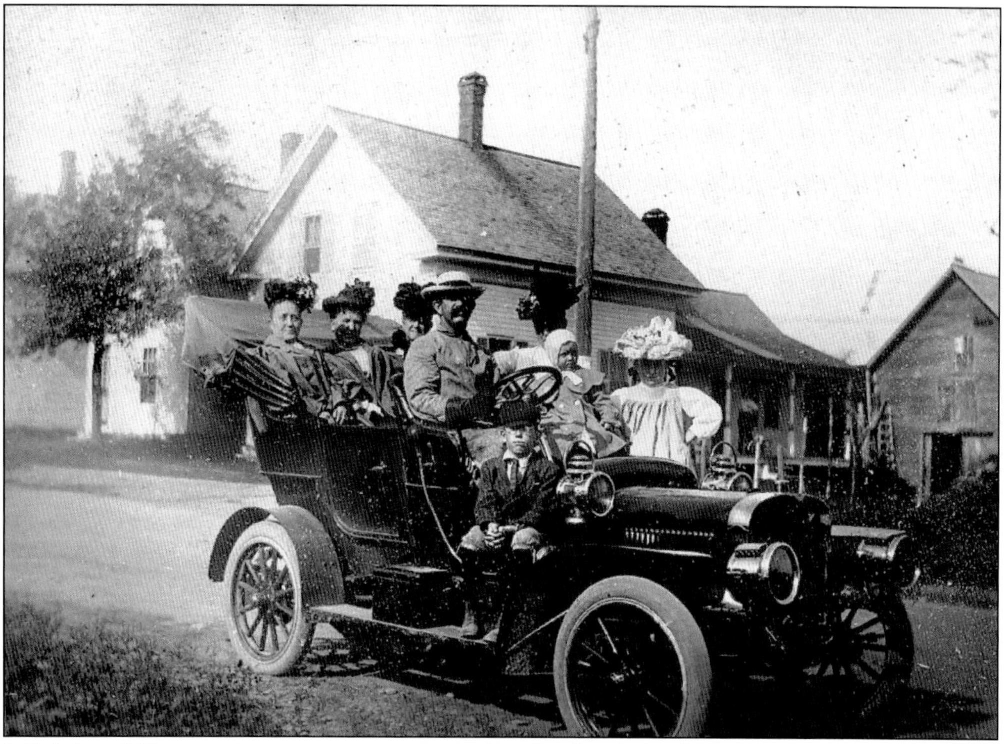

J. Ralph and Florence Bean were a prominent Detroit family in the early 1900s, owning a large automobile in 1910 complete with the necessary gauntlets and dusters to shake off the road residue. The Bean's daughter Achsa became a doctor and served with the British Army before the United States joined World War II.

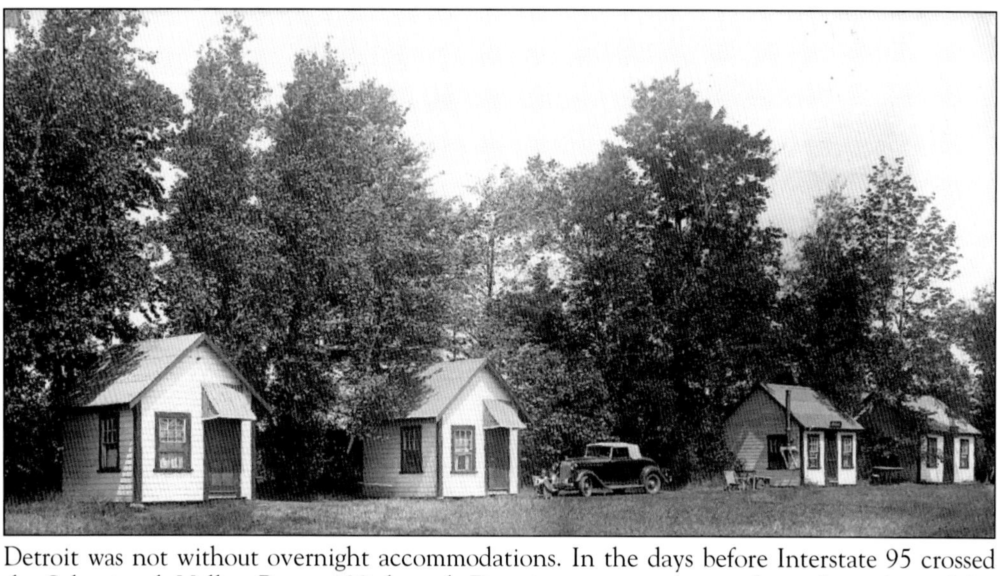

Detroit was not without overnight accommodations. In the days before Interstate 95 crossed the Sebasticook Valley, Route 100 through Detroit was a popular north-south roadway. John and Irene Braley opened a lunchroom and added cabins in the orchard to create Orchard Inn on the North Road. The location was across the road from the former Agway fertilizer plant and around the corner from Palmyra's Oxbow Cabins.

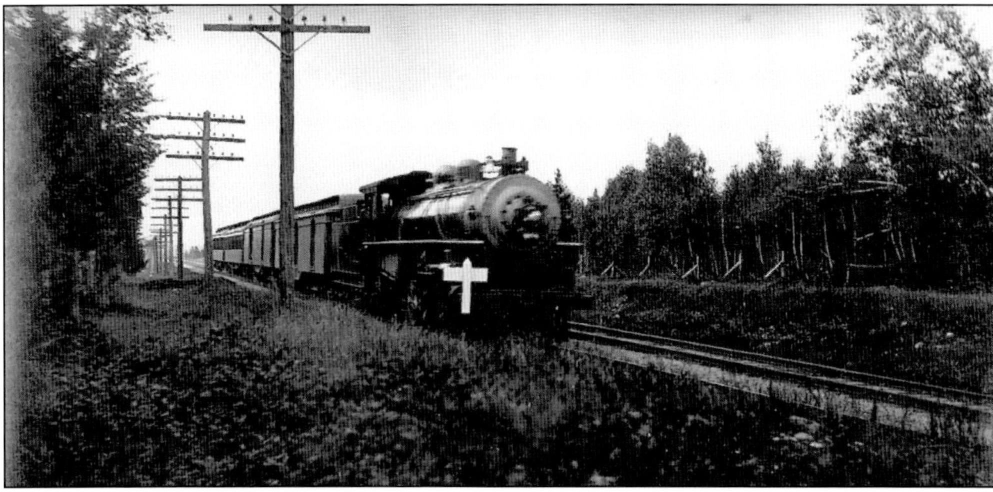

Train travel was a common mode of transportation for Detroit residents until passenger service was suspended in 1960. In the 1920s, Anna Field used the train daily to attend classes at Newport High School. She went on to get her teaching degree and became a popular and well-known teacher in Detroit and Pittsfield. The last steam locomotive, No. 470 (similar to the one pictured above), made its final trip on the Maine Central Railroad lines in 1954.

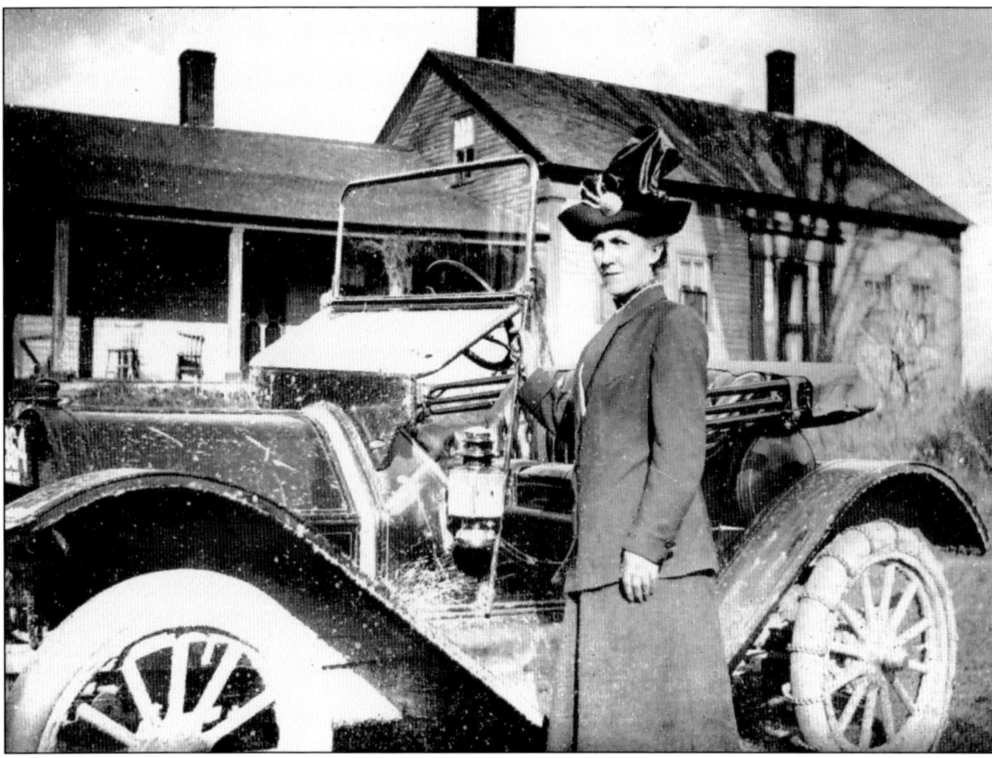

Rose Libby may have been born in Detroit, but she apparently lived most of her life out of state in New York and Massachusetts. She is pictured here in front of the Libby homestead on the North Road during one of her many visits. The trip from New York or Massachusetts could have been an interesting ride, if the mud spatters on her car are any indication. Or perhaps the spatters are more demonstrative of the roads she found once she arrived in Maine.

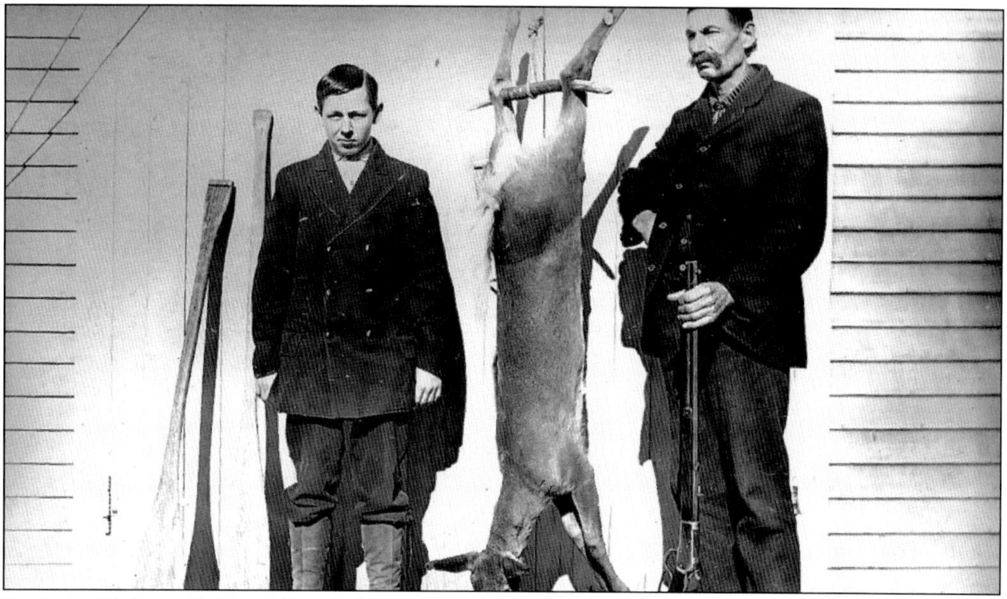

Fred A. Nelson (left) of Pittsfield apparently had success hunting with his brother-in-law Aaron C. Libby (right) on the Libby farm in Detroit sometime after 1906. Aaron and his brothers were avid outdoorsmen, often spending weeks hunting in the Moosehead Lake region as members of the Sabattus Club.

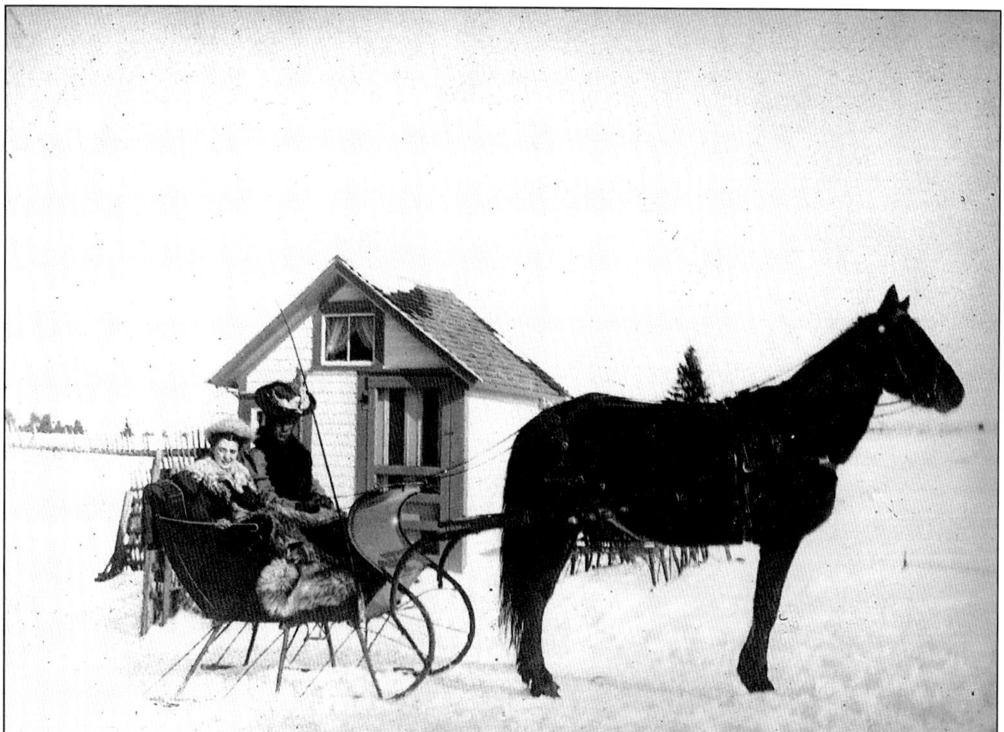

Mary Head Harding enjoyed taking her daughter Minnie for a sleigh ride. The duo is shown here stopped in front of Minnie's playhouse.

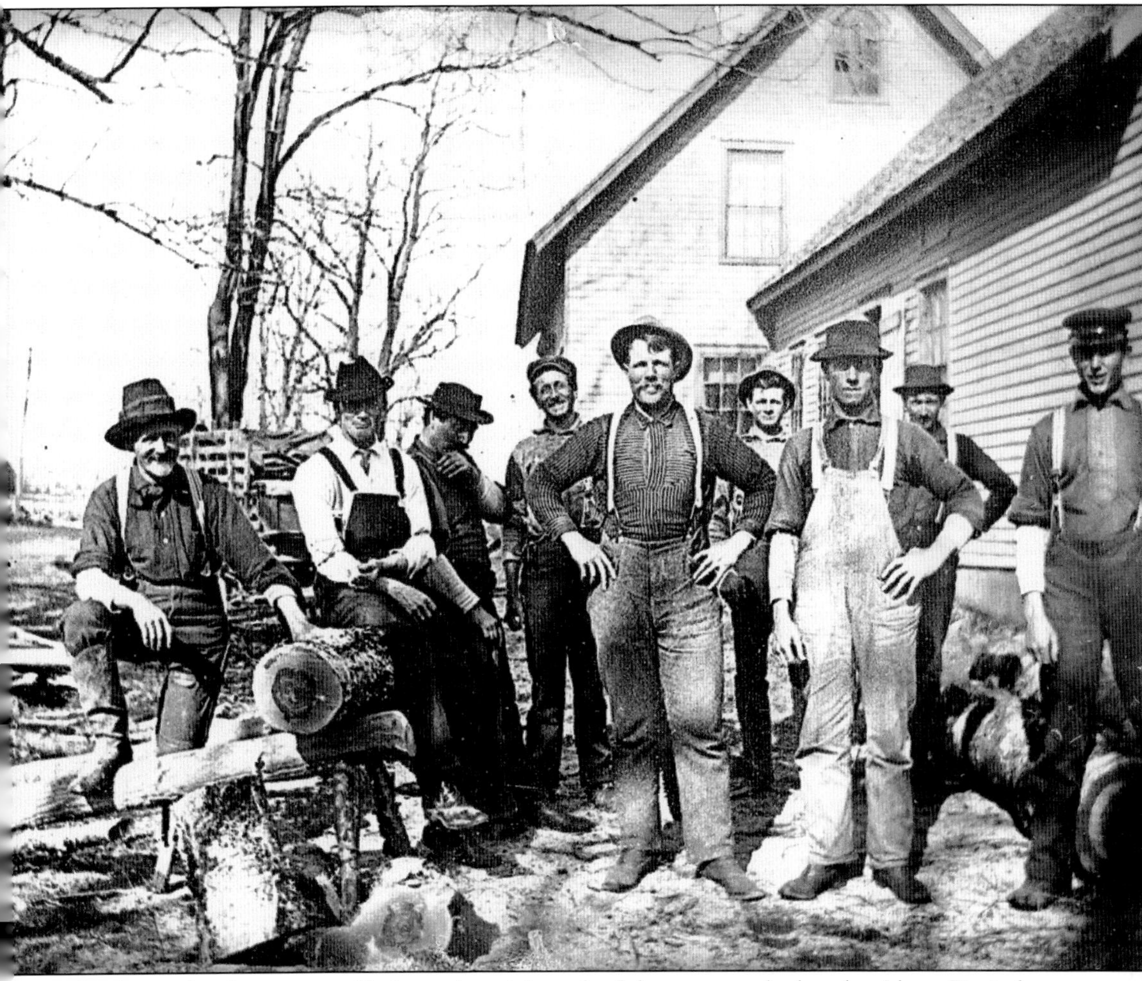

This hearty lumbering crew likely made quick work of the trees stacked at the Almer Davis farm on the North Road *c.* 1905. Unfortunately, none of the men in the photograph are identified.

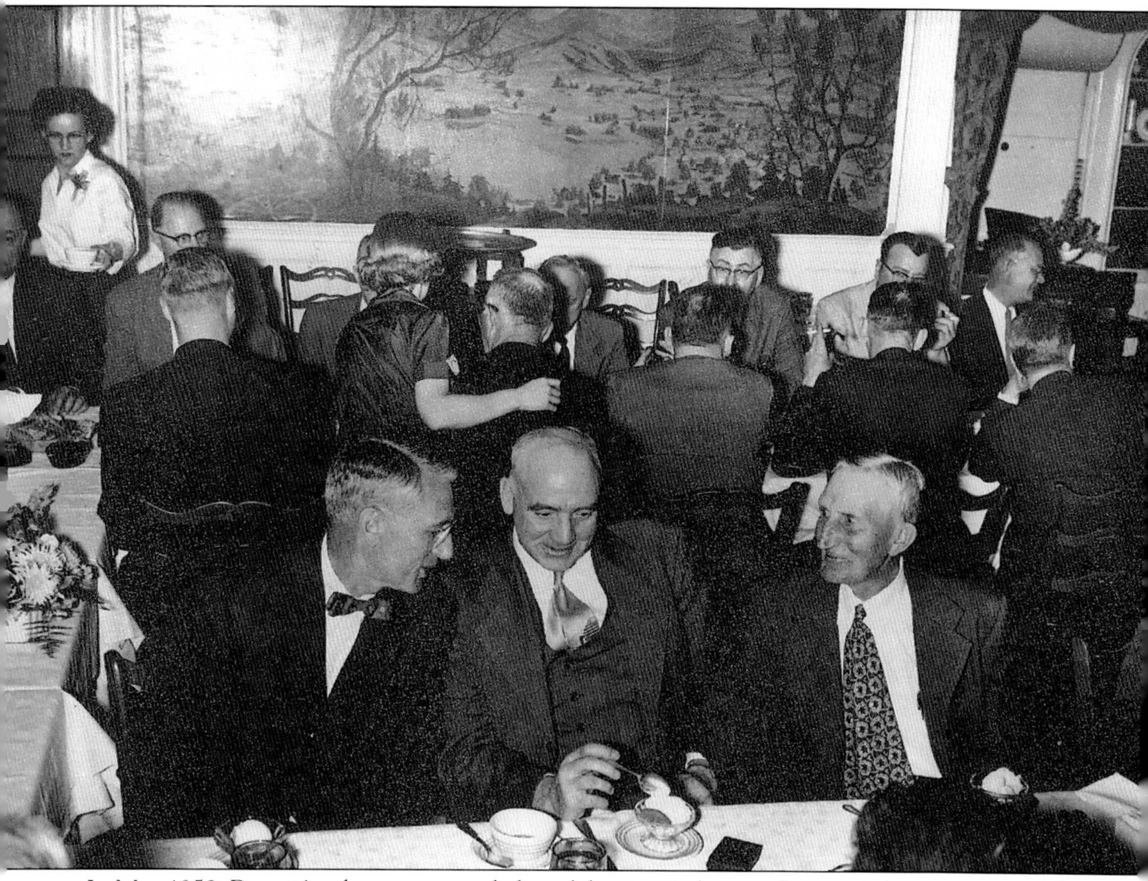

In May 1958, Detroit's selectmen attended a celebration in honor of a new industry in town. The event was held at Pittsfield's famed Lancey House in recognition of the new Eastern States (eventually Agway) fertilizer plant on Route 100. The selectmen shown here are, from left to right, as follows: (front) Wendell Bickford, first selectman, George Fernald, second selectman, and Fred Bagley, third selectman. In the back row and to the far left, two Pittsfield business leaders are visible; they are J. R. Cianchette, owner of a large road-construction company, and Sanger M. Cook, the author of *Pittsfield On the Sebasticook* and a former state legislator from Pittsfield.

Four
St. Albans

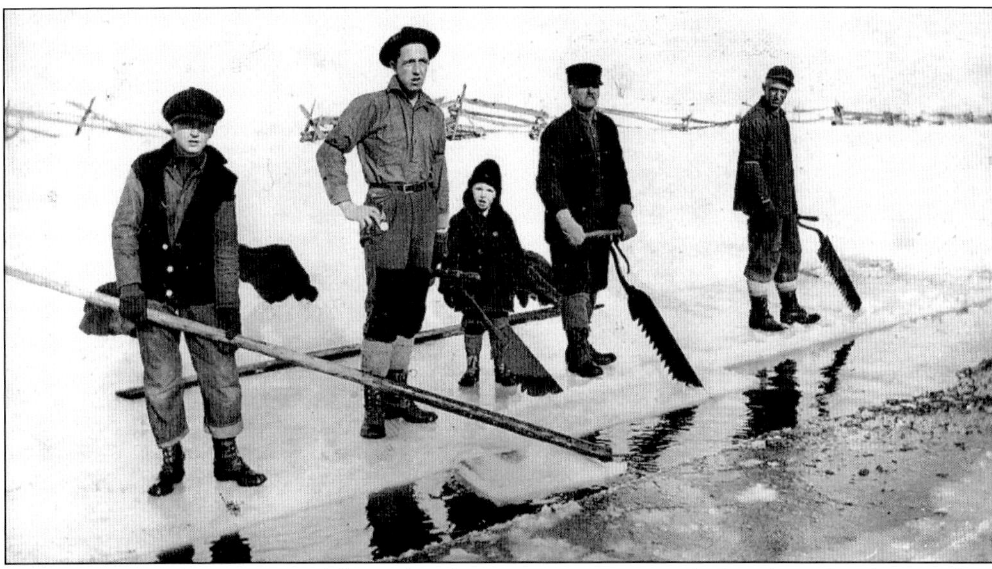

Throughout its history, St. Albans has been a community of close-knit families working together for common goals. The annual ice harvest was part of that collaboration. Many families would gather on the ice each year to share the chore. Often it was on Big Indian Lake, although occasionally it was held on a nearby frog pond closer to the families' respective icehouses. In this scene from 1922, three of the Seekins brothers gathered to share the ice chores with their father and grandfather. Shown in this photograph are, from left to right, Harold, Joe, and Jim Seekins, who share the work with grandfather Stephen and father Wesley. When the *History of St. Albans, Maine, 1799 to 1981* was written in 1982, authors Ruth M. Knowles and Gladys M. Bigelow found family connections and collaborations a common theme and a continuing practice as they strived to assemble information for a comprehensive history. While Knowles collected research, Bigelow collected memories. The efforts of families in the St. Albans Historical Society continue that work today. Without their photograph and data collections, much of local history might still be scattered among the town's many families.

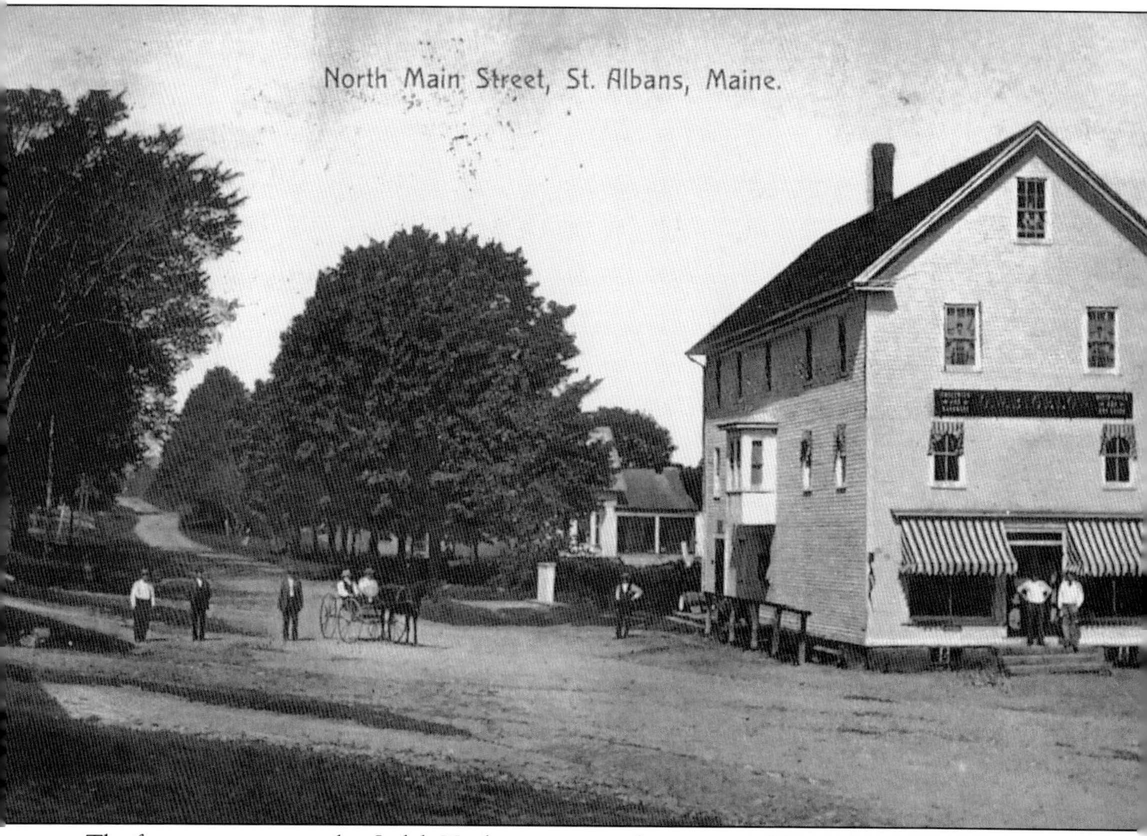

The first permanent settler, Judah Hackett, came to the portion of Township No. 5 that became St. Albans in 1800, building a log cabin about two miles north of the area where the village eventually developed. The Hacketts were joined in 1804 by Joseph Watson. By 1810, there were 22 families (116 individuals) recorded in the census. By the late 1800s, a bustling community was offering goods, services, and employment. This *c.* 1900 scene displays a sample of that business, with Prescott and Hurd doing business on the corner. At that time, the stores sold hardware, dishes, dress materials, yard goods, and a variety of necessary wares to meet the needs of their customers. St. Albans families, like most rural residents of the time, were self-sufficient, growing and preserving their own food as much as practically possible and relying on their local stores to supply whatever they might lack. In the 1880s, Calvin and Melvin Bigelow ran a store on the opposite corner. By 1895, it was operated as Bigelow and Goodwin and was run by A. P. Bigelow and Othello Goodwin. Recently the former East St. Albans library was moved to the site to be restored by the St. Albans Historical Society.

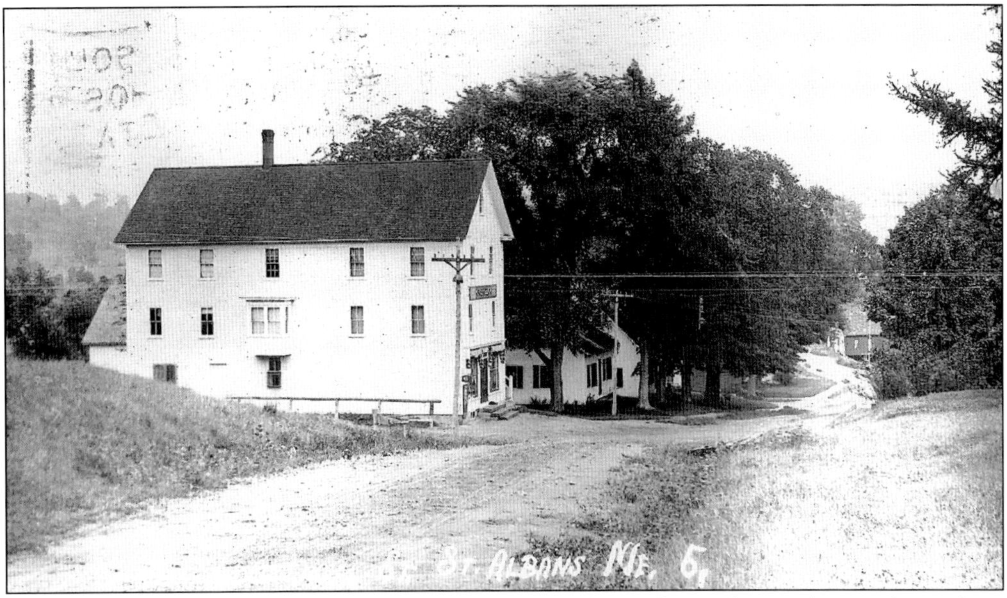

By 1900, only one store remained at the corner, and it still stands. Bigelow and Goodwin burned in 1899 and was never replaced. In 1912, the remaining corner store was operated by C. C. Hanson, and the Hanson family operated it well into the 1970s. At the bottom of Commercial Street (now Corinna Road), another general store operated from as early as 1851. It was located opposite the dam at the foot of Big Indian Lake. Built by T. B. Seekins, it was run under many owners, including James Seekins, a second cousin to T. B. Currently, that store is known as Indian Lake Market.

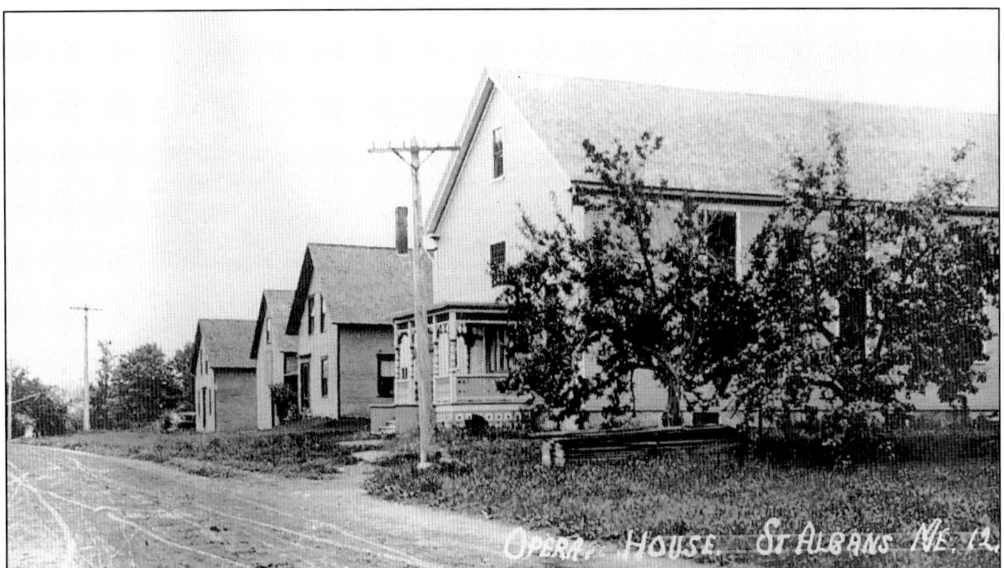

This scene from Water Street c. 1910 shows the town hall–opera house before it burned and the grange hall at the far end before its renovations. The town hall burned in 1910, taking with it several prized artifacts from the St. Albans Grange. Members of the grange were holding meetings in the town hall while renovations were underway on their own building. The hall was replaced in grand style with the help of local attorney D. D. Stewart. That building stands today.

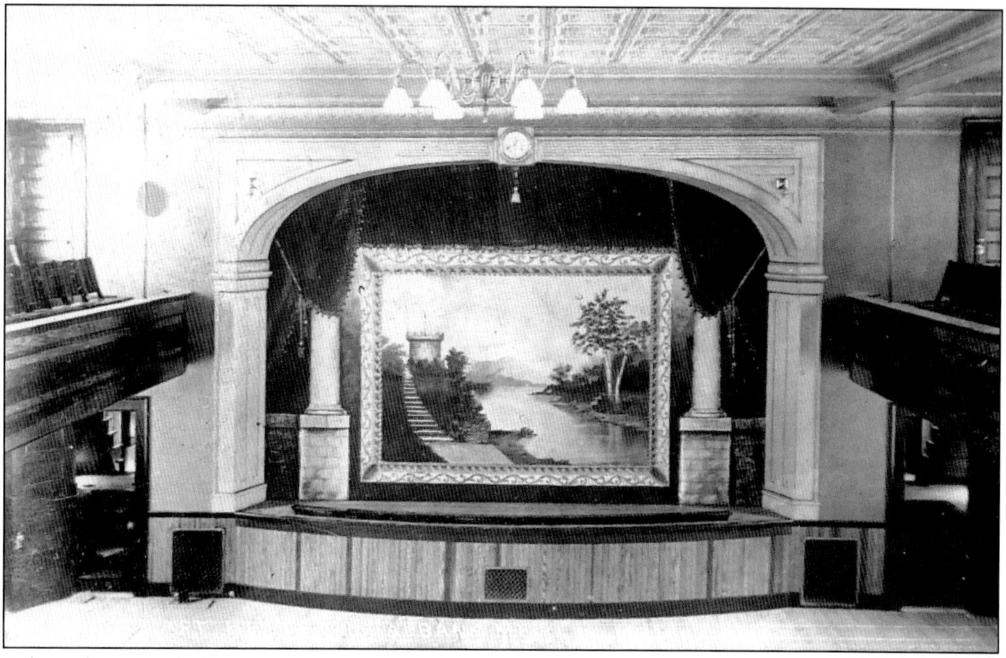

When the town hall–opera house was rebuilt in 1911, it was much grander inside and out, and the main hall was named in honor of D. D. Stewart. In the last years of the 20th century, a restoration project renewed the main hall's original grandeur of 90 years before.

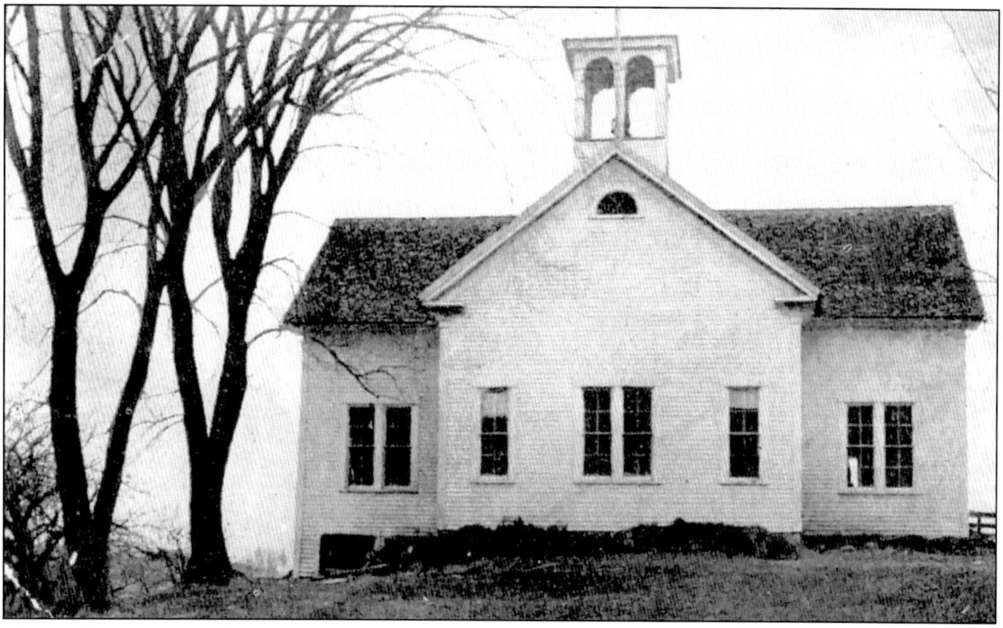

The Village School, the town's second two-room schoolhouse, was constructed in 1883 on the hill overlooking the village center, replacing an earlier structure from 1846 that had burned. The building was moved to its hillside location in 1904 to allow for a larger and safer lot. In the 1800s and into the 1900s, the town supported as many as 17 schools in addition to the Village School. By the mid-1930s, only four of the outlying one-room schoolhouses remained. The village school stood until it was replaced by new construction on the Hartland Road in 1981.

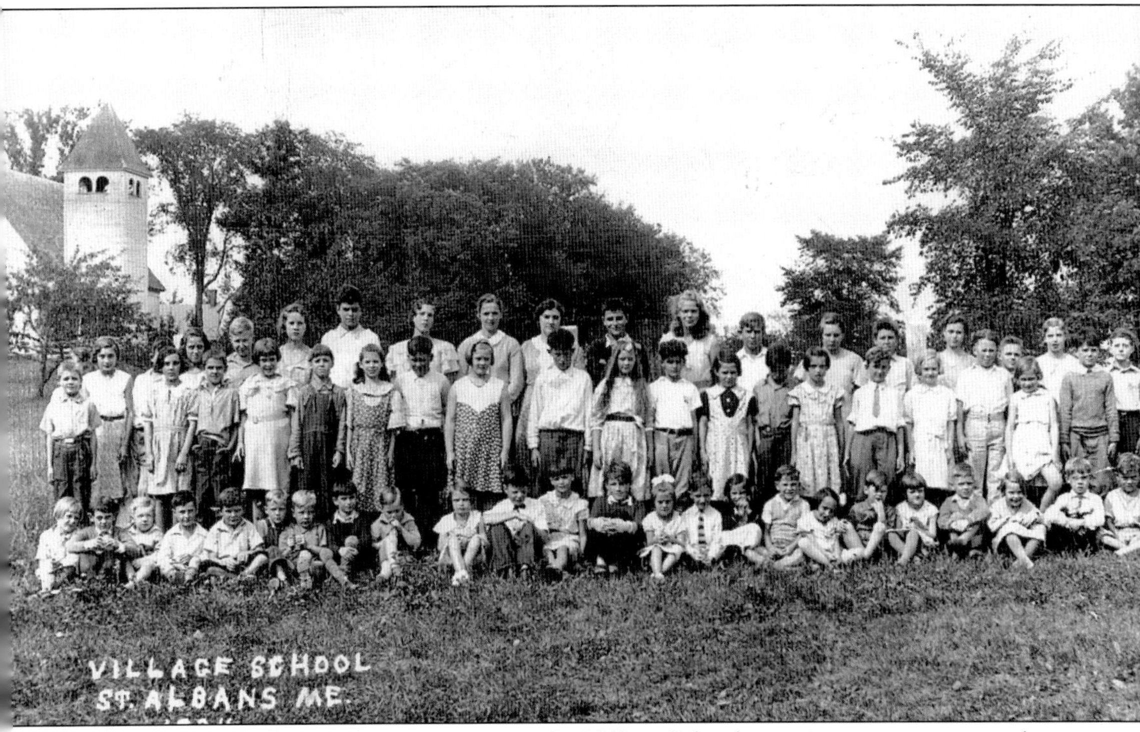

In the 1930s, with the population growing at the Village School, creative measures were taken to house the growing student body and plan for an addition to the school. In 1934, this group attended the original school, but by 1936 the classes were moved out as work began on a much-needed addition to the Village School. The school was the beneficiary of President Franklin Delano Roosevelt's New Deal and a Works Progress Administration program that created a two-story addition. People shown in this 1934 group photograph are, from left to right, as follows: (first row) Irene Patten, Arthur Chapman, Ivan Welch, Richard Lucas, Paul Hughes, two unidentified people, Wendell Bubar, James Mills, Ina Knowles, Adrian Knowles, Alice Frost, Colby Emery, Evangeline Powers, Gerald Nadeau, Mary Chapman, unidentified, Lois Seekins, Charles Ross, Vivian Bowman, Charles Russell, Lillian Hart, Tom Ellingwood, and Harlow Powers; (second row) Arthur Dewey, Marjorie Lowell, Jean Lucas, Alfred Welch, Mildred Bishop, Alfred Frost, Ena Bubar, Edward Patten, Barbara Martin, Milton Osborn, Pauline Martin, Edwin Mower, Evelyn Patten, Everett Nichols, Virginia Bowman, Clayton Cook, Barbara Ross, Leon Patten, Marilyn Mills, and unidentified; (third row) unidentified, Mary Hart, Gareth Hanson, Jeannette Ellingwood, Henry Parkman, Dorothy Spencer, Florice Green, two unidentified people, Emily Crocker, three unidentified people, Wilfred Parker, unidentified, and Gerald Robertson.

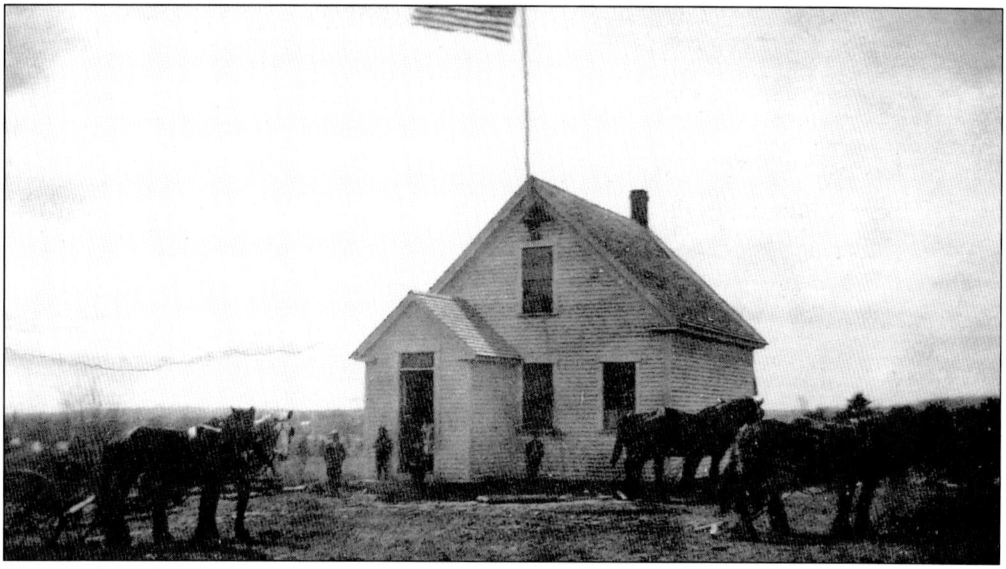

The rural landscape of Maine, including the Sebasticook Valley and St. Albans, was dotted with tiny one-room neighborhood schoolhouses in the 1800s and well into the 1900s. The Pond Road School, at the corner of the Pond Road near the St. Albans-Hartland town line, received a lot of support from its families and, perhaps, from alumni. Teacher Irene Libby appears to have been a resourceful instructor and organizer for the benefit of the tiny school. A scrapbook of her service and activities at the rural school is in the possession of the St. Albans Historical Society.

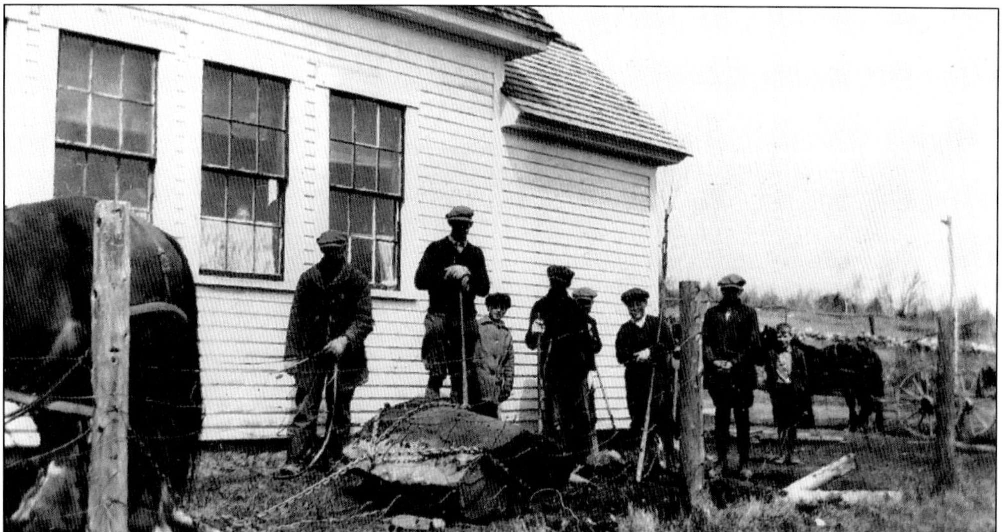

On April 28, 1922, Libby organized an "Improvement Day" at the school with the support of students and parents alike. While the children were busy with cleanup activities, the men of the community went about removing a large rock from the school grounds. Ultimately, the rock could only be moved so far, and the men proceeded to destroy the mass with a well-timed explosion that was caught on film, preserved in a blurry photograph, and retained in the school scrapbook. The efforts of the school were recognized in the local newspaper as follows: "Pond School, St. Albans Proves Pride of the Countryside Improves."

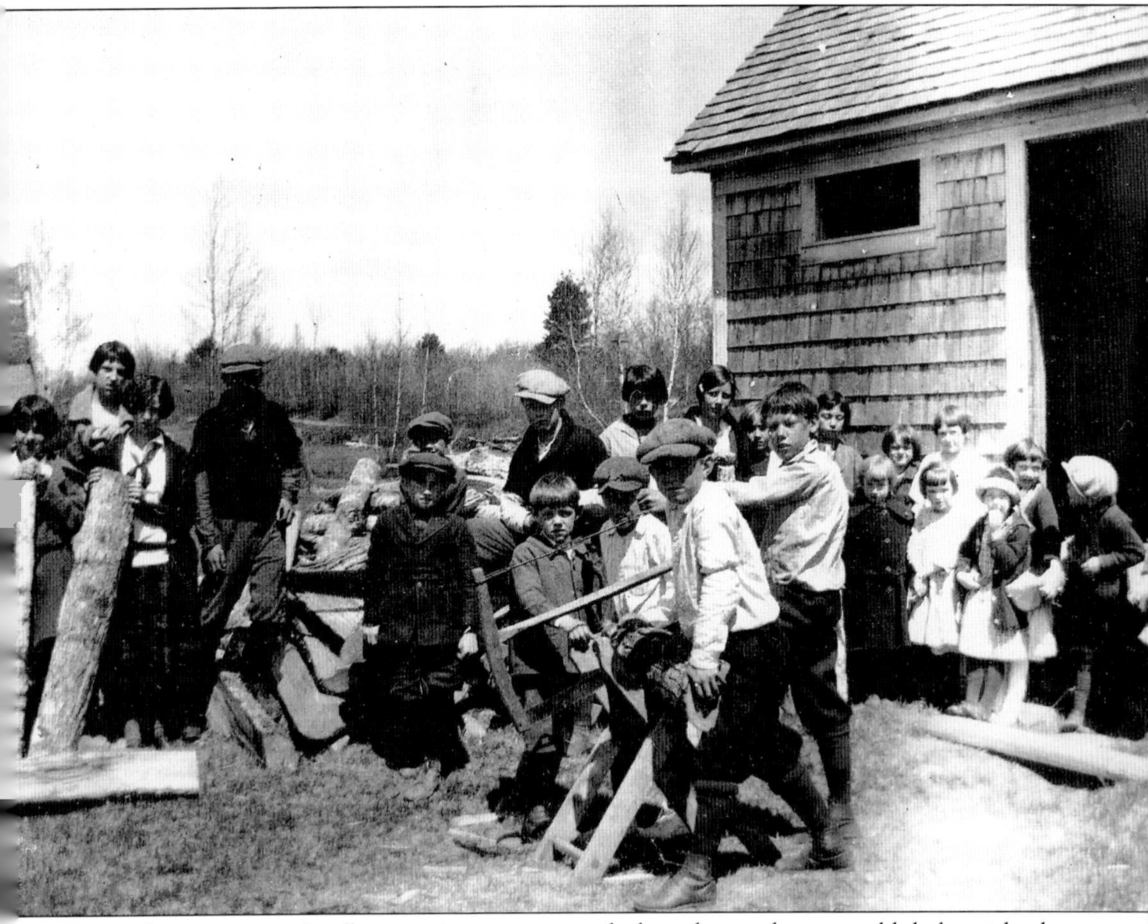

In rural one-room schoolhouses, it was expected that the students would help with the maintenance chores, including bringing in the firewood. At the Pond Road School, however, teacher Irene Libby saw the opportunity for her students to earn additional revenue for the school. As part of the Improvement League Fund, the children earned money by cutting firewood for community members, as they are pictured doing in this scene from the spring of 1925. The funds bought extra supplies for the school. In one year, it appears that the fund raised about $264, which Libby used to buy a Victrola (phonograph) for $64, two rubber balls at 25¢ each, a flag for $3.20, a "fireless cooker" for $2, and many other things. At another time, Libby reported using improvement funds to purchase a teacher's desk. The Pond Road School was among the last of the one-room schoolhouses in St. Albans. It operated into the 1930s.

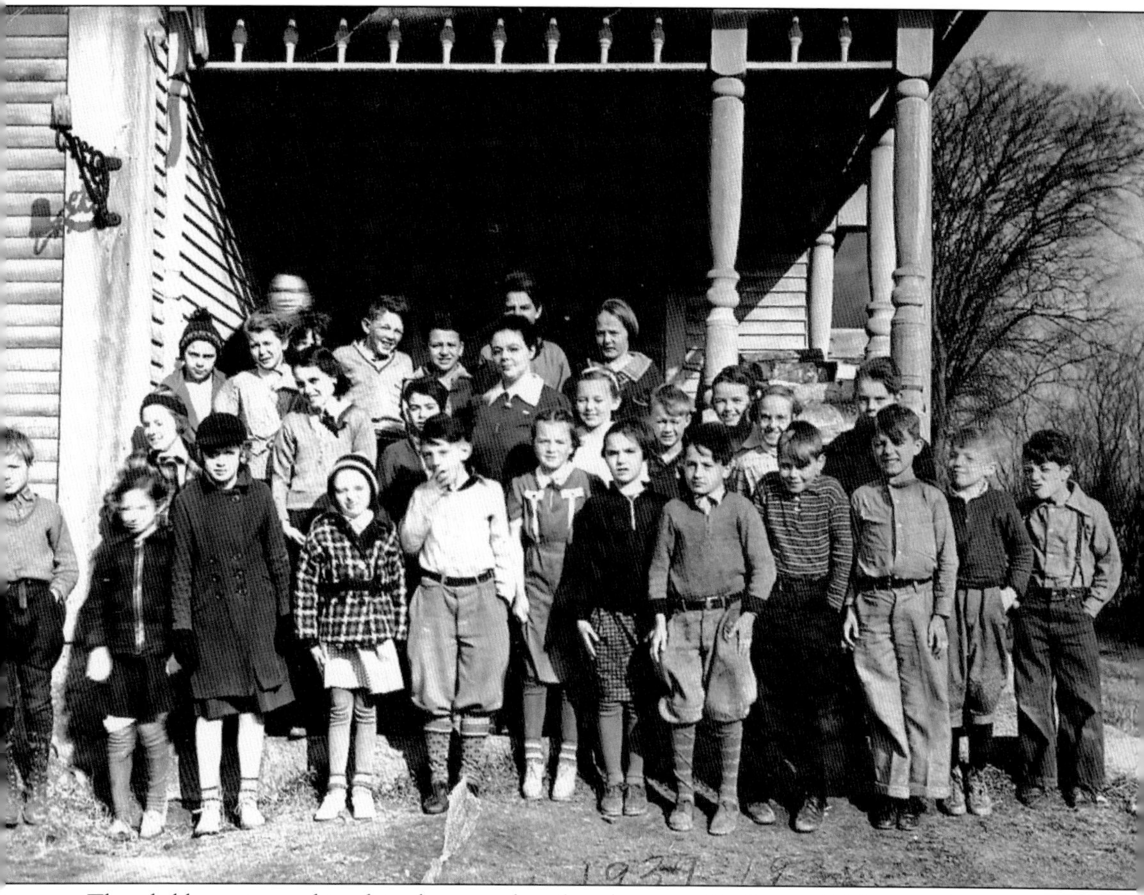

The children pictured in this photograph, taken between 1937 and 1938, attended classes at the Friends Church, now known as the Chatterbox Club. Some classes were held at the town hall before they were able to return to the Village School's new two-story addition in 1939. The children pictured here are, from left to right, as follows: (first row) Elton Knowles, Mary Chapman, Marilyn Mills, Lois Seekins, Arthur Chapman, Pat Lord, Sarah Parker, Richard Lucas, James Mills, Harlow Powers, Ivan Welch, and Earl Jones; (second row) Evangeline Powers, Lillian Hart, Florence Knight, Virginia Bowman, Wendell Bubar, Hilda Bishop (teacher), Elizabeth Peakes, Benjamin Knight, Edith Lord, Maxine Jones, and Tom Ellingwood; (third row) Harold Field, William Lord, Charles Green, Alfred Welch, and Irene Patten.

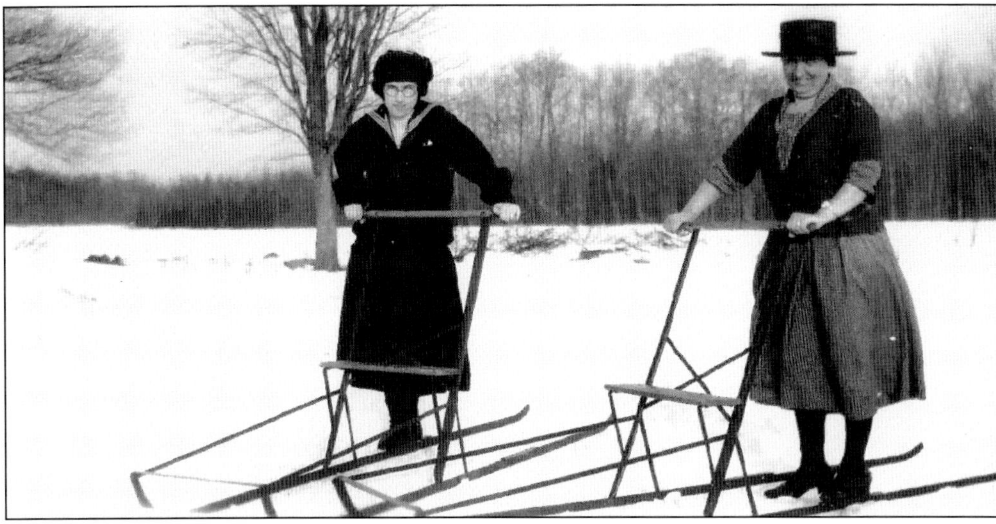

Kick sleds were popular entertainment, as well as transportation, in the 1920s, as Almeda "Meda" (Neal) Seekins and Bertha (Seekins) Davis demonstrate. Participants could walk, run, or ride the runners from the back. The more adventurous participants sat on the seat and took their chances, holding on for the ride or carrying goods home from the store. It was more than just a little scary when the light and wobbly contraptions got a good start on a slippery slope, according to some participants.

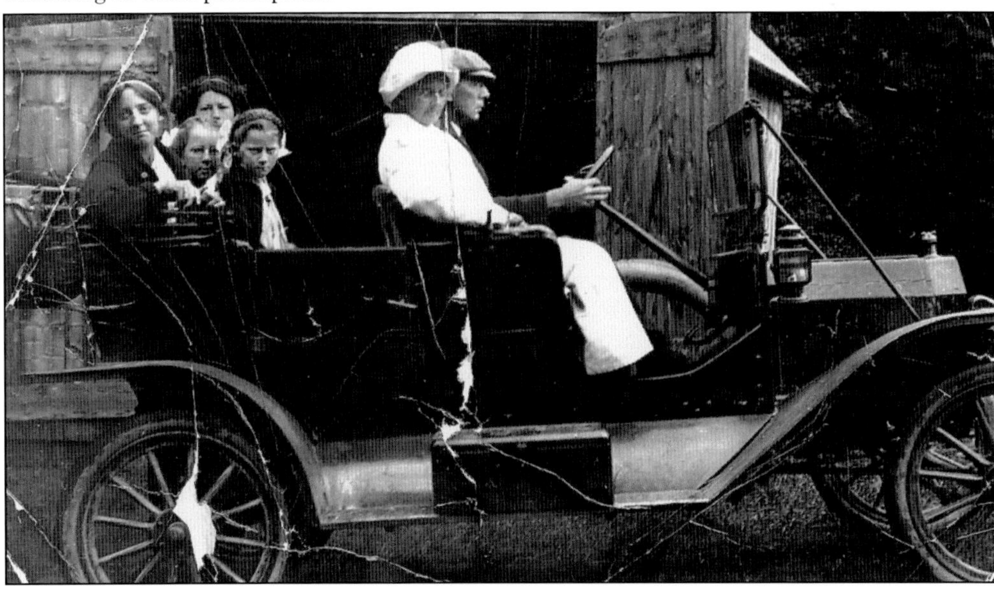

Recreation takes many forms and seasons in St. Albans, both in the past and the present. The Childs family operated a business in Pittsfield and became regular summer residents on the St. Albans shore of Great Moose Lake in 1903. They continued vacationing there long after moving to southern Maine, and new generations followed the annual trek to "Moose Pond." St. Albans residents have the benefit of sharing the shoreline of two major lakes: within the town's borders are "Moose Pond" and Big Indian Lake. Descendants of the Childs family still own property on Great Moose, and several have retirement homes on the Hartland shores of the lake. Edwin and Jennie Childs brought their children Helen, Marion, and Edna (the other passenger is unidentified) to camp in their new auto *c.* 1910.

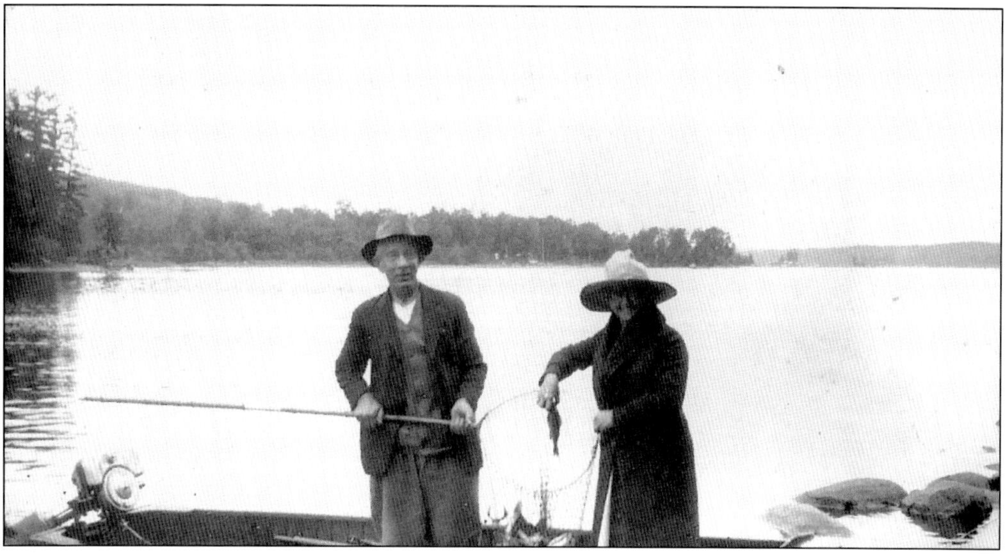

Fishing was a popular vacation pastime when Edwin Sr. and Jennie Childs came to camp on the St. Albans shore of Great Moose Lake in the 1920s. They began a tradition that their descendants continue today, 100 years after their ancestors first visited in 1903.

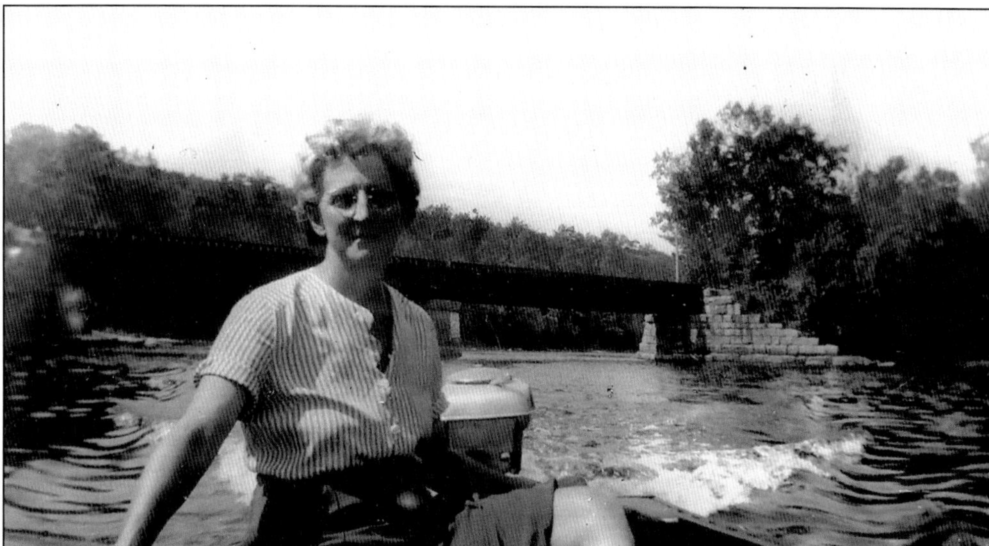

Many summers on the lake made Helen Childs Shorey as adept a "boatsman" as anyone in her family, as this scene from 1947 demonstrates. The Childs descendants remember playing in and under the old train trestle that once carried a branch of the Maine Central Railroad over the west branch of the Sebasticook, just below the outlet of Great Moose Lake. The train brought summer residents to camp, took them to town for shopping, and allowed the breadwinners of the family to make weekly commutes to their summer quarters. The train routinely stopped for passengers when flagged down on the tracks along the lake. The train was a daily presence along the shores of the lake until the Harmony line was discontinued in 1966; the trestle and tracks disappeared soon after. The train from Hartland to Pittsfield continued for several more years, ultimately ending with the removal of the tracks and a transformation to a trail system for use by off-road vehicles in all seasons.

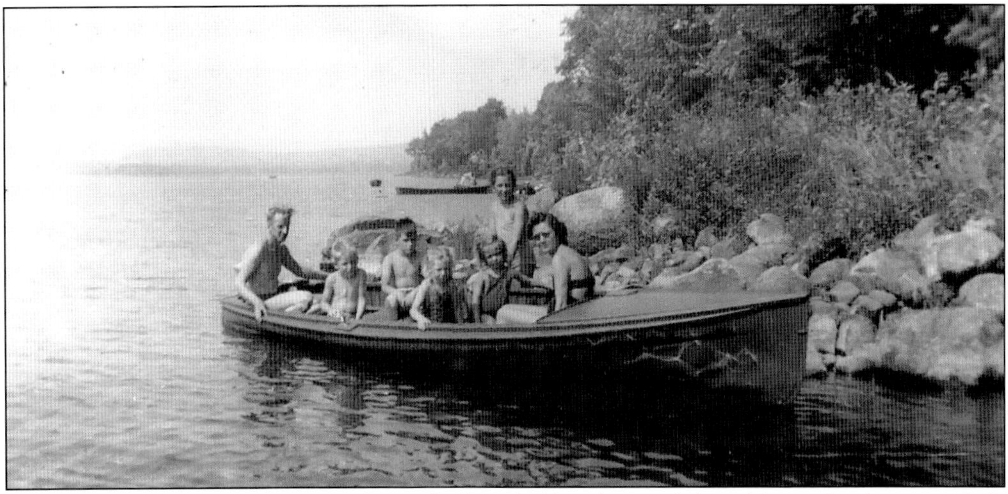

Boating was slow, but it was popular with the Childs, who used this old wooden boat in 1947. Shown in this photograph are, from left to right, as follows: Ned, Donnie, Peter, Connie (Thies), Bettie Jayne (Frosch), and Effie Childs. Cousin Mary Ellen Ferrucci (Bossom) stands on the shore. Their experiences were similar to those of the many seasonal residents that flocked to the shores in the Sebasticook River Watershed.

By 1952, the Childs's Camp Hemlocks was shrinking as the family was growing and continuing to enjoy their lakeside retreat. The fun-loving family decided there was only one way to make more room in the rustic old cabin: the unused and out-of-tune keyboard had to go. It's size versus the size of the old camp, however, meant it went in pieces. Shown here are, from left to right, Ned Childs, Ralph Ferrucci, and Bill Ferrucci, who were only too happy to oblige.

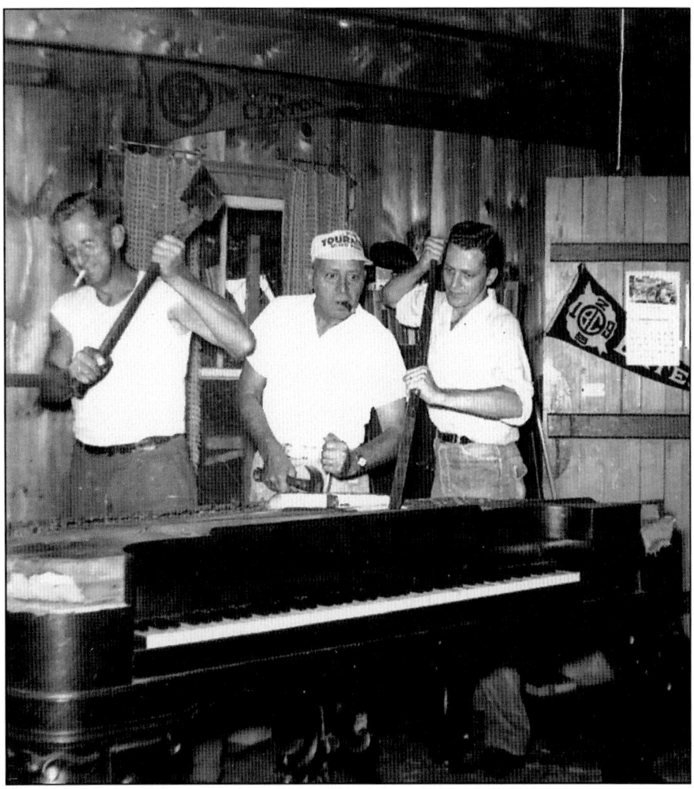

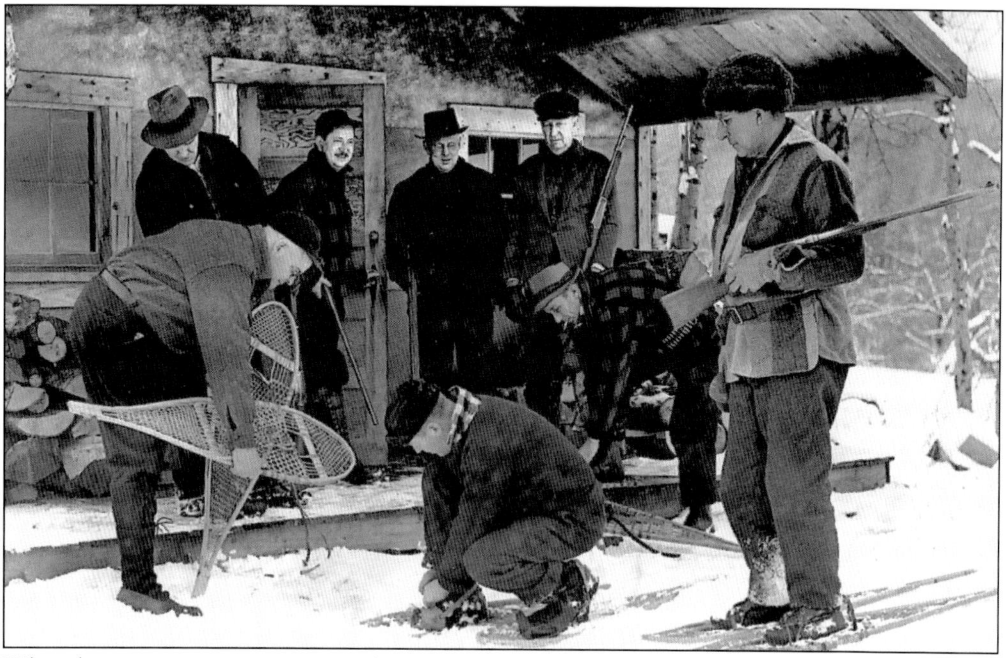

When hunting season comes to Sebasticook Valley, the men of the region, past and present, take to the woods. This group of Hartland and St. Albans men enjoyed a stay at a hunting camp on St. Albans Mountain in the 1930s. Seen here, from left to right, are the following: (front) Ervin Martin, Lloyd "Red" Hubbard, and Paul Brown; (back) Rae Randlett, George Loignon, Bill Steeves, Melvin Martin, and Willis Nichols.

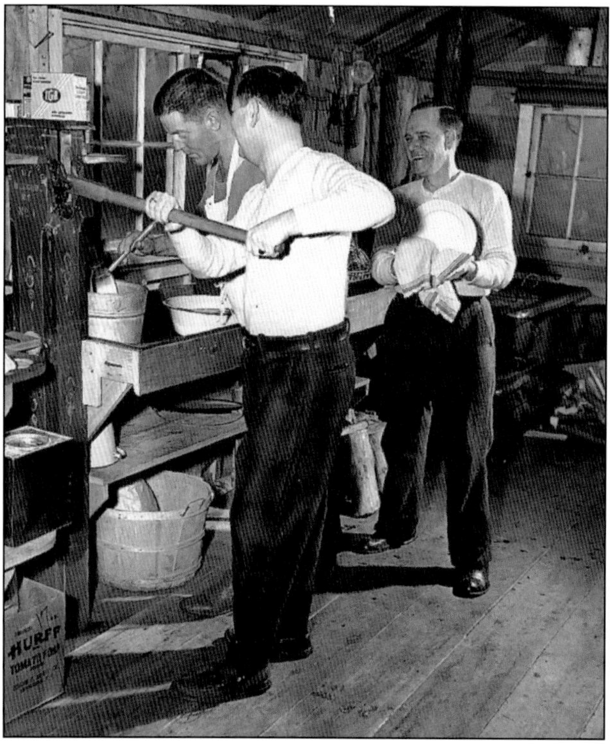

With the fun comes the work, as this trio finds out when it is time to do dishes. It is just like old times, with George Loignon manning the pump while Lloyd "Red" Hubbard rinses and Rae Randlett wipes.

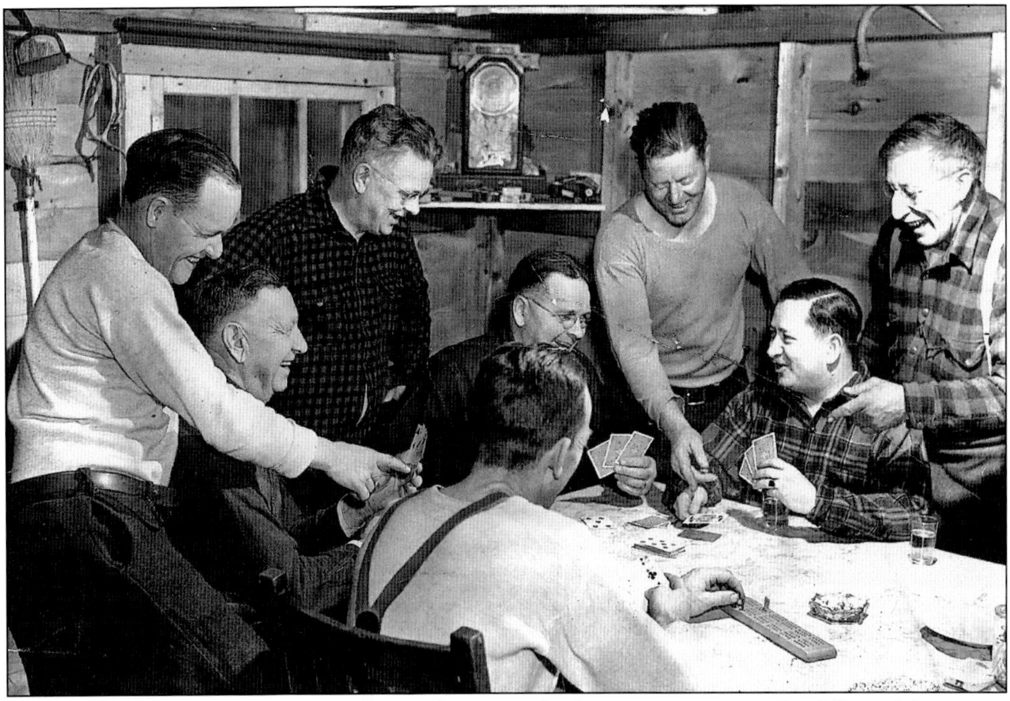

A friendly game of cribbage is still a tradition at the hunting camps on St. Albans Mountain, as it was in the 1930s. Shown enjoying this game are, from left to right, as follows: Rae Randlett, Melvin Martin, Bill Steeves, Willis Nichols, Ervin Martin, Lloyd "Red" Hubbard, George Loignon, and Paul Brown.

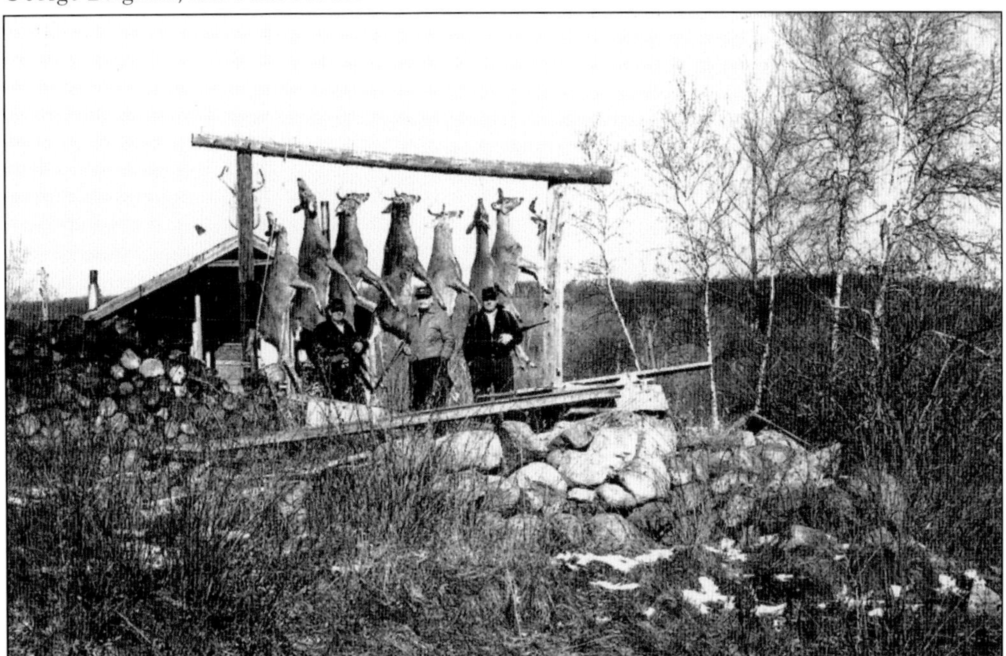

There was no argument that this trip was well worth the effort for the fun, the companionship, and the game.

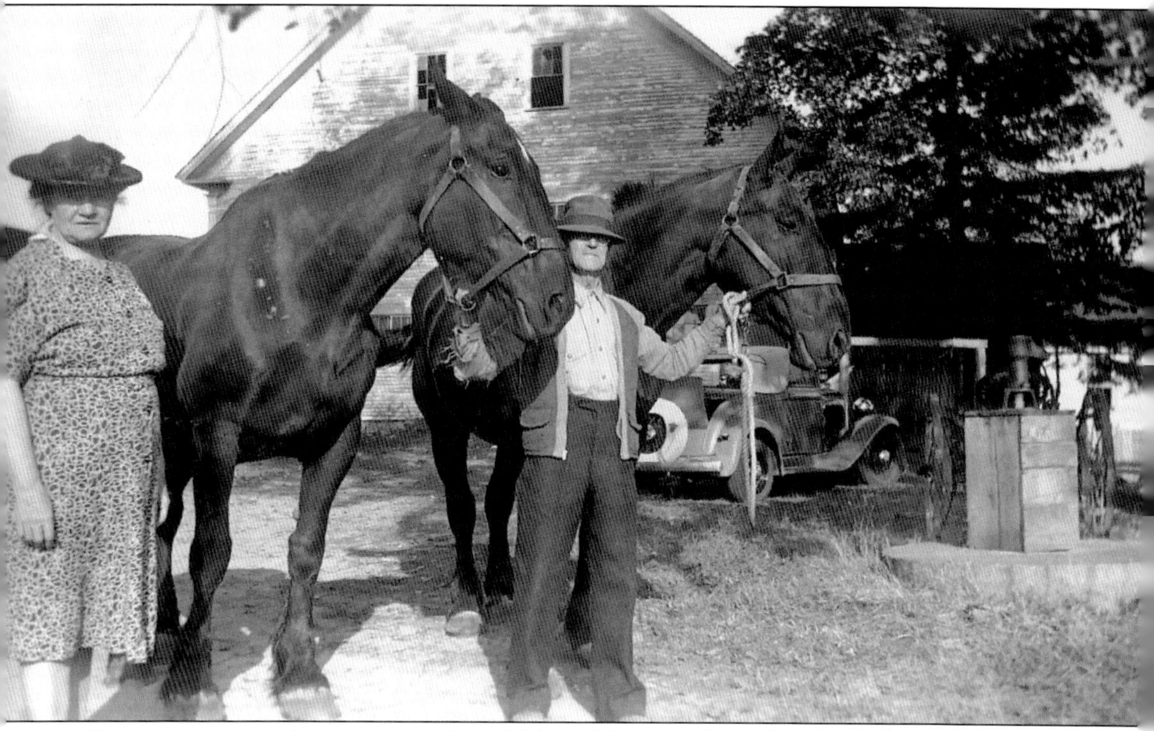

Horses were as much a mainstay of rural life in Maine in the early part of the 20th century as they were in the 19th century. Margaret and Thomas Randlett took pride in the horses they kept at their farm on the Mountain Road. Tom also was an ice dealer in the St. Albans and Hartland area long after electricity had replaced most iceboxes.

Five

HARTLAND

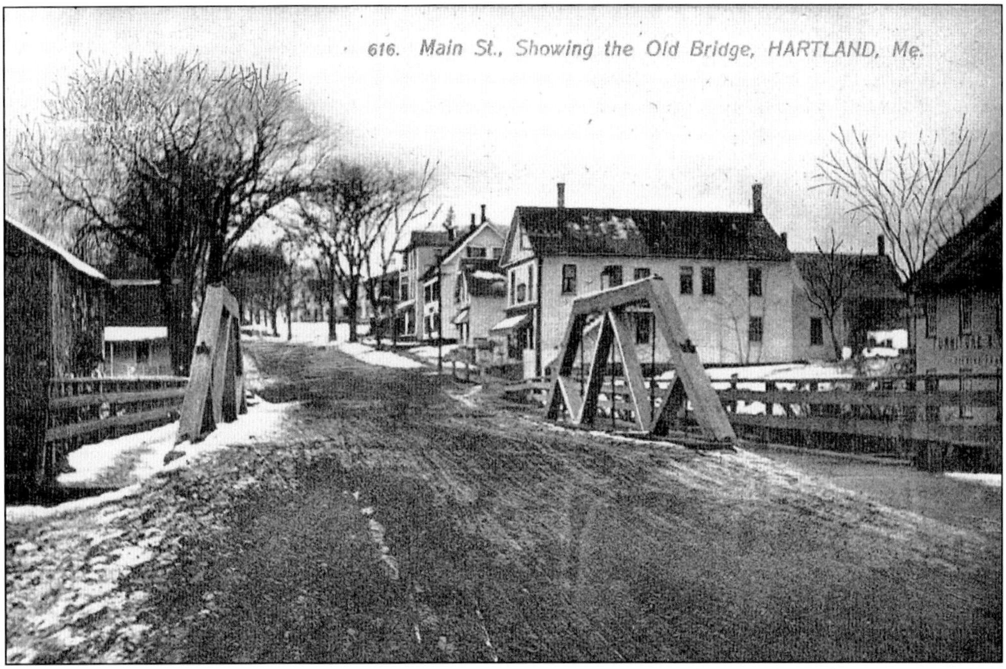

Main Street, Hartland, in the early 1900s was a great deal different from how it is today. However, it is likely a sharp contrast from the view that William Moore and James Fuller found when they arrived in 1800. Moore had visited the area for years before, but did not return to settle until he had married. Eventually, he built a frame house on what is now Commercial Street. Fuller, age 16 at the time, tried farming, and eventually turned to running a tavern at Fuller's Corner in West Hartland to take advantage of the county road traffic that crossed his land. The Fuller's Corner Road at that time continued on to cross the Sebasticook and connected with the Warren Hill road when there was a bridge that was known for many years as "nigger bridge." The name was applied by local residents when the slaves from Warren Hill in Palmyra were freed in the mid-1800s and moved to the river's edge on the "old county road" near the bridge. The families apparently thrived by creating a business that moved goods on the river. Although Maine outlawed place names using the racist term in 1977, Palmyra's "nigger bridge road" escaped scrutiny until an investigative college student brought the oversight to the attention of local officials in 1995. By a vote of the people at the annual town meeting that year, the name was changed to Gale Road.

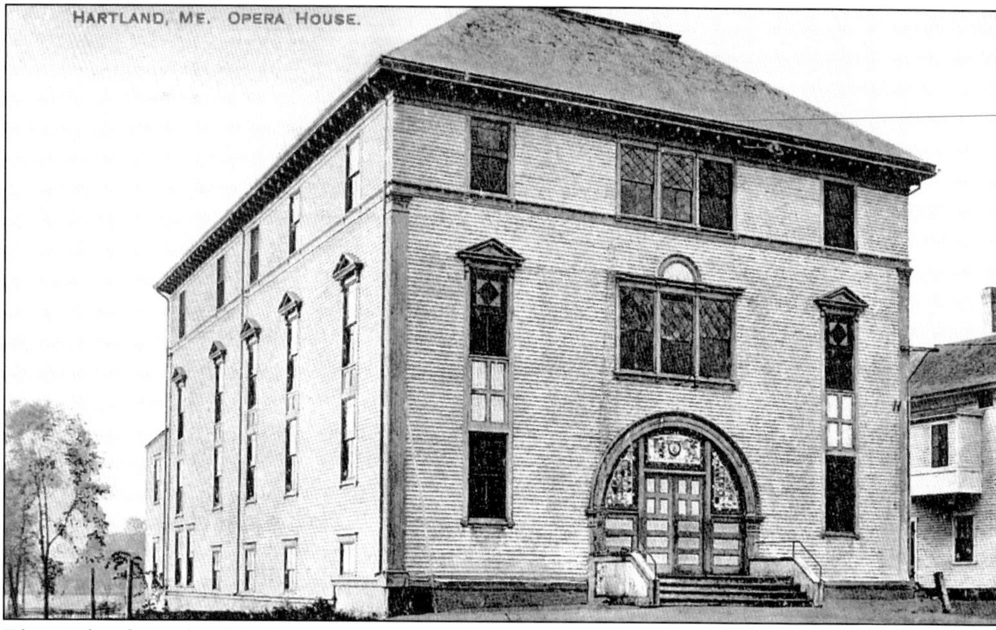

The pride of Hartland is displayed in two of its historic buildings: The Opera House (above) and Hartland Academy (below). In 1890, after nearly 40 years of waiting, the town hall–opera house was built in conjunction with the International Order of Odd Fellows and the Masonic Lodge. The town's share was $2,000, with the International Order of Odd Fellows owning the largest share. The first town meeting was held there two years later. The building burned to the ground five years after that and was rebuilt the next year. Over its 100-plus years, it has housed a variety of activities and historic events. In 2002, the town offices vacated the building and relocated to the former Hartland Academy building. After a 150-year history, the aged school had outlived its usefulness as a school and was returned to the town. Built originally in 1856, the building survived fires, overcrowding, and remodeling; it was eventually deemed too expensive to modify or maintain. The town has taken on the task of preserving the building and, with it, part of history. Several generations of Hartland-area children have been educated in the old hall.

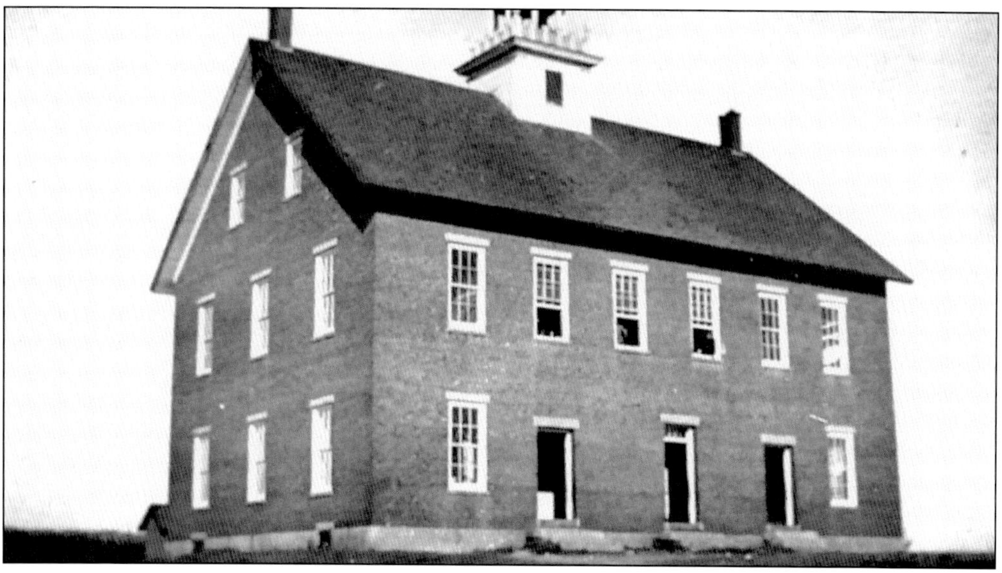

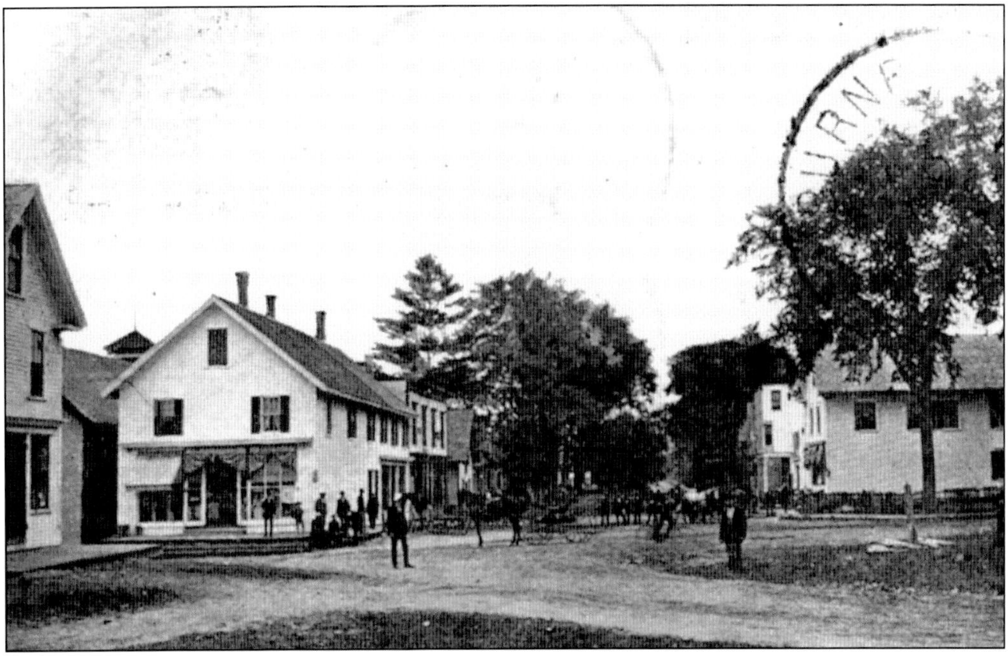

In the 1880s, Commercial Street and most of Hartland's business district were a vibrant and self-sufficient community. Horses ruled the road and cars were not yet invented, although the train was on its way. The Sebasticook and Moosehead Railroad was opened to Hartland in 1886.

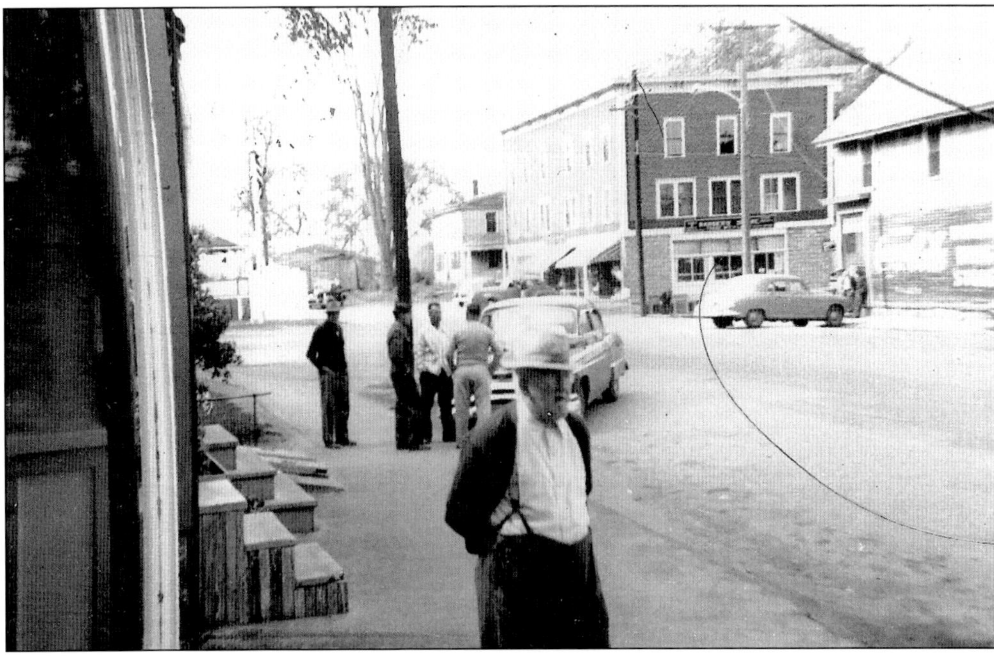

Wesley Harrington owned Harrington's Market on Main Street, later known as Lewis's, for many years. On this day, sometime in the 1950s, Wes was visiting Commercial Street businesses. The drugstore and the former Barden's Block, also home to the former Wright's Market and IGA at one time, can be seen in the background. The town's bandstand and honor roll can be seen in the far back, and to the left.

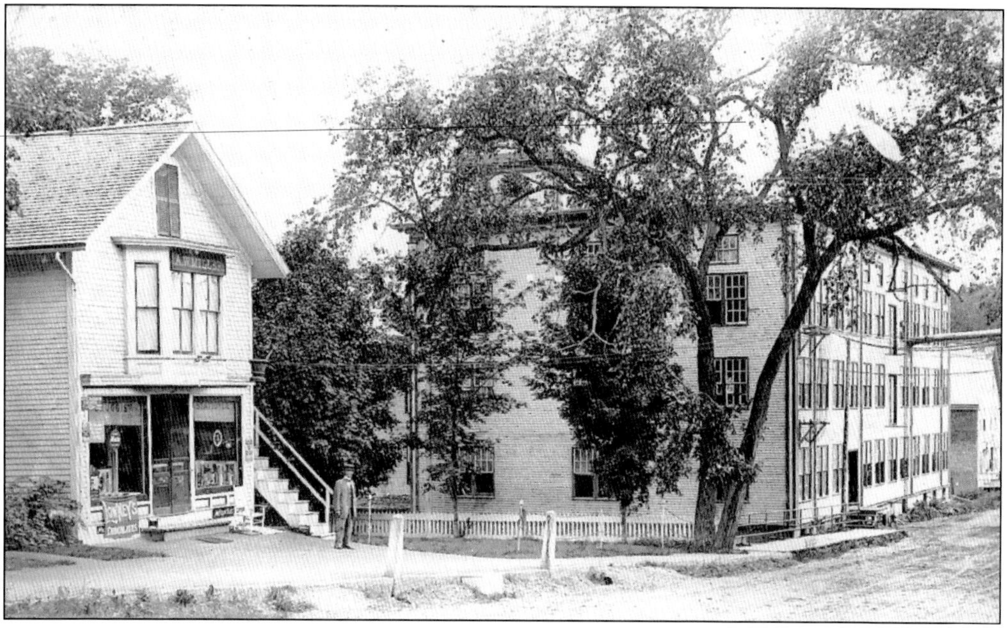

Early in the 20th century, Al and Myra Miller operated a drugstore on Main Street just up the hill from the Linn Woolen (later American Woolen) Mills. The drug store has disappeared. The mill is now part of the tannery, and the store site is part of the tannery parking lot.

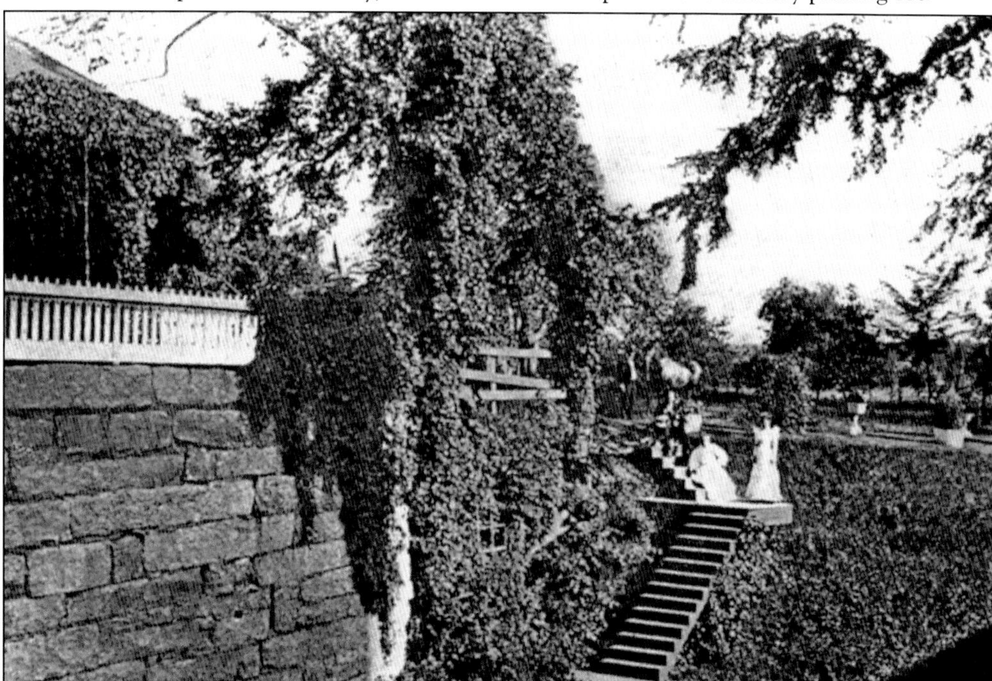

At some point in the late 1800s and early 1900s, a picturesque inn called Woodbine Terrace was located on the east shore of the Sebasticook River, just south of Main Street. Some reports indicate Captain Parsons's steamer *Winthrop* made a daily stop nearby on its round trip from Ringwood Park on the Sebasticook in Palmyra.

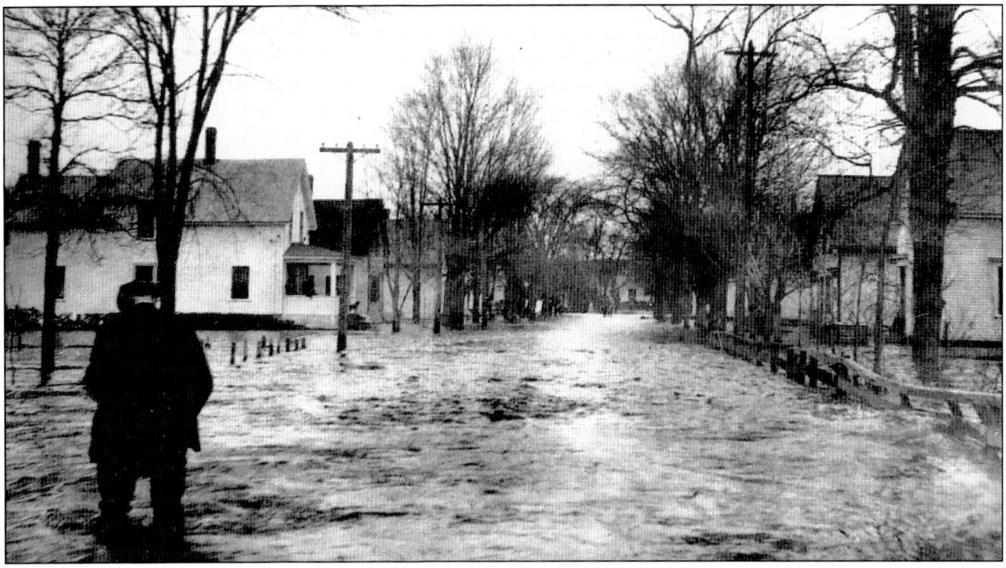

Hartland's Water Street was aptly named, as this 1923 photograph demonstrates. At the time, the area was known as Georgetown. Some locals believe the name was given due to the fact that several men named George lived in the area, but there is no firm evidence to that effect. The man walking is identified as Owen Emery, who was reported to be over six feet tall. He was trying to make his way to his sister's house farther down the street, where she and her family were stranded on the second floor.

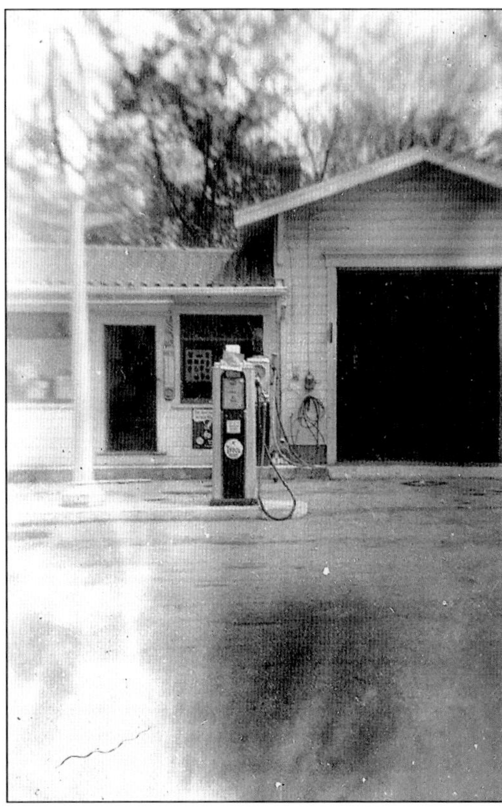

In 1943, the Tydol station on Pittsfield Avenue was a primary source of auto service and gas. The station was operated by Bert Lovely for more than 20 years for Butterfield's of Dexter. The station eventually burned and was replaced by the current Citgo station.

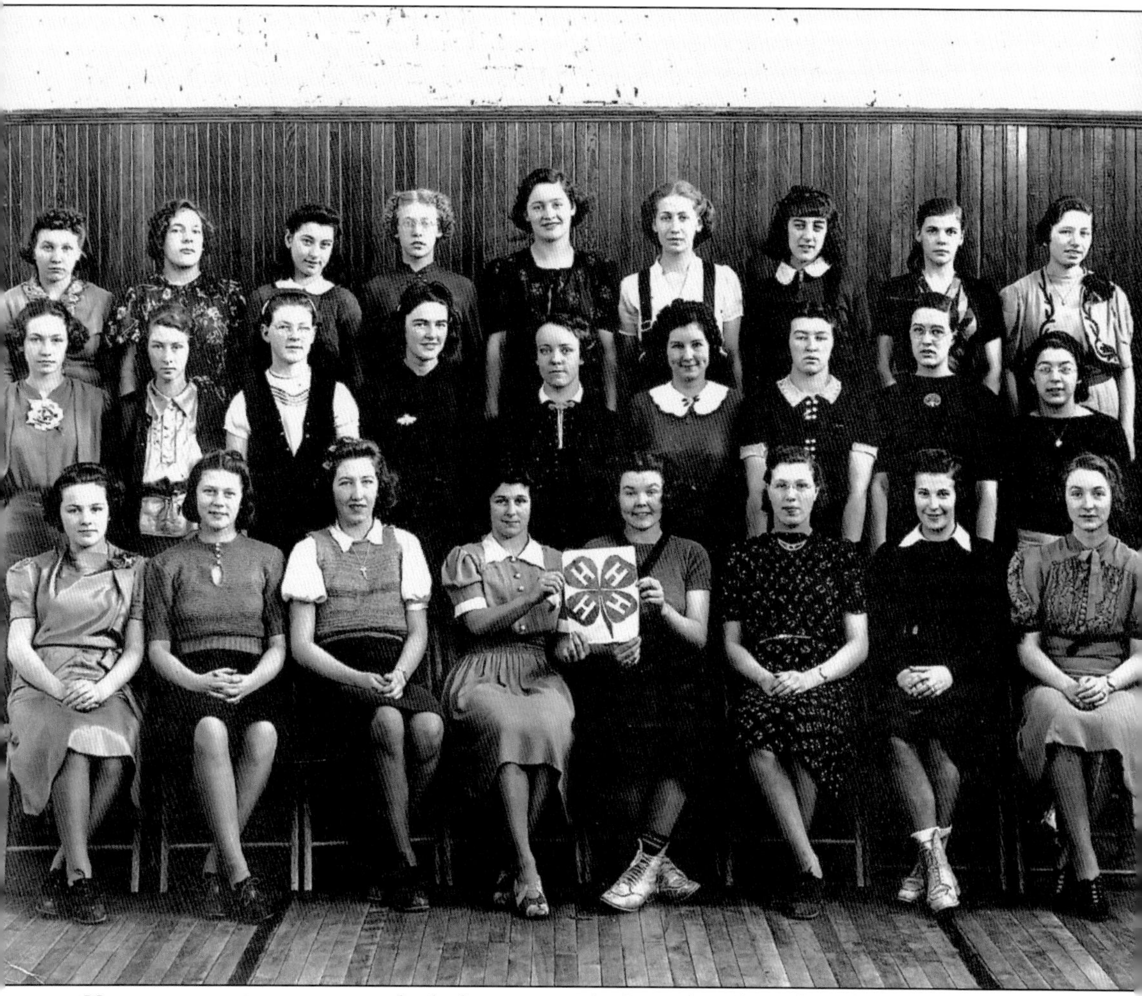

Home economics was a standard class, primarily for girls, when this photograph was taken during the 1938–1939 school year. The girls at Hartland Academy also participated in the 4-H program as part of the class. The participants shown here are, from left to right, as follows: (first row) Lucille Nichols, Marnie Moore, Norma Emery, Bea Wilbur, Pat Gee, Dorothy Spencer, Becky Rediker, and Meredith Knowles; (second row) Doris Libby, unidentified, Margaret Lord, Grace Lord, Rena Allen (teacher), Dorothy Ford, Isabel Cook, Eunice Millett, and Madeline Cook; (third row) Florence Bishop, Nellie Baird, June Gee, Edith Cooley, Marguerite Walker, Jeannette Smith, Virginia Millett, Fern Kimball, and unidentified.

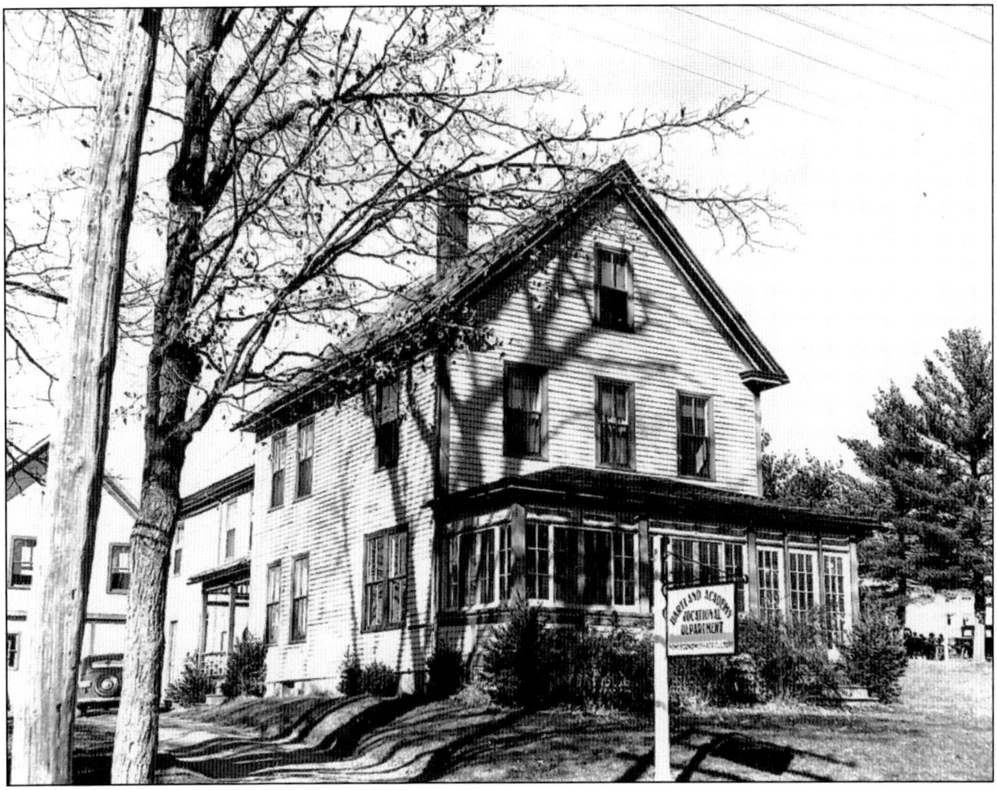

In 1938, Hartland Academy needed more space for its vocational programs. The home just west of the academy was purchased and renovated. The agricultural and shop programs were housed in the barn, with the shop on the first floor and classrooms on the second. The boys' shop class did many of the renovations.

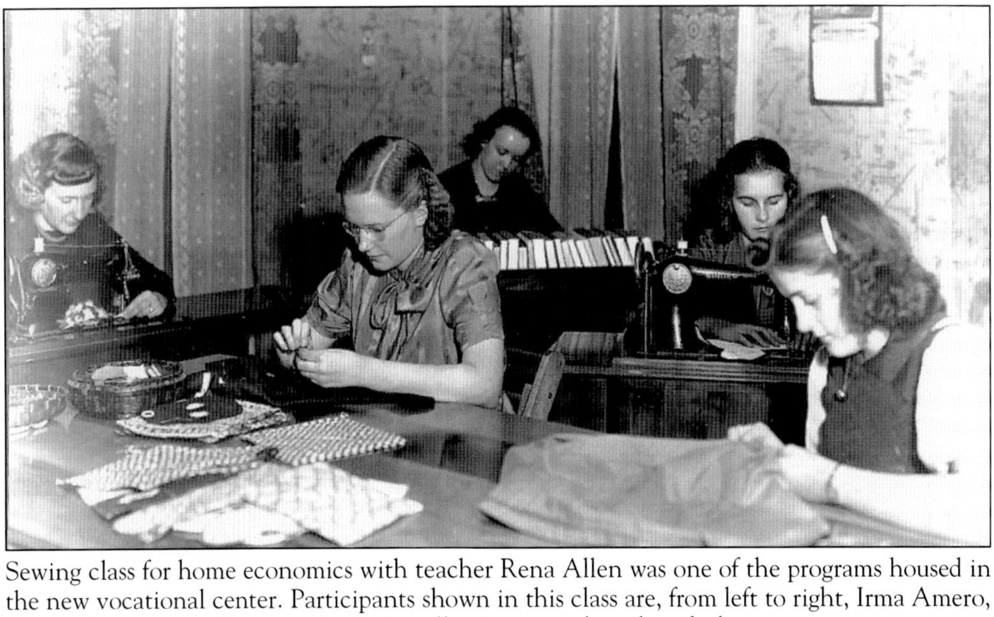

Sewing class for home economics with teacher Rena Allen was one of the programs housed in the new vocational center. Participants shown in this class are, from left to right, Irma Amero, Patty Libby, Rena Allen (teacher), Priscilla Moore, and unidentified.

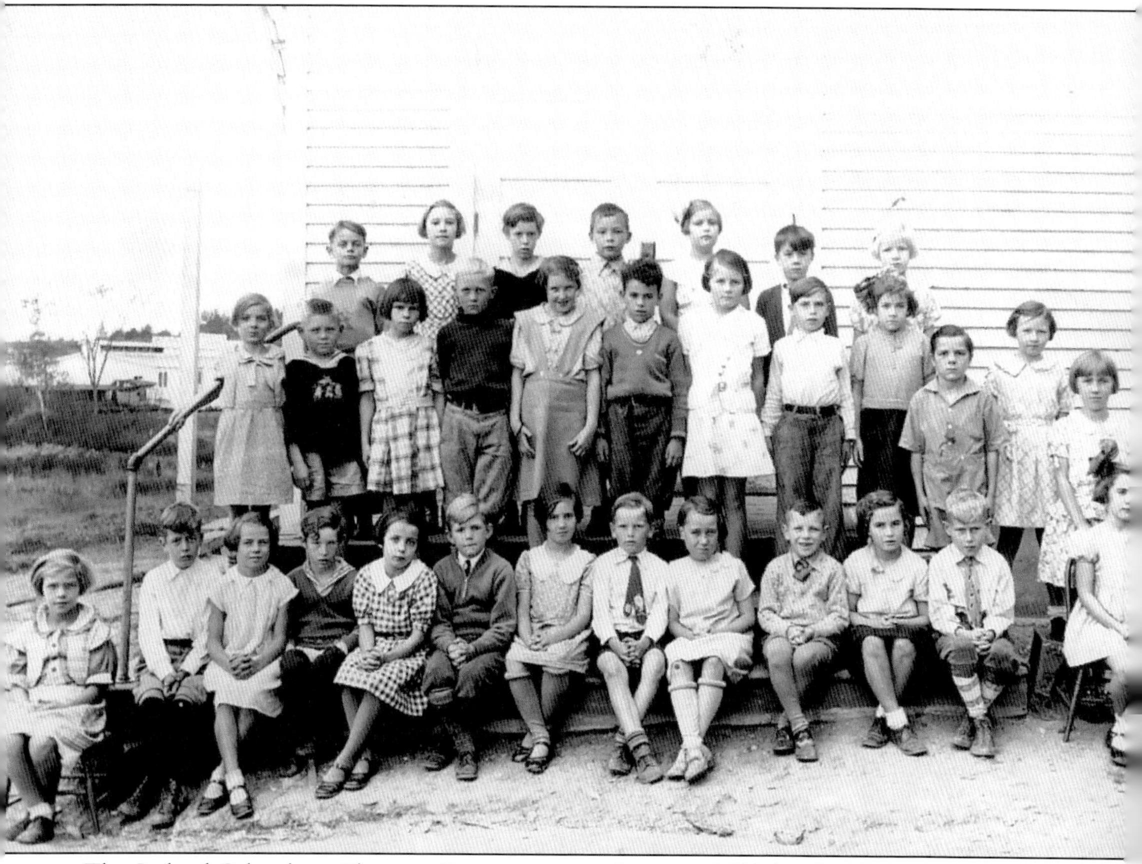

The Ireland School on Pleasant Street was torn down in 2003 by the Steeves-McCormack American Legion post. The building was in disrepair and the membership in the organization was not able to restore it. Many Hartland children got their primary education in its classrooms and posed for pictures on the steps. Included in this *c.* 1935 group photograph of second and third graders are, from left to right, as follows: (first row) Charlotte Stanhope, Douglas Austin, Glenice Withee, Alvira Graves, Virginia Inman, Wayne Varnum, Charlene Stedman, Floyd Austin, Effie Holt, Elwood Gray, Myrtle Lovely, Ivan Pearson, and Estelle Randlette; (second row) Ann Duncan, George Merrow, Gladys Deering, Buddy Gardner, Shirley Cooke, Donald Salisbury, Helen Moore, Leslie Sherburne, Virginia Wheeler, Donald Nichols, Delma Smith, and Joyce Emery; (third row) Dennis Walker, Hazel Devereaux, Herbert Groves, Donald Adams, Jackie Hogan, Billy Raymond, and Annie Wheeler.

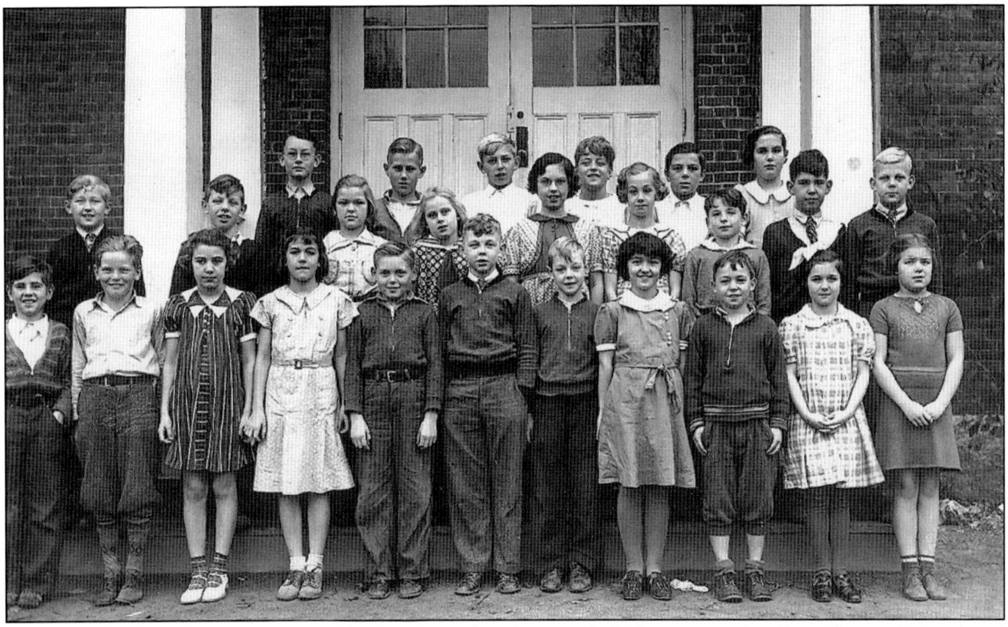

In the 1930s, fifth and sixth graders in Hartland attended classes on the first floor of Hartland Academy. Included in this *c.* 1938 group photograph are, from left to right, as follows: (first row) Alan Rowe, Floyd Austin, Estelle Randlette, Virginia Wheeler, George Merrow, James Moore, Mahlon Gray, Shirley Stedman, Alton Withee, Geraldine Sawyer, and RaeJean Randlette; (second row) Harlan Emery, Elwood Gray, Jeanette Stanhope, Ruth Pearson, Arlene Sands, Arlene McPherson, Charles Sherburne, Edwin Jordan, and John Moore; (third row) Clayton Harrington, Ivan Pearson, Charles Bell, Douglas Austin, Donald Nichols, and Myrtle Lovely.

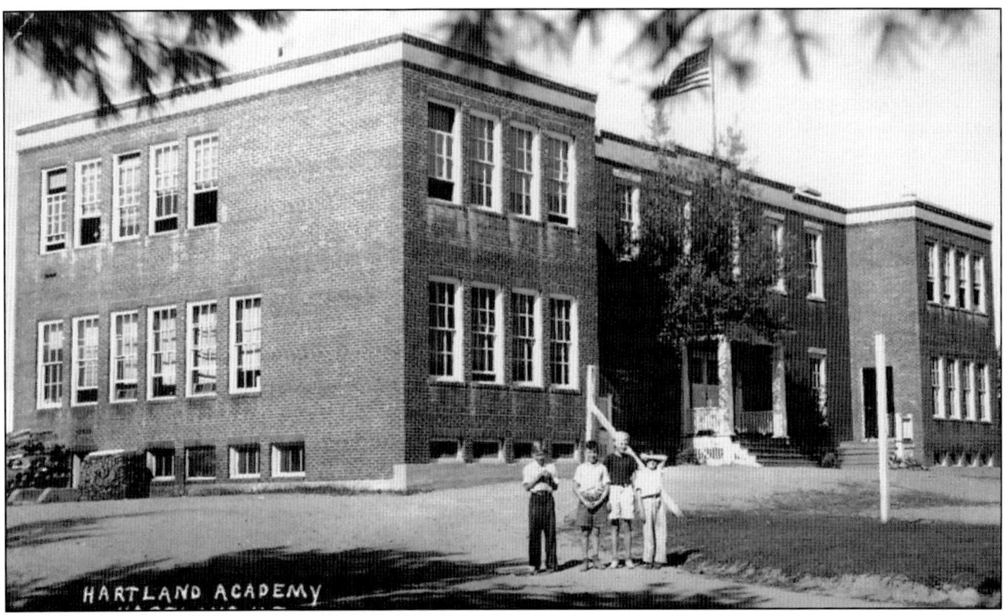

In the 1950s, the academy looked much as it does today, with the exception of the addition of a different entrance and energy-efficient windows.

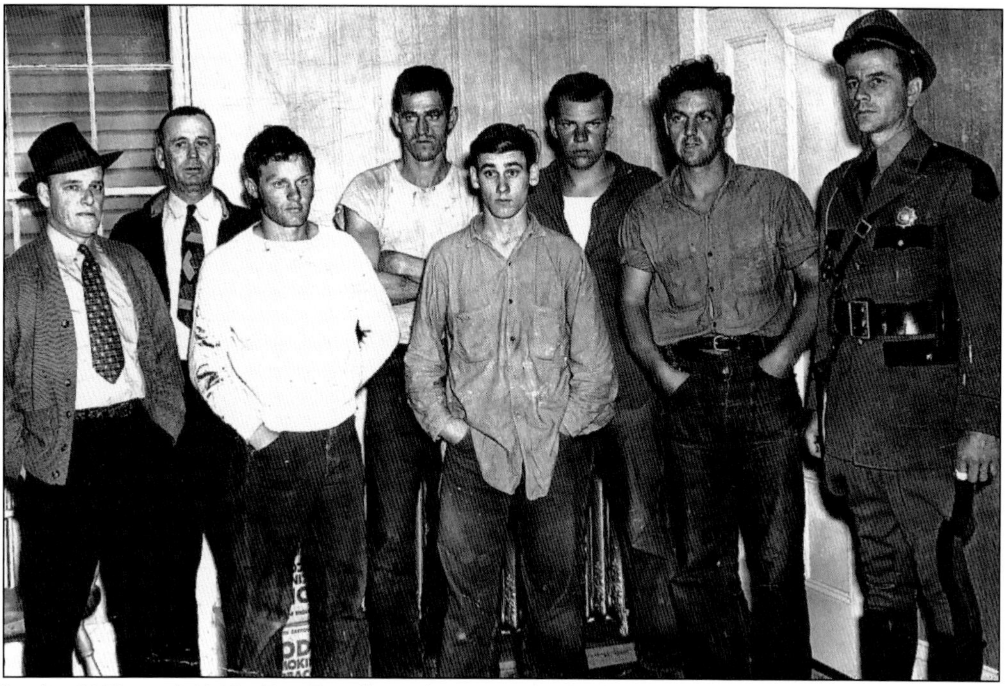

In the 1930s and 1940s, Rae Randlett, shown to the far left, was one of the youngest deputies on the Somerset County Sheriff's Department. He proved his worth early on, single-handedly capturing a quintet of prison escapees, reportedly from Windham. The group was apprehended near Ward's Corner and was eventually brought in with the help of another unidentified deputy and a Maine state trooper. This is a telling photograph of different times when criminals would pose for pictures after being arrested.

$25.00 REWARD!

On Monday Night, October 29th, 1888,

The Hardware Store of W. E. Bradley, of Hartland, Me., was entered by burglars. A large number of Jack Knives, Razors, and $40 00 in money, were stolen. Amongst the money, was one Silver Half Dollar, very badly scratched up.

Also, the Jewelry Store of Wm. Furber, several watches and other small articles were stolen. One Open Faced Stem Wind Nickel Cased Swiss Lever Pacific Watch Co., No 64436. Pivot gone in scape wheel. One Hunting Case, Small Silver plated Swiss, No 47539, movement out of the case. Hair Spring gore from movement. One Small Open Faced Silver Key Wind, (Lever movement) Engraved, No. of case, 31404.

Also, the Millinery Store of Miss A. A. Withee, where the following articles were stolen: Pink Baby's Hood, trimmed with white swans down. Cut Steel Buckles and other ornaments. Two Hair Forks, with rhine stone centers. Jet Ornaments, Black Ribbons, and some Jewelry, Cu. Steel Brown for Hair.

The above reward will be paid for the arrest and conviction of the thief or thieves. If found, arrest and notify

Ira M. True, Licensed State Detective, Hallowell, Maine.

Hallowell, Nov. 3, 1888. or R. S. Williams, Dep. Sheriff, Hartland, Me.

In early times, it appears that local law enforcement relied on the aid of the public. In 1888, the deputy and detective involved with a burglary investigation issued postcards soliciting information from local citizens and offering a $25 reward.

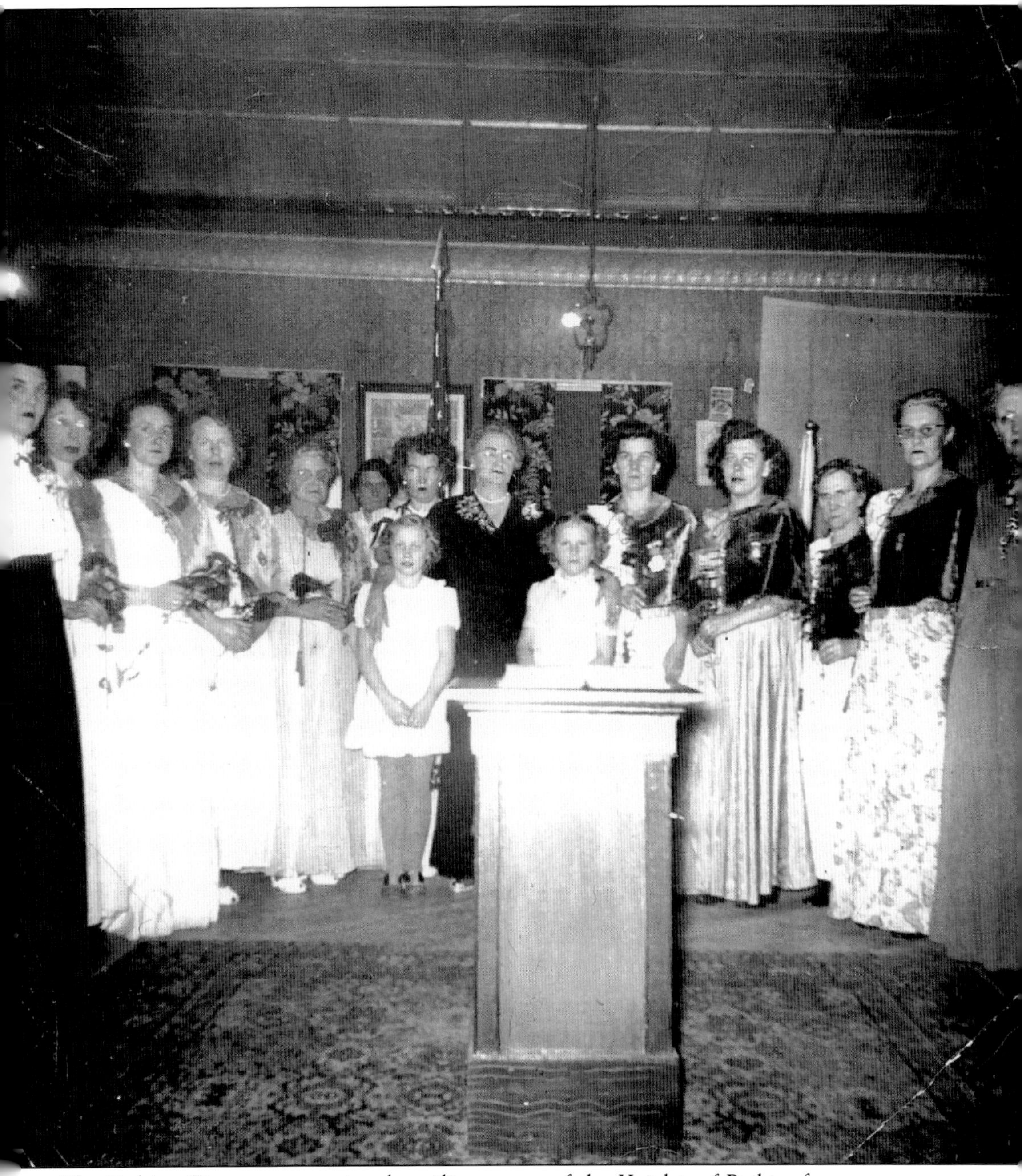

The Pythian Sisters was a regional auxiliary group of the Knights of Pythias for many years. While the lodge is still active in other Maine communities, the knights hall is now used by the local Masonic Lodge. Members of the sisters are shown here in the 1940s. Beginning with the second woman from the left, identified members are Dolly Green, Meredith Randlett, Lenora Morgan, and Vivian Morgan Davis. The others are not identified.

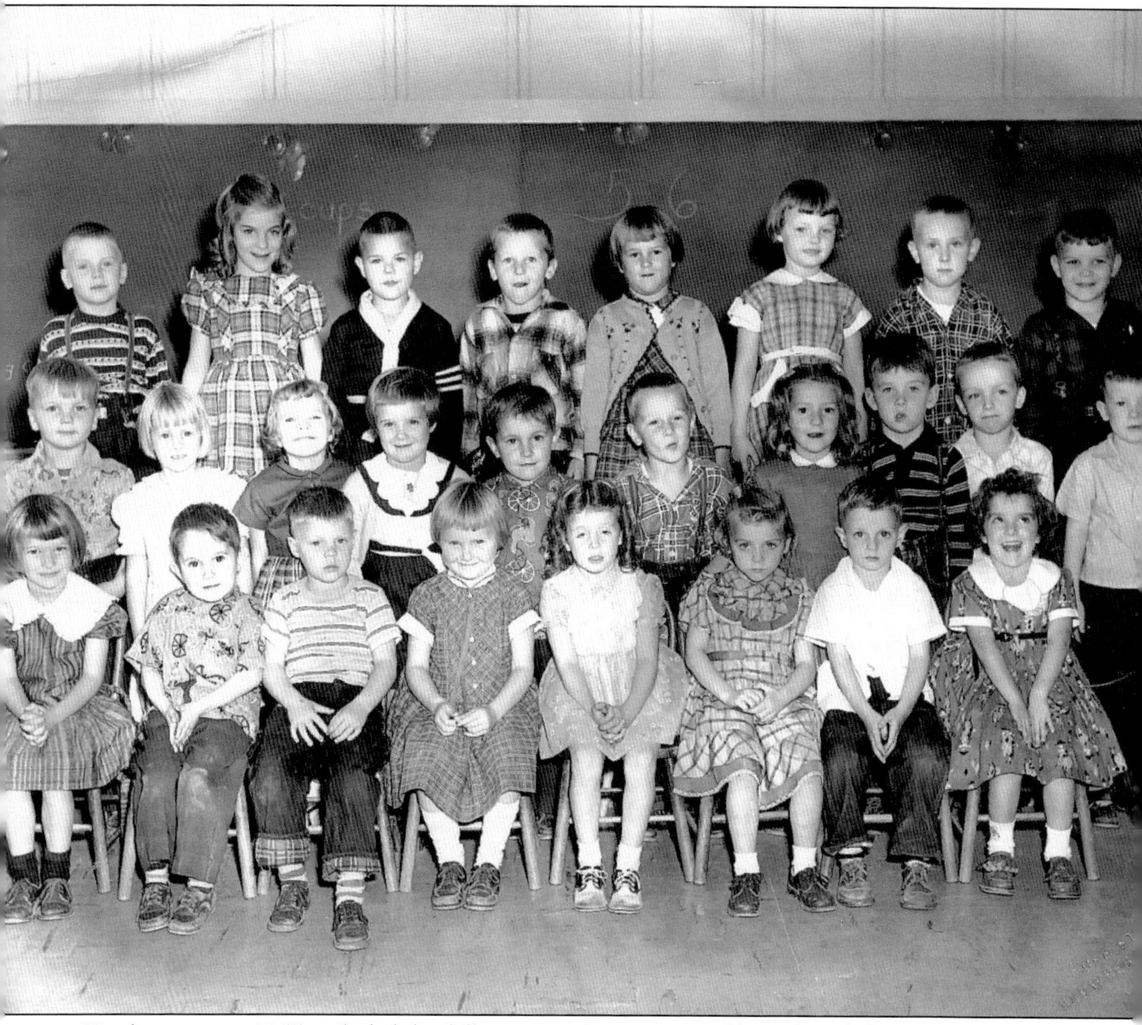

Kindergarten in 1955 included the following students, pictured here from left to right: (first row) Sylvia Stedman, unidentified, Bruce Taylor, Daphne Randlett, Mary Elizabeth Bartlett, unidentified, Phil Ripton, and Edwina Mower; (second row) unidentified, Rose Reynolds, Sherry Tapley, Ginger Towle, two unidentified people, Kathy Perkins, Mike Babnaw, Malcolm Burrill, and Michael Scott; (third row) Darryl Gordon, Arlene Wyman, Jerry Wheeler, Preston Wentworth, Peggy Morgan, Dixie Moore, Malcolm ?, and unidentified.

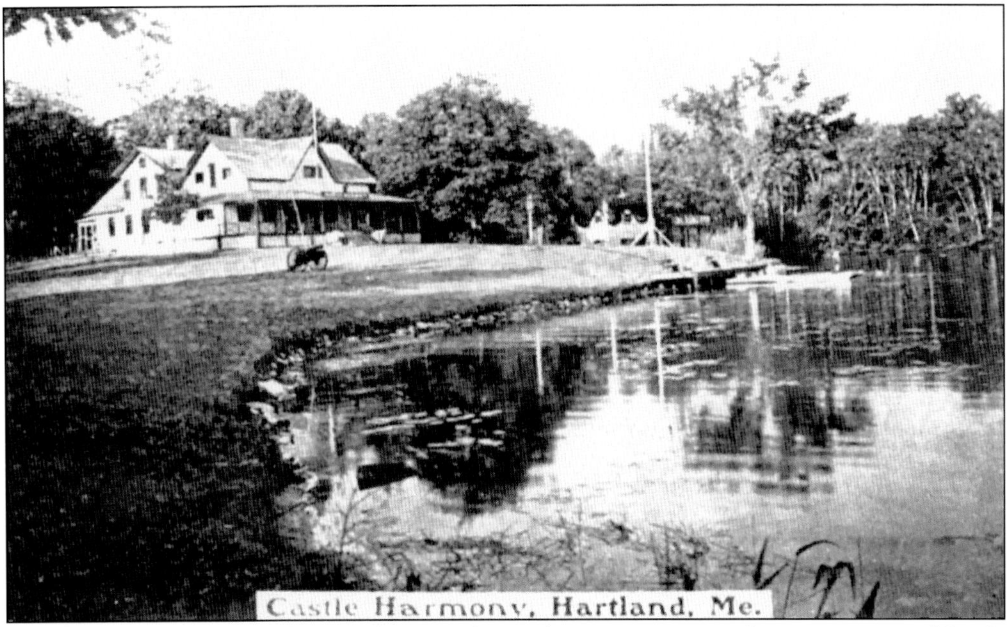

The identities printed on the two photographs on this page are contradictions in terms. "Castle Harmony, Hartland, Me." is not exactly true. The early 20th century hunting lodge at Main Stream is not in Hartland, but in neighboring Harmony. Its history is so interlocked with Hartland, however, that many people have thought of it as being in Hartland. From 1956 to 1995, the castle operated as Wild Goose Camp for Boys; however, long before, beginning in 1878, much older boys were taking the train to Maine to a wilderness lodge that served them in grand style for weeks of hunting and fishing. The trip required changing trains at Pittsfield for the Hartland to Harmony line. Some sportsmen also came up Great Moose Lake by boat from Hartland, no doubt watching with eagerness for the lighthouse that marked the entrance to Main Stream. The exclusive club actually began with pigeon hunting and was limited to 35 members. The guest list over the years included some very famous men, including president Warren G. Harding.

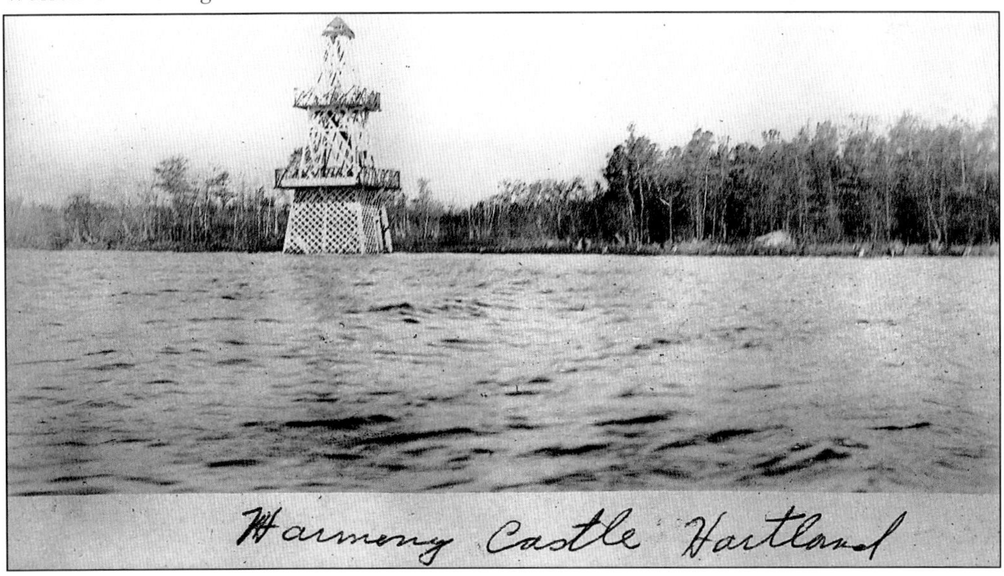

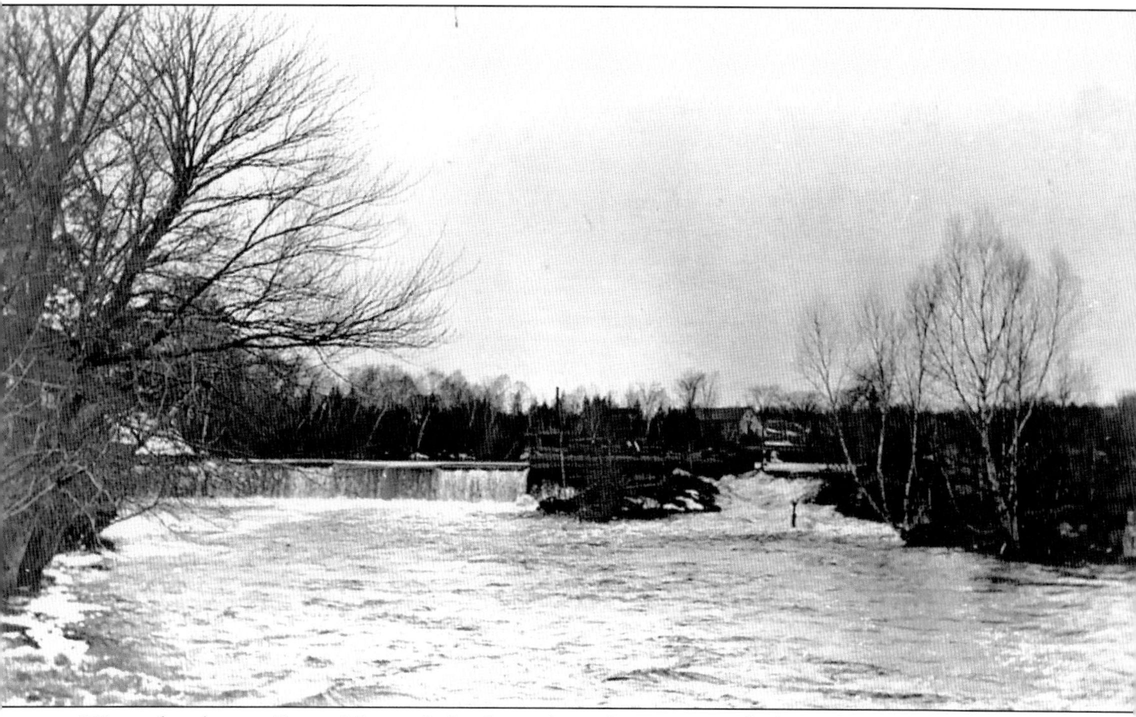

Water levels on Great Moose Lake have long been controlled at the outlet. A log dam controlled the flow for power use at Shaw's sawmill *c.* 1906, and later a concrete and stone dam was used. The flood of 1987 knocked more than three feet off the top of the old dam, and it was replaced with federal grant money. The new dam is electronically controlled and is named in honor of longtime town manager Peggy Morgan.

Six

PALMYRA

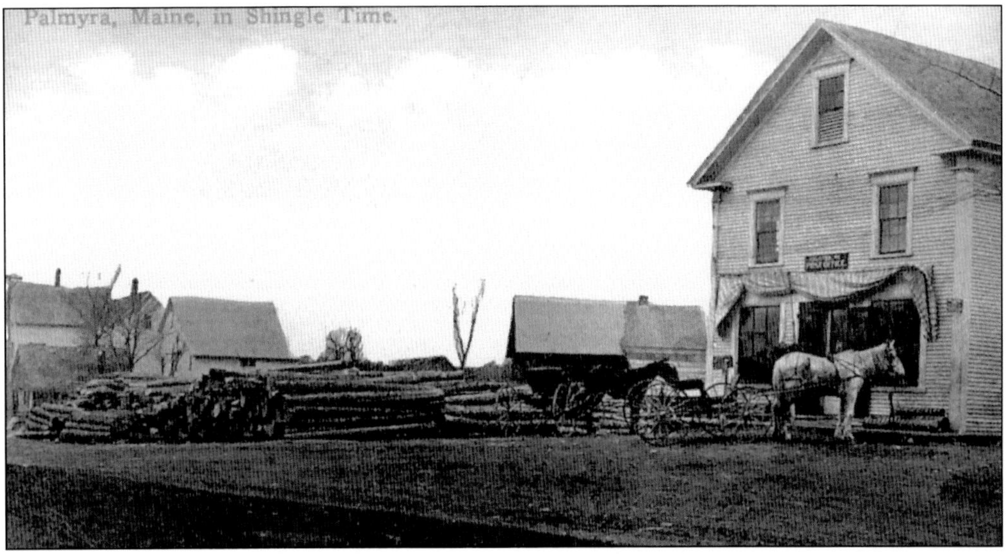

The old general store on Route 2 has long been recognized as Palmyra's center. But it was many years after this photograph was taken, showing the store and the adjoining shingle mill, that Route 2 became a federal highway, and Palmyra was a sleepy village in its path. John Harvey acted as a judge and ran the first general store, which included a post office. Like its neighbors, Palmyra traces its roots back to the initial surveying in 1792 by Ephraim Ballard and Samuel Weston. It was known as Township No. 5, third range, north of the Waldo Patent. However, it was Dr. John Warren of Revolutionary War fame that gave the town its start. Warren was the area's largest landowner, purchasing 28,200 acres for $7,666. The land he purchased would encompass four towns in the valley, three of which are featured in this publication: Palmyra, Hartland, and St. Albans. (The fourth town was Corinna.) Warren had five years to settle 20 families on the land. Within one month, he sold acreage to Benjamin Shepard that became part of Palmyra and St. Albans. The first Palmyra settler was Daniel Gale, who built the first log cabin near Gale Corner. Other early settlers included Caleb Shaw, Jeremiah Robinson, Eban Nay, and Joseph Warren (Dr. Warren's son and his local agent). By 1813, Joseph Warren had built the largest home and had cleared Warren Hill with the help of his slaves. It was the DeLancey family of Normandy, France, that settled the village area. Later known by the last name Lancey, the family built the first gristmill and sawmill in the village. The town was incorporated in 1807 after a meeting at Lancey's Tavern. Other members of the Lancey family settled in Pittsfield and also ran a tavern.

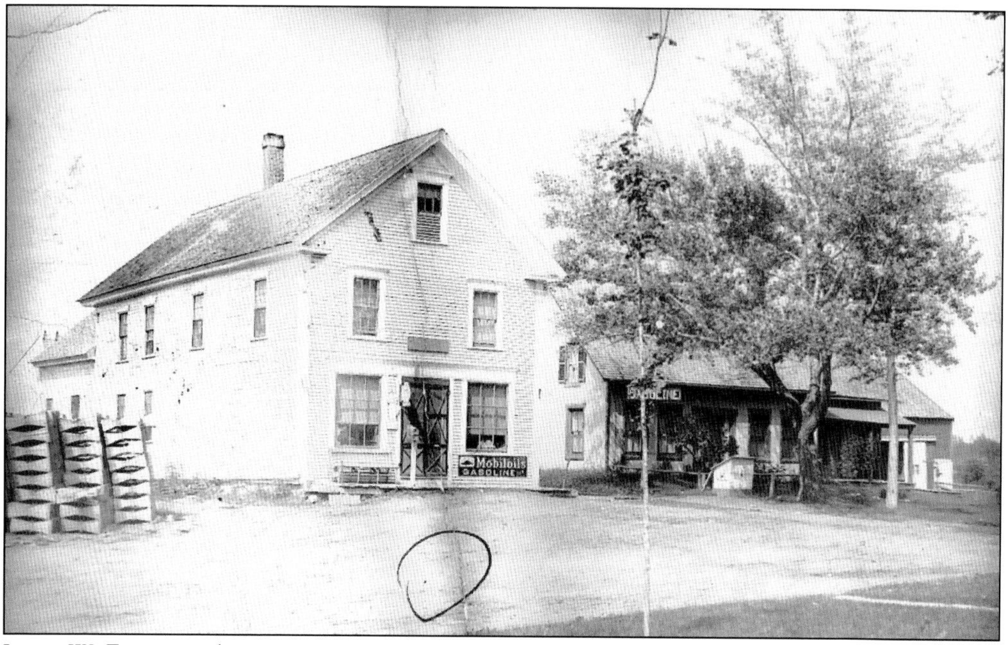

Lewis W. Frost was the town postmaster and owner of the village store *c.* 1900. He also had the distinction of owning the first automobile.

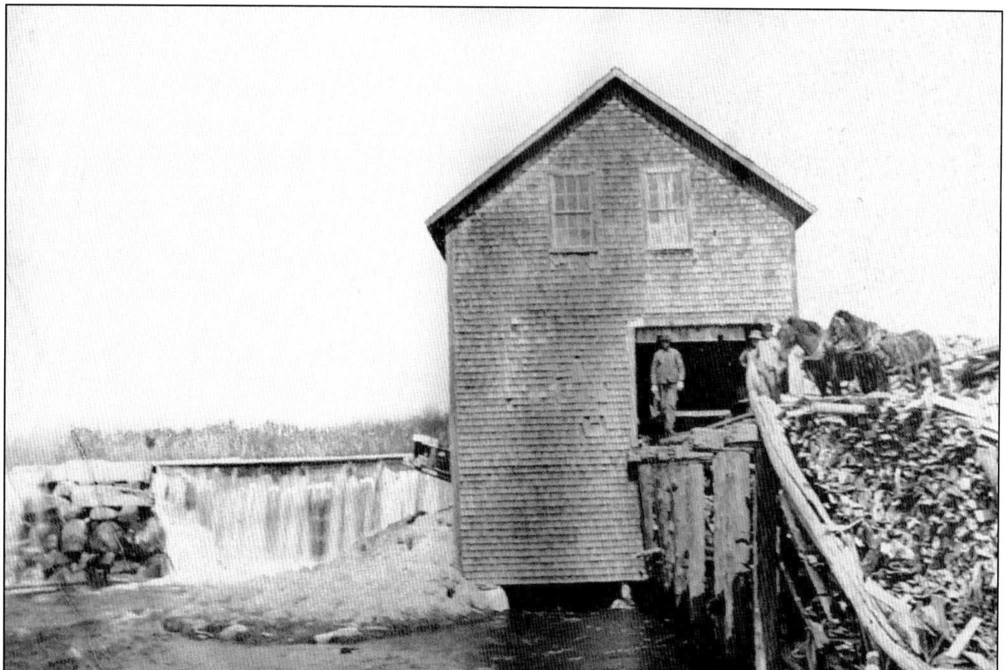

Timothy Homstead built the first mills in the village *c.* 1832. However, it was Hollis Weeks who was known as the longtime owner-operator of the shingle mill in the village. The mill burned in 1946. The Weeks boys apparently were fond of sliding down the sawdust pile in the summer and landing in the stream below. Many pictures of the village show logs and finished shingles stockpiled between Hollis Weeks' home and the village store.

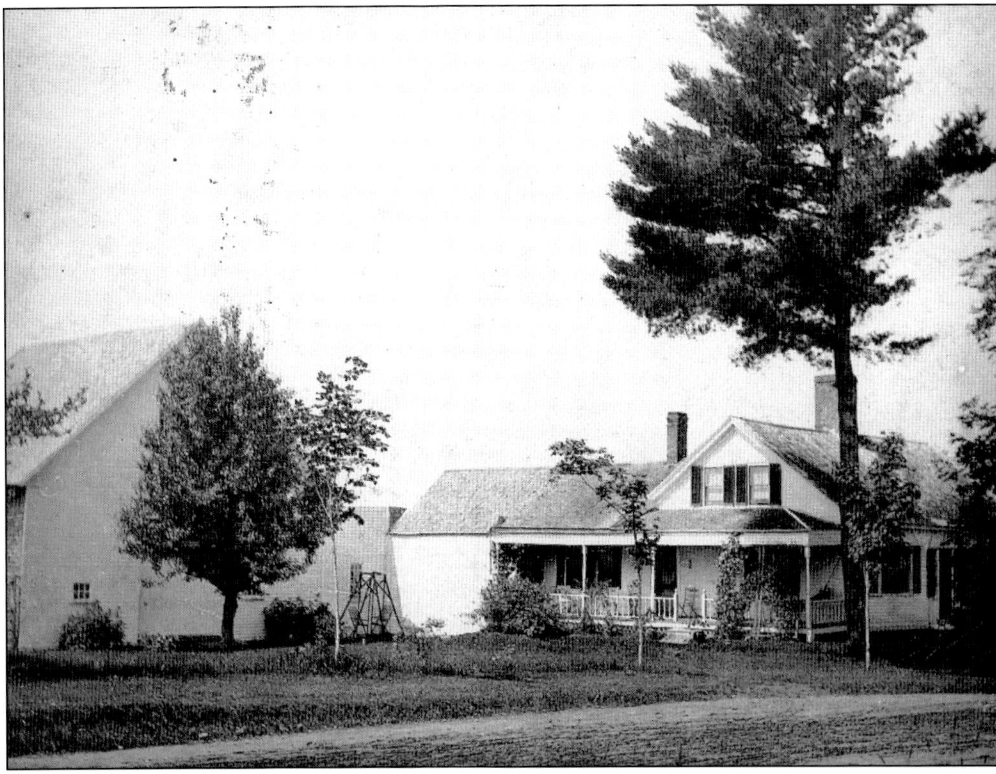

Louis and Cora (Weeks) Frost operated the general store on the north side of the Route 2, but lived on the south side. In later years, Eunice (Millett) and Louis Harper Sr. lived in the home.

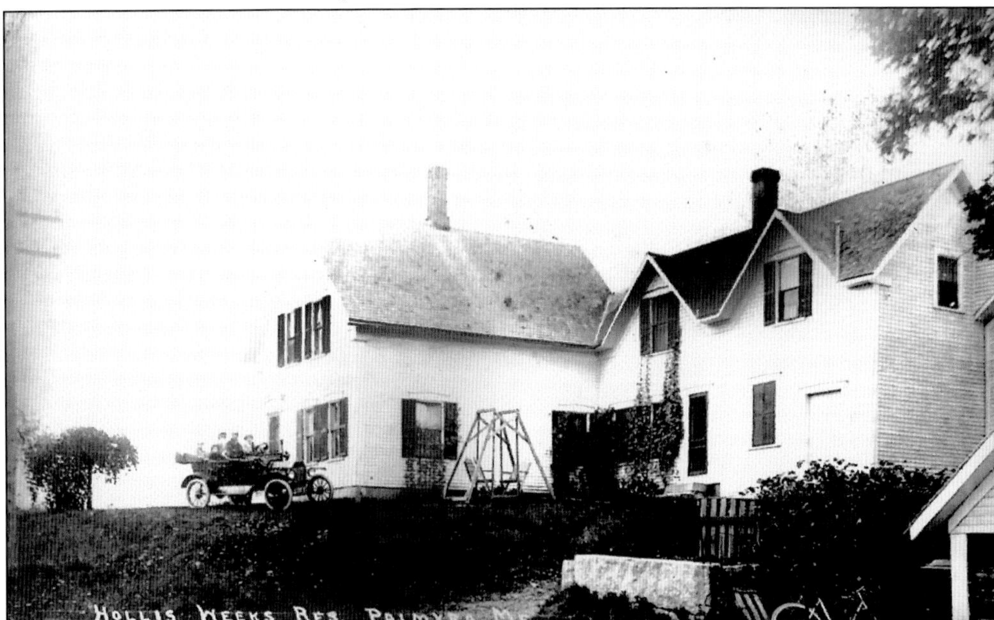

The Hollis Weeks home was located west of the mill, and stands today as the home of Millard Varney.

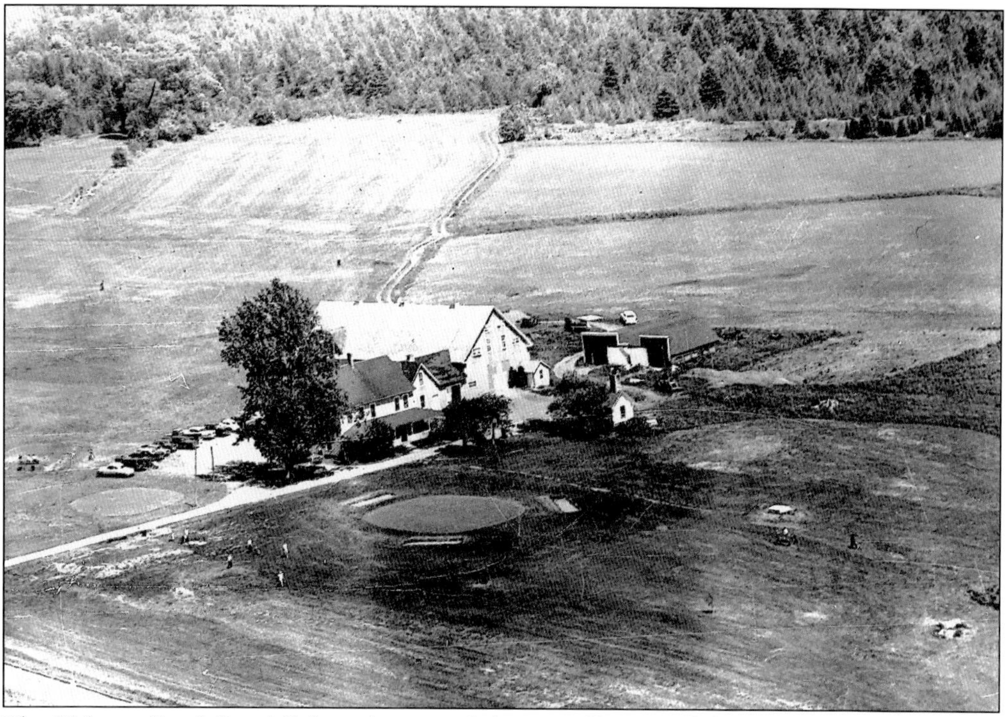

The 375-acre Frank Randall farm dominated the top of Lang Hill for much of the 1900s until it was developed into a golf course. Today the area is the Palmyra Golf Course and RV Resort.

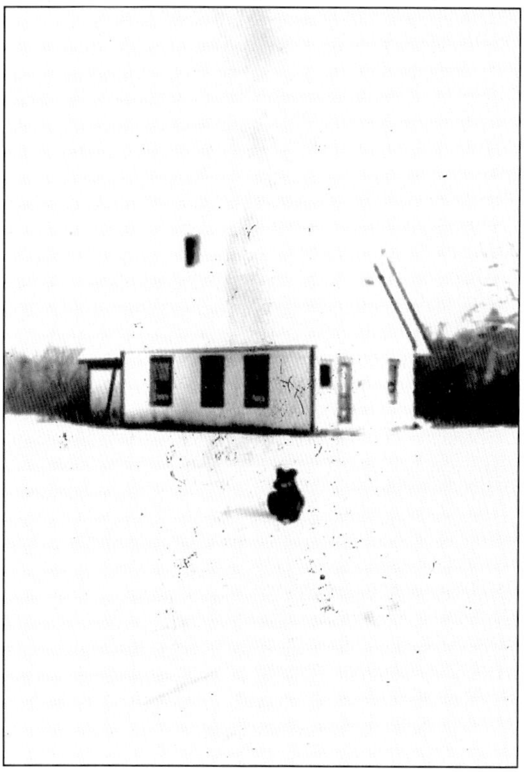

The Egypt School on the Spring Hill Road was one of approximately 17 one-room schoolhouses in the village until the 1950s. Others included Ell Hill, Gale, March, Adams, Madawaska, Dogtown, South Ridge, Warren Hill, Goodrich, Carr, South Union, and Village, to name a few. Several still exist as private homes.

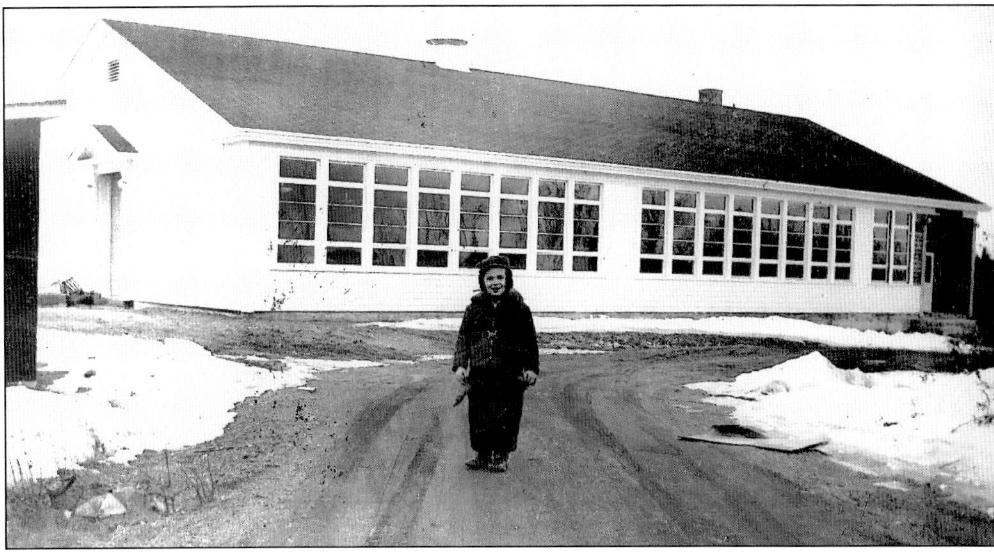

Palmyra's Consolidated School opened in 1954 to house grades one through five. Sixth through eighth grade were taught at Ell Hill, Egypt, and Gale Schools. By 1960, an addition was ready at the Consolidated School to house all of Palmyra's elementary students. High school students had the option of attending Newport High School, Hartland Academy, or Maine Central Institute. When this 1956 photograph was taken, young Lewis Harper Jr. was in his first year at the Consolidated School.

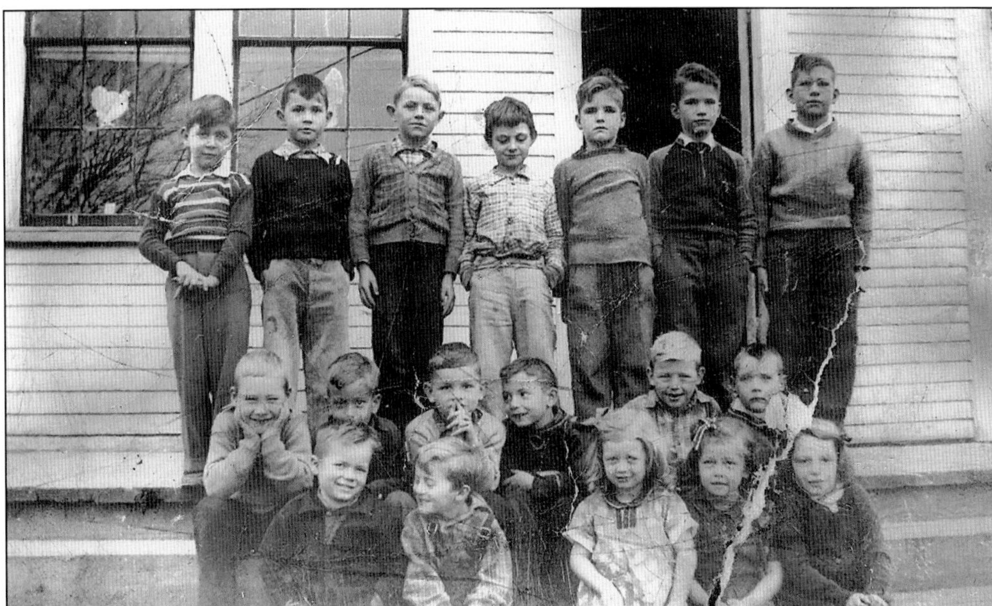

This group attended the village school across from the church *c.* 1945, sometime before classes were consolidated in the new multi-room school. Shown in this photograph are, from left to right, the following: (first row) Stanley Willey, Bill Small, Jolene Tompkins, Charlene Nickless, and Marilyn Shaw; (second row) Skipper Gordon, Gene Temple, unidentified, Ken Weeks, Bruce Tompkins, and Martel Gordon; (third row) two unidentified people, Ronny Peterson, Harold Emerson, ? Rideout, ? Rideout, and ? Rideout.

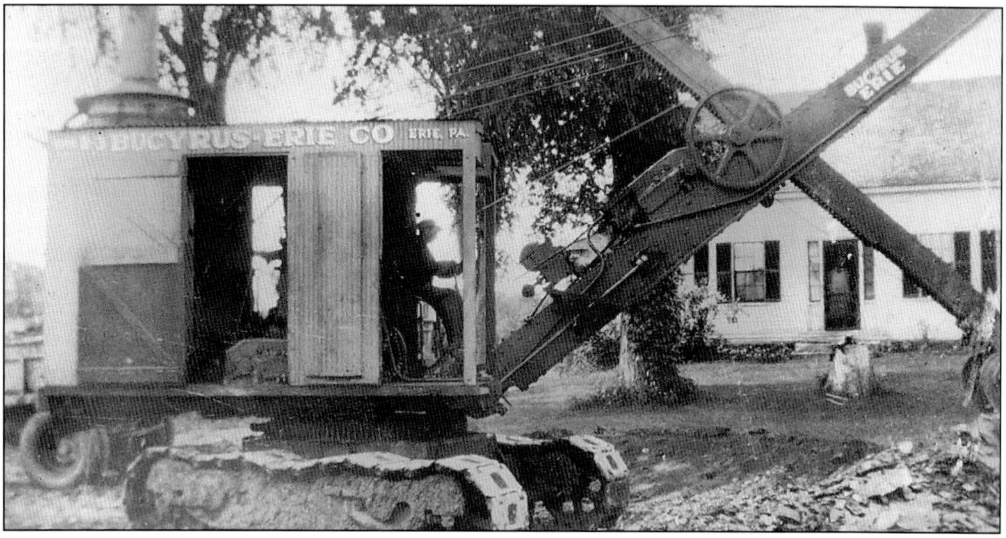

In 1931, federal funds were used to reconstruct the main road through the village, and Route 2, and one of Maine's primary east-west highways, was born. The large steam shovel that dug up the old roadbed was an attraction for young and old alike.

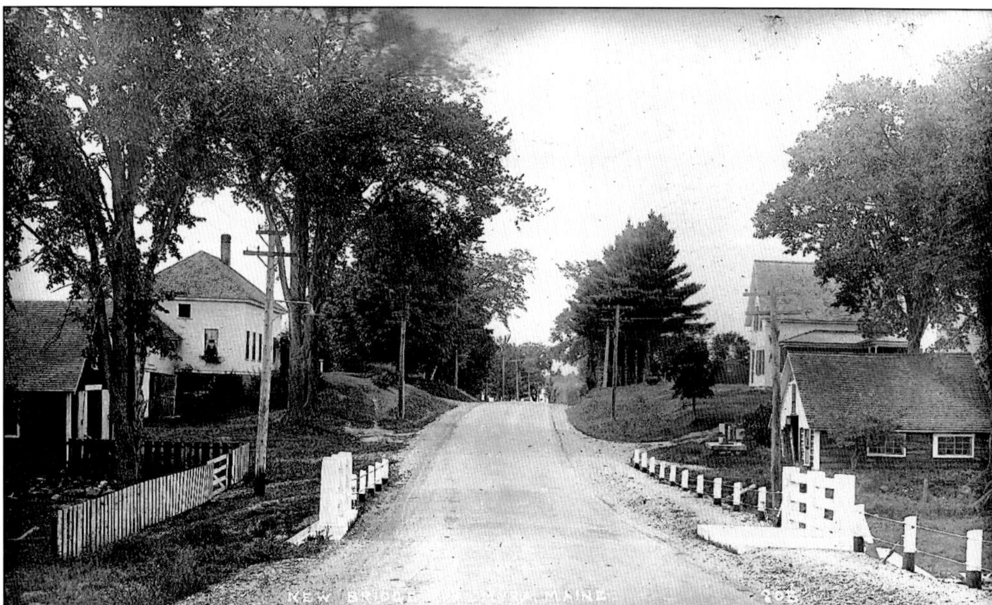

A new concrete bridge across the mill stream also was constructed in 1931, as can be seen in this photograph looking west. Bridges were a primary problem and expense in the early days of the village. The first bridge of concern was over the Sebasticook, although it was not in the current path of Route 2. In the early days, the county road crossed the village by way of Warren Hill and connected to a road over the Sebasticook farther north than today's Merry Memorial Bridge. Once called the Bridge of the Sebasticook, it came to be known locally as "nigger bridge" (see page 101).

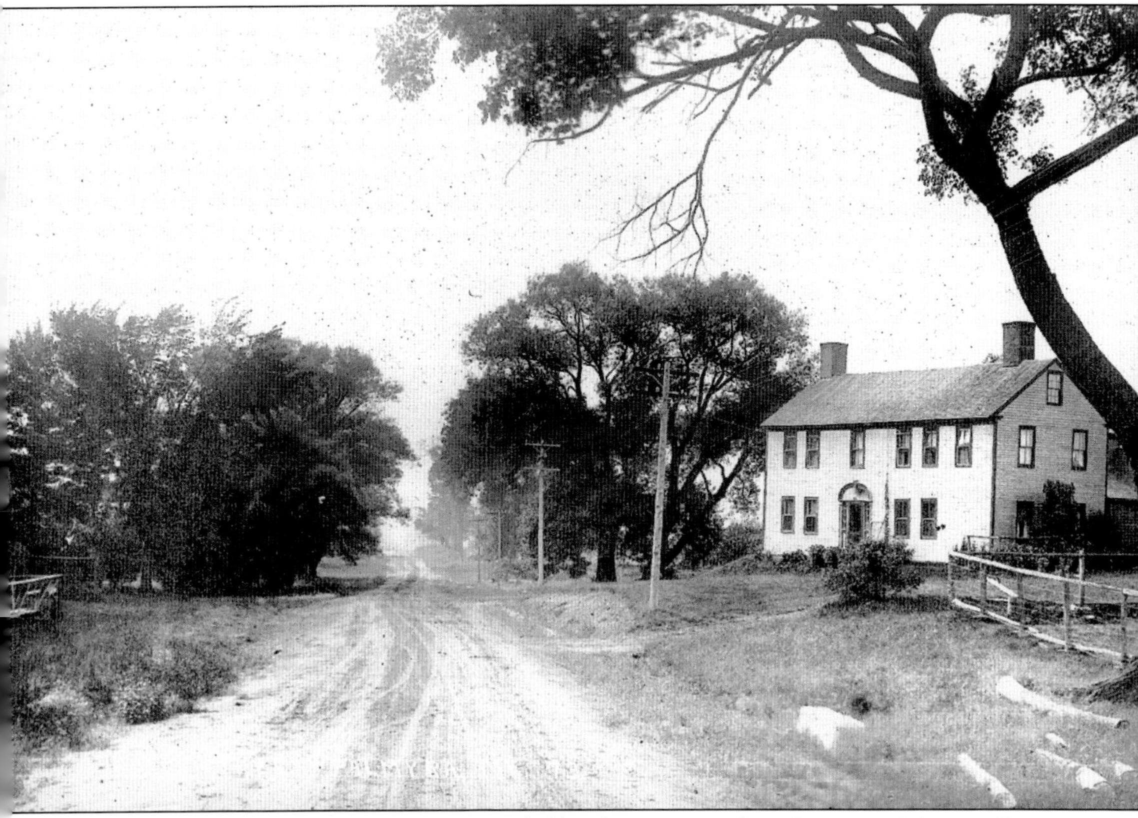

Before reconstruction, Main Street was much like the streets and roads in most Maine villages. The town tavern stood at the corner of Main Street and the Warren Hill road. It was the home of the Donald Curtis family for many years. It has since been removed and replaced by a new U. S. post office.

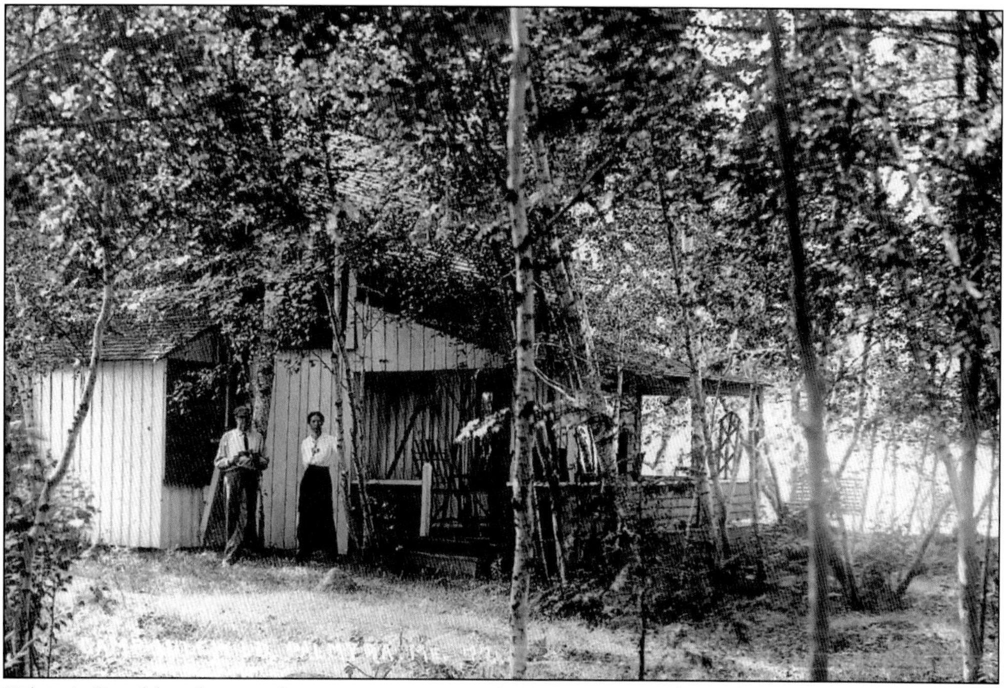

White's Pond has been a favorite vacation and recreation site for Palmyra residents for many years. L. W. Weeks, seen here with Jen Weeks, owned Camp Idlewild, which was one of the first camps.

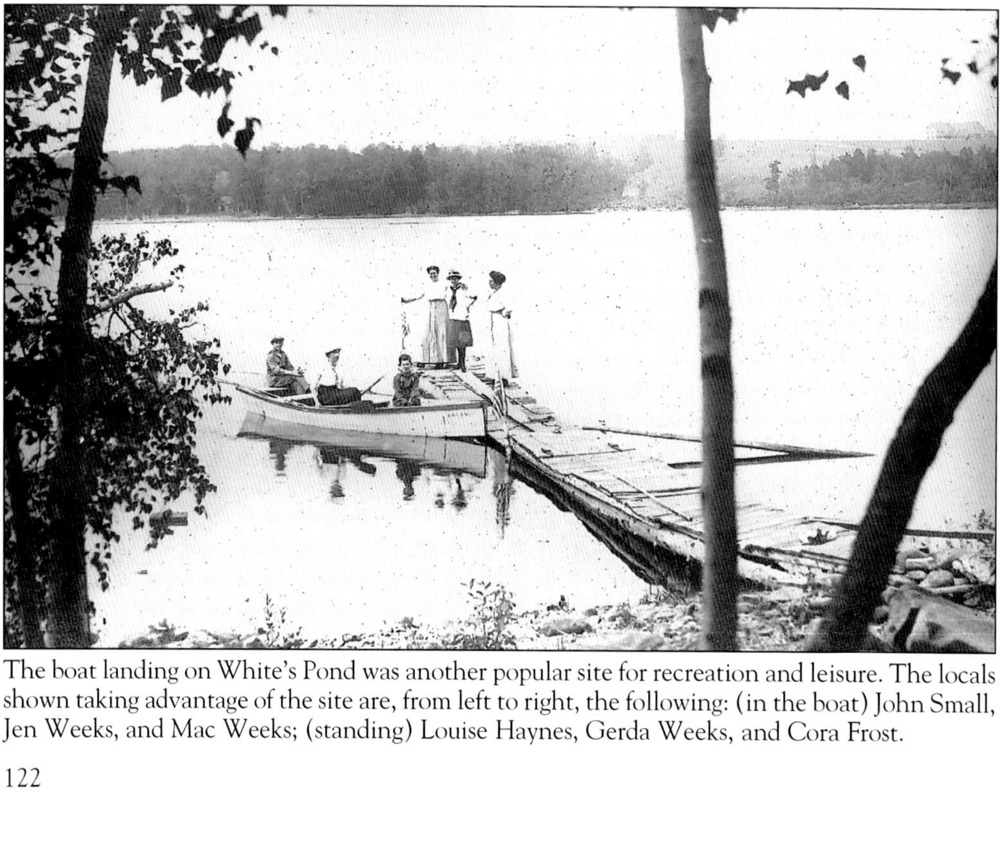

The boat landing on White's Pond was another popular site for recreation and leisure. The locals shown taking advantage of the site are, from left to right, the following: (in the boat) John Small, Jen Weeks, and Mac Weeks; (standing) Louise Haynes, Gerda Weeks, and Cora Frost.

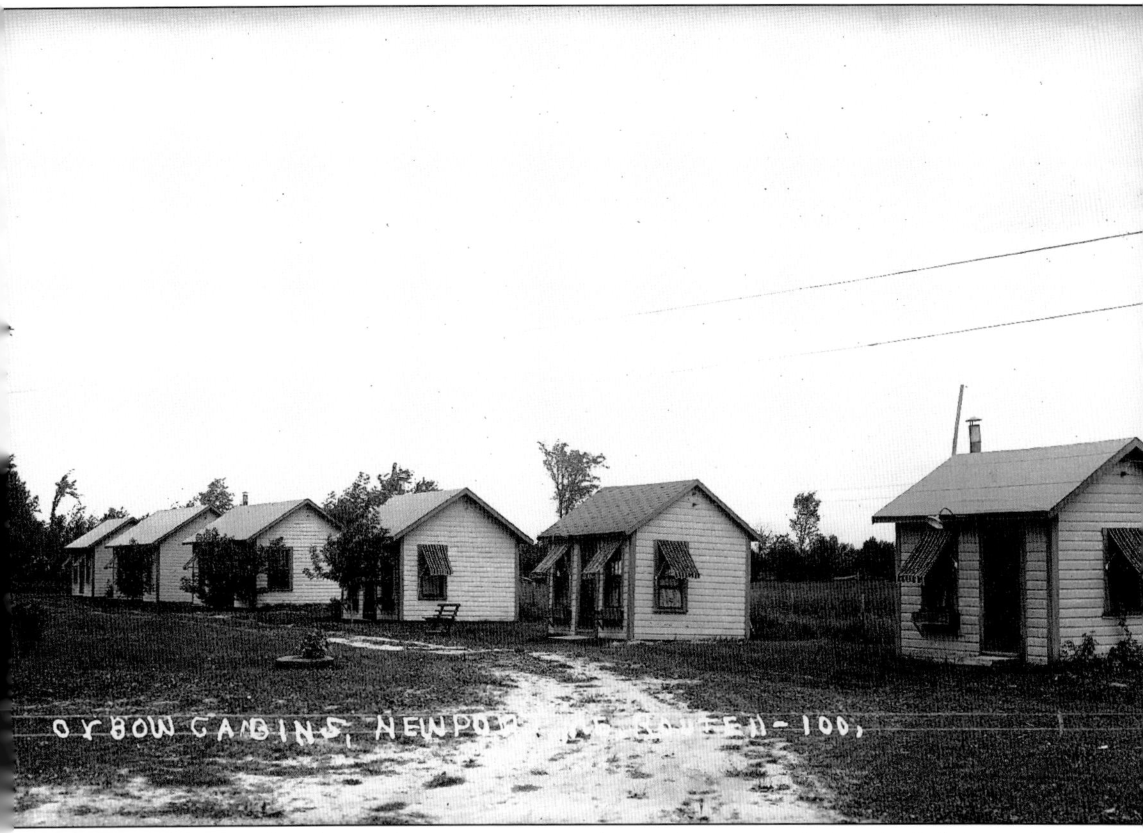

In the 1930s, traveling by car became more popular, and accommodations included popular roadside cabins, such as these on Route 100. The Oxbow Cabins, once located near the Smith Road, are the reason that section of Route 100 in Palmyra is currently named Oxbow Road.

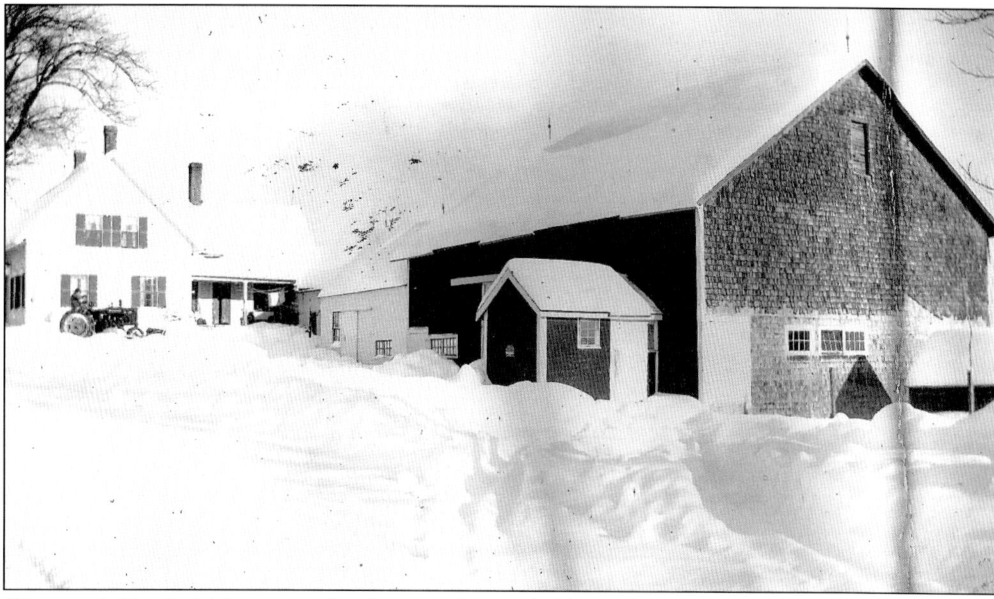

Obed and Gerda Millett raised a family of five children, Eunice, Virginia, George, Joe, and Tom, on the Millett farm off the Spring Hill Road. The property was converted in the 1970s, becoming the home of Hardwick Fence, but was lost to fire in the 1980s.

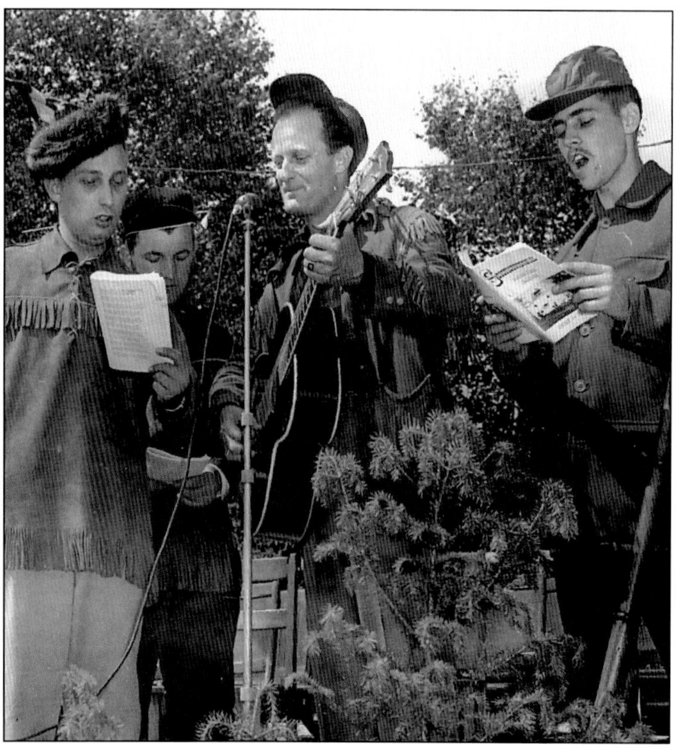

In 1957, Palmyra celebrated its sesquicentennial, a 150th birthday. Entertainment included a well-known personality accompanied by local residents. Maine's own "Yodelin' Slim" Clark from neighboring St. Albans provided the guitar and led the singing with help from Richard Brown of Newport (left), Terry Perkins, and Dana Fields (far right).

Participation is what makes small communities function. In 1959, this group shared duties on a town committee. Shown in this photograph are, from left to right, the following: (seated) Alley Howes, a longtime moderator of town meetings, and his wife, whose name is unknown; (standing) Helen Johonnett, Carl Emery, Frances Goodrich, and Gerda Millett.

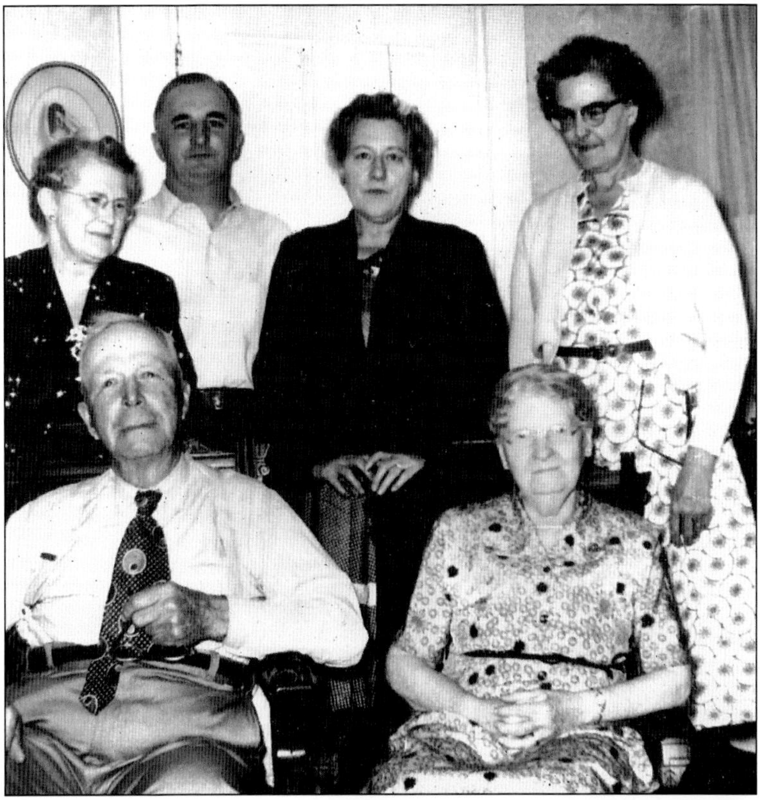

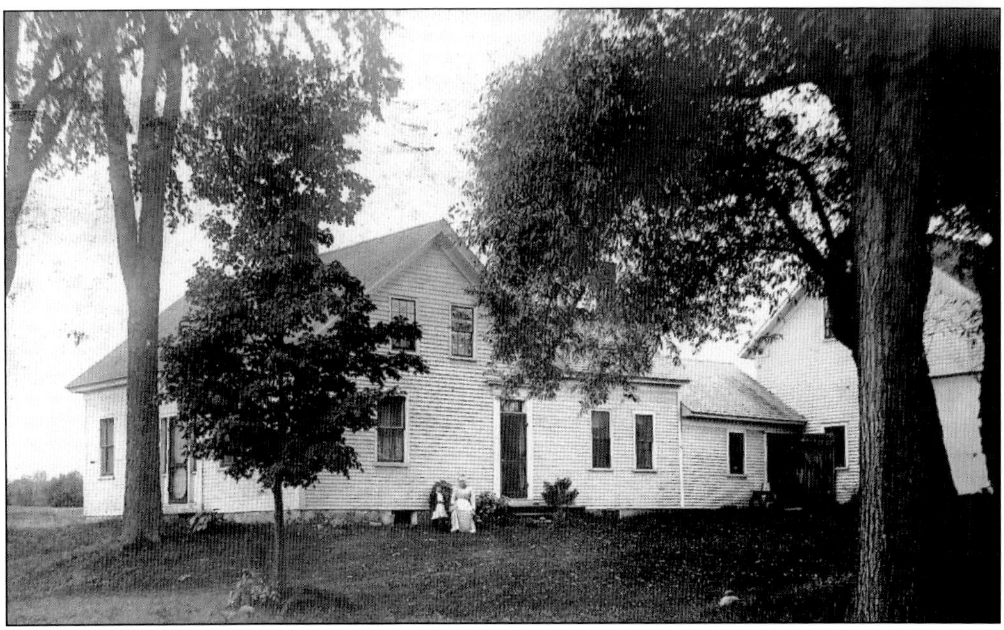

Reuben Homstead came to Palmyra in the early 1800s and was one of the first settlers. His descendants remain in the village and surrounding areas. In 1870, the town voted, after many years of delay, to build a town hall, and purchased land from the Homsteads. In the early 1900s, Jennie Homstead lived in this home on Main Street between the town hall and Warren Hill Road.

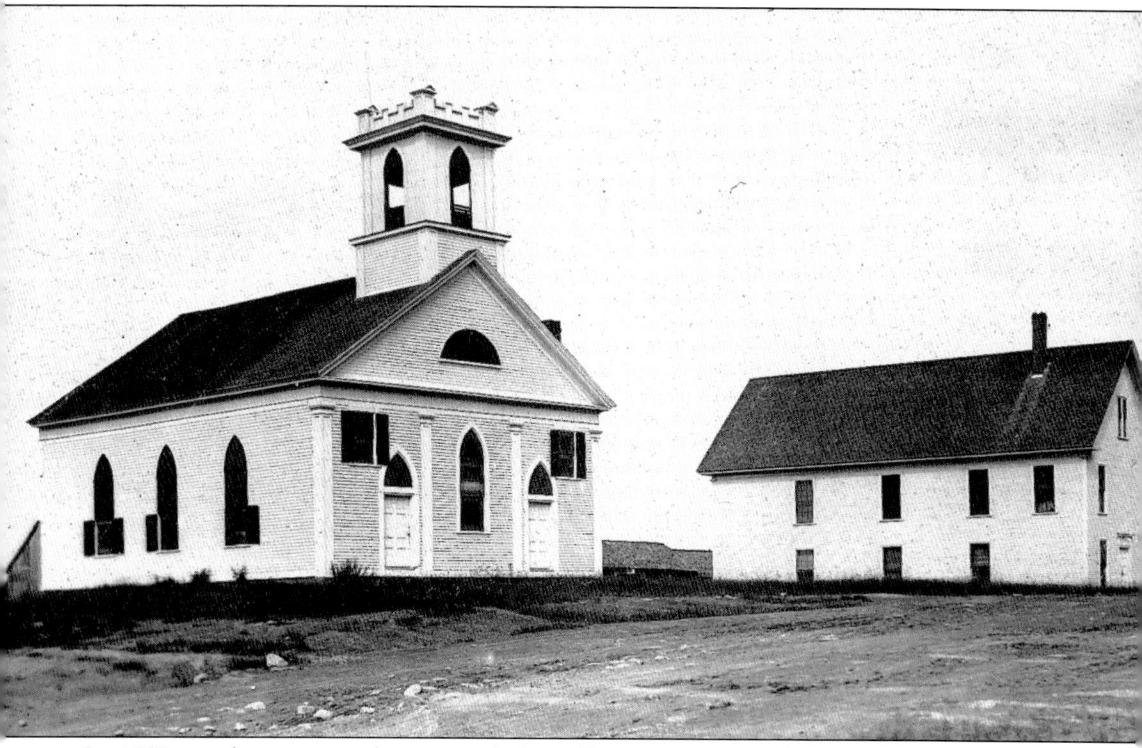

In 1832, a religious revival motivated the villagers to raise a church by first selling pews. Stephen Robinson swapped land for one of the pews. George Lancey contracted to build the structure and hired Lewis Williams as head carpenter to work with volunteers including John White, Levi Judkins, Hill Judkins, Titus Johonnett, Thomas Lancey, Samuel Lancey, Samuel Lang, Freeman Holway, and Benjamin Daggett Paine. Jeremiah Robinson supplied the pine for the pews. The same building serves the community today as St. Martin's Episcopal Church. Its parish hall was once the Palmyra Grange Hall.

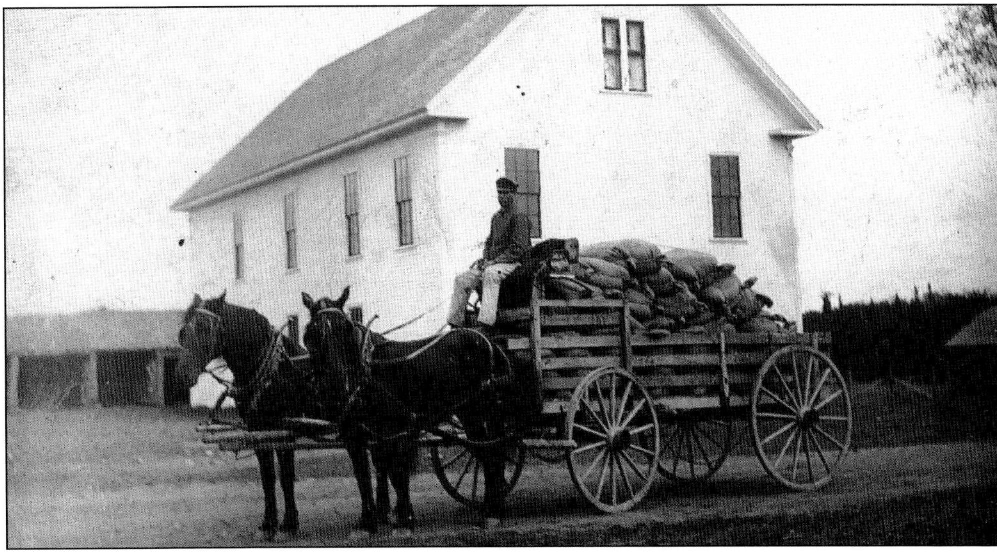

The Palmyra Grange Hall has been a fixture in the village since before 1900. Palmyra's agricultural past is apparent in this photograph, and with the town's construction of a large meeting hall for "the Patrons of Husbandry," as the National Grange was called when it was founded. The organization became an important part of many rural communities' social and political life in the late 1800s and early 1900s. It was often routine for whole families to find activity and socialization at the grange on a Saturday night. Although the grange has long since disbanded in Palmyra, the building is still used by St. Martin's Episcopal Church for suppers, fairs, and other functions.

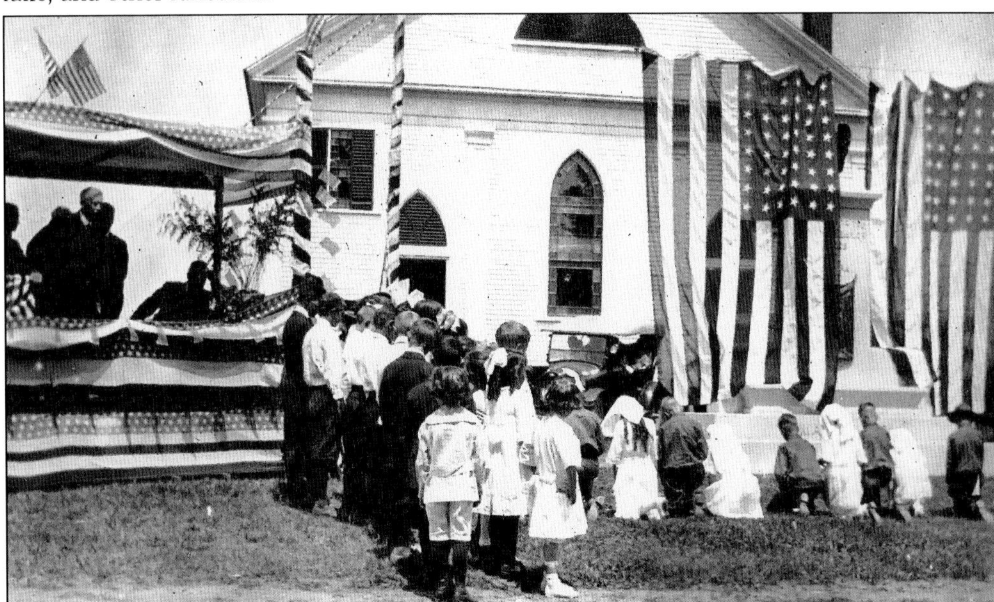

On May 30, 1921, the children of Palmyra gathered to participate in the dedication of the war memorial outside the village church on Route 2. In recent years, attempts were made to relocate the memorial because of its location on a hill near the reconstruction of the highway. The plan was abandoned, however, when local residents objected. A new memorial to the soldiers of subsequent wars was constructed at the new town park near the town hall.

BIBLIOGRAPHY

Background information also was gleaned from the published histories of the Sebasticook Valley towns, including the following:

Bigelow, Gladys M. and Ruth McGowan Knowles. *History of St. Albans, Maine*. Bowie, Maryland: Heritage Books, 1995.

Cook, Sanger Mills. *Pittsfield on the Sebasticook*. Bangor, Maine: Printed by Furbush-Roberts Print Company, 1966.

Fernald, Douglas Ira. *Detroit, Maine, 1828-1978: Saga of a Sebasticook Town*. Thorndike, Maine: Hutchins Brothers, 1977.

Hill, Donald A. and Kent Higgins. "Palmyra, 175th Anniversary, 1807 to 1882."

Mitchell, William H. A *Brief History of Newport, Maine, 1814-1914*. Newport, Maine: A. W. Lander, printer, 1914.

Seekins, Brenda. "Milestones and Memories, Pittsfield 1819 to 1994."

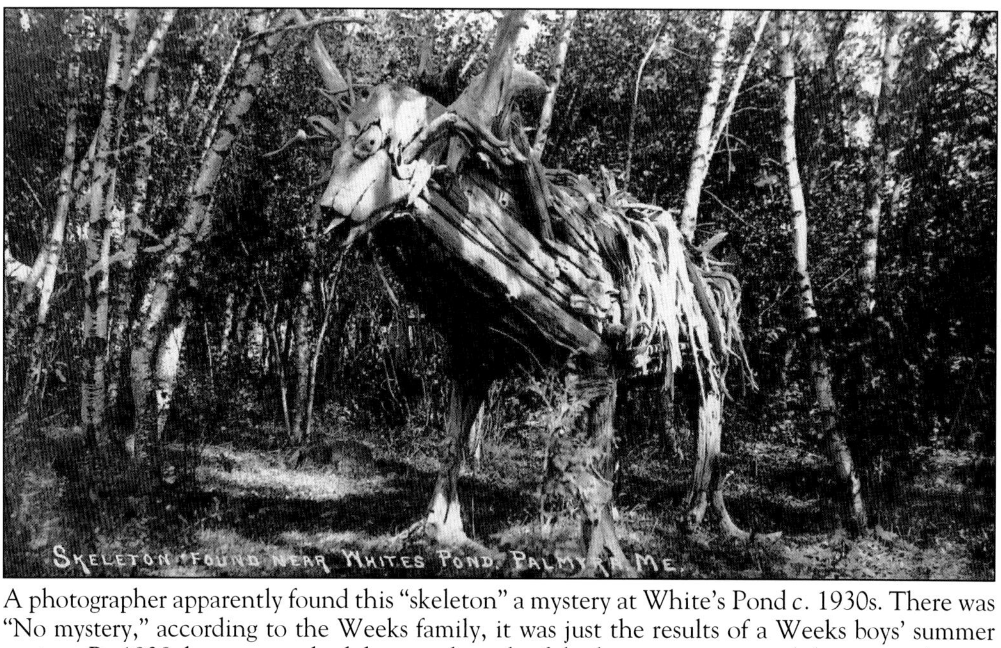

A photographer apparently found this "skeleton" a mystery at White's Pond c. 1930s. There was "No mystery," according to the Weeks family, it was just the results of a Weeks boys' summer project. By 1938, heavy snow had destroyed much of the large structure, and the remainder was destroyed by fire.